Reveille for
a new generation

Reveille for
a new generation

ORGANIZERS AND LEADERS REFLECT ON POWER

Compiled and Edited by
GREGORY F. AUGUSTINE PIERCE

REVEILLE FOR A NEW GENERATION
Organizers and Leaders Reflect on Power
Compiled and edited by Gregory F. Augustine Pierce

Design and typesetting by Patricia A. Lynch

Published by ACTA Publications, 4848 N. Clark Street, Chicago, IL 60640, (800) 397-2282, www.actapublications.com

Library of Congress Number: 2020945927
ISBN: 978-0-87946-683-1

Printed in the United States of America by Total Printing Systems
Year 35 34 33 32 31 30 29 28 27 26 25 24 23 22 21 20
Printing 10 9 8 7 6 5 4 3 2 First

♻ Text printed on 30% post-consumer recycled paper.

Contents

Dedicated to

Jim Drake

1938-2001

Rev. Vernon Dobson

1924-2013

Ed Chambers

1930-2015

Carmelia Goffe

1948-2016

Andy Sarabia

1940-2019

Sr. Christine Stephens

1940-2019

And all past, present, and future
leaders and organizers
of the Industrial Areas Foundation

INTRODUCTION

You Can't Take Anything without Organization

by Gregory F. Augustine Pierce

Writing is to organizing as preaching is to religion: You've got to do it well if you want to persuade others to act together in a certain way. "The ability to act together in a certain way" is a good definition of power, and power is why organizers and leaders organize.

Hence this book. And hence this book now.

When Saul Alinsky founded the Industrial Areas Foundation (IAF) in 1940, there was real question whether democracy itself could survive—not only in the United States but around the world. Today, that same question has become real again. The answer then, as it is now, depends on whether people and the institutions they control can be organized into what Alinsky called "People's Organizations" to exercise the power they already have.

The Industrial Areas Foundation today is still at the business of helping local communities organize for power in over sixty affiliated organizations throughout the United States and in a few other countries. In celebration of its 80th anniversary in 2020, these stories, poems, sermons, eulogies, and essays reflecting on power (and powerlessness) by leaders and organizers are collected here in one place for the first time. Each piece of writing is accompanied by information about the author or authors and followed by three questions for discussion and reflection by readers. Permission is hereby granted to copy and distribute with proper attribution single chapters of this book at no charge for training and educational purposes by not-for-profit organizations.

The purpose of this collection is three-fold:

- To inspire new leaders and organizers (especially young adults, people of color, and members of unorganized communities) about why, when, where, and how to organize People's Organizations.
- To convince religious institutions of all faiths and denominations and non-religious associations of all philosophical stripes that it is in their immediate and long-term self-interest to join together in People's Organizations that have enough power to create pockets of the "world as it should be" right in the midst of the "world as it is" in order to help "repair the fabric of the world."
- To explain to politicians and government officials, corporate and foundation leaders, the media and academia that democracy can and does work best when there are plenty of independent, self-supporting, non-partisan, diverse, action-oriented People's Organizations that can get at the root causes of the problems that face us as local communities, states, the nation, and the world.

The book is divided into three parts, with an epilogue, containing some fifty-two entries. Part One looks at the roots of organizing in the

United States through the eyes of some of the forebearers of modern IAF organizing. Part Two contains pieces by or about the founders of the IAF and a few of its historic leaders and organizers, and Part Three is composed of reflections from the current and future crop of IAF leaders and organizers. The Epilogue is an excerpt from the important and widely praised book, *The Heartbeat of Wounded Knee: Native America from 1890 to the Present* by David Treuer, which brings this book of reflections on the organized power of oppressed people in American history full circle.

Virtually all the contributors to this book have declined payment for their work, or their writing has been deemed to be either in the public domain or fair use. Instead, a royalty of twenty-five percent of all the money received from the sale of the book will be paid into a special fund for recruitment, training, and tryouts of people who want to actualize in their own lives what one of America's foremost black labor and civil rights leaders, A. Philip Randolph, the founder of the Brotherhood of Sleeping Car Porters who helped conceive and initiate the 1963 March on Washington for Jobs and Freedom, preached: "At the banquet table of nature there are no reserved seats. You get what you can take, and you keep what you can hold. If you can't take anything, you won't get anything; and if you can't hold anything, you won't keep anything. And you can't take anything without organization."

Gregory F. Augustine Pierce
Chicago, Illinois
Election Day, November 3, 2020

A note on my editorial decisions.

I have been an editor and publisher for thirty-five years, and my goal is to never cause the reader to stop reading because of inconsistencies, lack of clarity, or grammar or punctuation errors. This book, because of its large number of authors and wide historical scope, presented several challenges in this regard. I have tried to apply these rules in this case:

1. I tried to apply a unified style on spelling, punctuation, and grammar—even to the older essays. I also corrected or adapted without noting any frank errors or lack of clarity I discovered. So do not consider the historical essays in this book to be the "original" writings but rather adaptations.

2. I have tried to honor the use of the writers' original words and name choices, except where it was my opinion they would have updated them if they could. For example, often writers meant to be inclusive in the use of pronouns but were following the usage of the time. In that case (the use of "men" to mean "all human beings") I simply substituted a more inclusive term without noting it, unless it was in a famous saying, for example, "All (people) are created equal," in which case I used parentheses to alert the reader to the change.

3. One current question is the use and capitalization of the word "Black" to mean the particular race of people. In the historical pieces in the book, I stayed with the author's original choices on this matter, e.g., "Negro" or "African American." In the more contemporary articles and my own comments, I capitalized "Black" as both an adjective and a noun, as that seems to be the current usage in many (but not all) respected periodicals.

PART ONE

Roots of Organizing

Roots of Organizing

Powerless people organizing in the United States is not a contemporary phenomenon but rather a rich tradition that began with the American revolution; the resistance of Native Americans; the fight for the abolition of slavery and the passage of the 13th, 14th, and 15th amendments to the U.S. Constitution; the opposition to segregation, Jim Crow laws, and voter suppression; the efforts to organize labor unions, farm cooperatives, social service agencies, and public and parochial education; the campaigns for women's suffrage and equality; the movements for civil and LGBTQ rights; the early and current fights for immigrant rights and acceptance; and many other social initiatives.

Part One contains fourteen excerpts from the writings, some of them not well-know, of a few people who represent the roots of this rich organizing tradition: Omar bin Said, Frederick Douglass, Sojourner Truth, Lucretia Mott, Emma Lazarus, Lucy Gonzáles Parsons, Ohiyesa, Mother Jones, John L. Lewis, Stoyan Pribichevich, Pauli Murray, leaders of the Student Nonviolent Coordinating Committee, Ella Baker, and John R. Lewis.

Not all leaders and organizers from these early roots of American organizing wrote their thoughts about power, and not all who did can be included here. People who were or became elected officials were mostly excluded, not because they did not do good organizing work but because their choice to be an elected official undermines the "iron rule" of organizing: "Never do for others what they can do for themselves."

■ ■ ■ ■

"O Ye Americans"

by Omar bin Said

Omar bin Said (pronounced "Sayyid," c. 1770-1864) was born in Futa Toro (modern Senegal). He was a member of the famous Fulani tribe known for their Islamic literary traditions. About 1807, he was captured and taken to Charleston, South Carolina, to be sold into slavery. In 1810, he ran away from his owner and was captured in Fayetteville, North Carolina, where his plea for freedom written in the Arabic script on the wall of his jail cell brought him in the attention of James Owen, who eventually bought him. Omar bin Said lived enslaved for the rest of his life on Owen's plantation in Fayetteville and later in Wilmington, North Carolina when the family moved to that seacoast town. Said died in 1864, before the end of the Civil War, and was buried on the Owen plantation.

My name is Omar bin Said. My birthplace was Futa Toro (modern Senegal), between the two rivers (Senegal River and Gambia River). I sought knowledge under the instruction of a Sheikh called Mohammed Said, my own brother, and Sheikh Soleiman Kembeh, and Sheikh Gabriel Abdal. I continued my studies twenty-five years. Then there came to our place a large army, who killed many men and took me and brought me to the great sea and sold me into the hands of the Christians, who bound me and sent me on board great ship, and we sailed upon the great sea a month and a half, when we came to a place called

5

Charleston in the Christian language.

There they sold me to a small, weak, and wicked man, called Johnson, a complete infidel, who had no fear of God at all. Now I am a small man and unable to do hard work, so I fled from the hand of Johnson and after a month came to a place called Fayetteville.

There I saw some great houses. On the new moon I went into a church to pray. A lad saw me and rode off to the place of his father and informed him that he had seen a black man in the church. A man named Handah (Hunter) and another man with him on horseback, came attended by a troop of dogs.

They took me and made me go with them twelve miles to a place where they put me into a great house from which I could not go out. I continued in the great house (which, in the Christian language, they called "jail") sixteen days and nights. One Friday, the jailor came and opened the door of the house and I saw a great many men, all Christians, some of whom called out to me, "What is your name? Is it Omar or Said?" I did not understand their Christian language. A man called Bob Mumford took me and led me out of the jail, and I was very well pleased to go with him to his place. I stayed at Mumford's four days and nights, and then a man named General Jim Owen, son-in-law of Mumford, having married his daughter Betsey, asked me if I was willing to go to a place called Bladen. I said, Yes, I was willing. I went with them and have remained in the place of Jim Owen until now.

■ ■ ■ ■

O ye people of North Carolina, O ye people of South Carolina, O ye people of America, all of you; have you among you any two such men as Jim Owen and John Owen? These men are good men. What food they eat they give to me to eat. As they clothe themselves, they clothe me. They permit me to read the gospel of God, our Lord and Savior and King, who regulates all our circumstances, health, and wealth, and who bestows his mercies willingly, not by constraint. According to his power I open my heart, as to a great light, to receive the true way, the way of the Lord Jesus the Messiah.

Before I came to the Christian country, my religion was the religion of Mohammed, the Apostle of God—may God have mercy upon him and give him peace. I walked to mosque before daybreak, washed my face and head and hands and feet. I prayed at noon, prayed in the afternoon, prayed at sunset, prayed in the evening. I gave alms every year: gold, silver, seeds, cattle, sheep, goats, rice, wheat, and barley. I gave tithes of all the above-named things. I went every year to the holy war against the infidels. I went on pilgrimage to Mecca, as all did who were able. My father had six sons and five daughters, and my mother had three sons and one daughter.

■ ■ ■ ■

When I left my country, I was thirty-seven years old; I have been in the country of the Christians twenty-four years. I reside in this our country by reason of great necessity. Wicked men took me by violence and sold me to the Christians. We sailed a month and a half on the great sea to the place called Charleston in the Christian land. I fell into the hands of a small, weak and wicked man, who feared not God at all, nor did he read (the gospel) at all nor pray. I was afraid to remain with a man so depraved and who committed so many crimes, and I ran away. After a month our Lord God brought me forward to the hand of a good man, who fears God and loves to do good, and whose name is Jim Owen and whose brother is called Colonel John Owen. These are two excellent men. I am residing in Bladen County.

I continue in the hand of Jim Owen, who never beats me nor scolds me. I neither go hungry nor naked, and I have no hard work to do. I am not able to do hard work for I am a small man and feeble. During the last twenty years I have known no want in the hand of Jim Owen.

■ ■ ■ ■

O ye people of North Carolina, O ye people of South Carolina, O all ye people of America. The first son of Jim Owen is called Thomas, and his sister is called Masa-jein (Martha Jane). This is an excellent family. Tom Owen and Nell Owen have two sons and a daughter. The first son is called Jim and the second John. The daughter is named Melissa. The younger Jim Owen and his wife Betsey have two sons and five daughters. Their names are Tom and John, and Mercy, Miriam, Sophia, Margaret, and Eliza. This family is a very nice family. The wife of John Owen is called Lucy and an excellent wife she is. She had five children. Three of them died and two are still living.

O ye Americans, O ye people of North Carolina. Have you among you a family like this family, having so much love to God as they? Formerly I, Omar, loved to read the book of the Koran the famous. General Jim Owen and his wife used to read the gospel, and they read it to me very much—the gospel of God, our Lord, our Creator, our King, he that orders all our circumstances, health, and wealth willingly—not constrainedly according to his power. Open thou my heart to the gospel, to the way of uprightness. Thanks to the Lord of all worlds, thanks in abundance. He is plenteous in mercy and abundant in goodness. For the law was given by Moses, but grace and truth were by Jesus the Messiah.

■ ■ ■ ■

Handwritten notes in Arabic by Omar bin Said in his personal bible:

Omar's benediction: My name is Umaru, son of Said; my mother is Umhan Yasnik. May God comfort her resting place.

When I was a Mohammedan I prayed thus: In the name of God the Merciful, the compassionate, may God have mercy on the Prophet Mohammed. Thanks be to God, Lord of all worlds, the merciful the gracious, Lord of the day of Judgment; thee we serve, on thee we call for help. Direct us in the right way, the way of those on whom thou hast had mercy, with whom thou hast not been angry and who walk not in error. Amen.

But now I pray "Our Father," etc., in the words of our Lord Jesus the Messiah.

■ ■ ■ ■

Editor's Note: Although Omar bin Said converted to Christianity in 1821, his Presbyterian pastor and later scholars concluded that he maintained his Muslim faith throughout his life. For while he encouraged other Muslim Africans to convert to Christianity, he also included Muslim prayers and texts in his writings, as in this 1831 autobiography, written in Arabic and translated into English, which begins with memorized passages from the Koran. These excerpts are taken and arranged from *The Autobiography of Omar bin Said, an Enslaved Muslim in the United States*, written in 1831 and found in the National Humanities Center Resource Toolbox under "The Making of African American Identity: Vol. I, 1500-1865" at the Library of Congress. An African American Muslim from Chicago, Derrick Joshua "Tariq" Beard, is credited with rediscovering a collection of writings and artifacts of Omar bin Said, which was purchased from Beard by the Library of Congress in 2018 and is now available online at: https://www.loc.gov/collections/omar-Ibn-said-collection/about-this-collection. "This unique collection is very important for several reasons: first because Omar bin Said's autobiography is the only known extant autobiography of a slave written in Arabic in America. The importance of this lies in the fact that such a biography was not edited by Omar bin Said's owner, as those of other slaves written in English were, and is therefore surmised to be more authentic. Second, it is an important document that attests to the high level of education and the long tradition of a written culture that existed in Africa at the time. It also reveals that many Africans who were brought to the United States as slaves were followers of Islam, an Abrahamic and monotheistic faith. Such documentation counteracts prior assumptions of

African life and culture. The collection was originally put together by Theodore Dwight (1796-1866), an abolitionist and founding member of the American Ethnological Society, in the early 1860s."

Questions for Discussion and Reflection

1. Why do you think those who are powerless sometimes defer to people in power who treat them kindly? Have you ever done this, or has anyone done it to you? Tell the story.

2. Why are religious faith and traditions so often important to those without power? Why do some people adopt the beliefs and/or political philosophies of their oppressors? Give examples from history or your own experience.

3. Does it surprise you to learn that as many as 30% of enslaved Africans in the United States may have been Muslims? What are the implications of this fact for present-day America polity?

The Power of Reading and Writing

by Frederick Douglass

Frederick Douglass (1818-1895) was born in slavery near Easton in Talbot County, Maryland, and was named Frederick Augustus Washington Bailey. As a young boy he was sent to Baltimore to be a house servant, where he learned to read and write with the assistance of his master's wife. In 1838, he escaped from slavery and went to New York City, where he married Anna Murray, a free woman of color whom he had met in Baltimore. Soon thereafter he changed his name to Frederick Douglass. In 1841, he addressed a convention of the Massachusetts Anti-Slavery Society in Nantucket, Massachusetts, and so greatly impressed the group that they immediately employed him as an organizer. He was such an impressive orator that numerous persons doubted if he had ever been enslaved, so he wrote *The Narrative of the Life of Frederick Douglass: An American Slave* in 1845. This is an excerpt from Chapter VII of that book.

I was now about twelve years old, and the thought of being a slave for life began to bear heavily upon my heart. Just about this time, I got hold of a book entitled *The Columbian Orator* [by David W. Blight, published in 1797]. Every opportunity I got, I used to read this book. Among much of other interesting matter, I found in it a dialogue between a master and his slave. The slave was represented as having run away from his master three times. The dialogue represented the conversation which took place between them, when the slave was retaken the third time. In this dialogue, the whole argument in behalf of slavery was brought forward by the master, all of which was disposed of by the slave.

The slave was made to say some very smart as well as impressive things in reply to his master—things which had the desired though unexpected effect; for the conversation resulted in the voluntary emancipation of the slave on the part of the master. In the same book, I met with one of [Arthur O'Connor's] mighty speeches on and in behalf of Catholic emancipation. These were choice documents to me. I read them over and over again with unabated interest. They gave tongue to interesting thoughts of my own soul, which had frequently flashed through my mind and died away for want of utterance. The moral which I gained from the dialogue was the power of truth over the conscience of even a slaveholder. What I got from O'Connor was a bold denunciation of slavery and a powerful vindication of human rights.

The reading of these documents enabled me to utter my thoughts and to meet the arguments brought forward to sustain slavery; but while they relieved me of one difficulty, they brought on another even more painful than the one of which I was relieved. The more I read, the more I was led to abhor and detest my enslavers. I could regard them in no other light than a band of successful robbers who had left their homes and gone to Africa and stolen us from our homes and in a strange land reduced us to slavery. I loathed them as being the meanest as well as the most wicked of human beings. As I read and contemplated the subject, behold, that very discontentment which my owner Master Hugh had predicted would follow my learning to read had already come—to torment and sting my soul to unutterable anguish. As I writhed under it, I would at times feel that learning to read had been a curse rather than a blessing. It had given me a view of my wretched condition, without the remedy. It opened my eyes to the horrible pit, but to no ladder upon which to get out. In moments of agony, I envied my fellow-slaves for their stupidity. I have often wished myself a beast. I preferred the condition of the meanest reptile to my own. Anything, no matter what, to get rid of thinking! It was this everlasting thinking of my condition that tormented me.

■ ■ ■ ■

There was no getting rid of thinking. It was pressed upon me by every object within sight or hearing, animate or inanimate. The silver trump of freedom had roused my soul to eternal wakefulness. Freedom now appeared, to disappear no more forever. It was heard in every sound and seen in every thing. It was ever present to torment me with a sense of my wretched condition. I saw nothing without seeing it, I heard nothing without hearing it, and felt nothing without feeling it. It looked from every star, it smiled in every calm, breathed in every wind, and moved in every storm. I often found myself regretting my own existence and wishing myself dead; and but for the hope of being free, I have no doubt but that I should have killed myself or done something for which I should have been killed.

While in this state of mind, I was eager to hear anyone speak of slavery. I was a ready listener. Every little while, I would hear something about

the abolitionists. It was some time before I found what the word "abolitionists" meant, but it was always used in such connections as to make it an
interesting word to me. If a slave ran away and succeeded in getting clear,
or if a slave killed his master, set fire to a barn, or did anything very wrong
in the mind of a slaveholder, it was spoken of as the "fruit of abolition."
Hearing the word in this connection very often, I set about learning what
it meant. The dictionary afforded me little or no help. I found it was "the
act of abolishing," but then I did not know what was to be abolished. Here
I was perplexed. I did not dare to ask anyone about its meaning, for I was
satisfied that it was something they wanted me to know very little about.
After a patient waiting, I got one of our city papers containing an account
of the number of petitions from the north praying for the abolition of slavery in the District of Columbia and of the slave trade between the States.
From this time, I understood the words "abolition" and "abolitionist" and
always drew near when that word was spoken, expecting to hear something
of importance to myself and my fellow-slaves.

The light broke in upon me by degrees. I went one day down on the
wharf of a Mr. Waters, and seeing two Irishmen unloading a scow of stone
I went, unasked, and helped them. When we had finished, one of them
came to me and asked me if I were a slave. I told him I was. He asked, "Are
ye a slave for life?" I told him that I was. The good Irishman seemed to be
deeply affected by the statement. He said to the other that it was a pity
so fine a little fellow as myself should be a slave for life. He said it was a
shame to hold me. They both advised me to run away to the north, that I
should find friends there, and that I should be free. I pretended not to be

interested in what they said and treated them as if I did not understand them; for I feared they might be treacherous. White men have been known to encourage slaves to escape and then, to get the reward, catch them and return them to their masters. I was afraid that these seemingly good men might use me so; but I nevertheless remembered their advice, and from that time I resolved to run away.

■ ■ ■ ■

I looked forward to a time at which it would be safe for me to escape. I was too young to think of doing so immediately; besides, I wished to learn how to write, as I might have occasion to write my own past. I consoled myself with the hope that I should one day find a good chance. Meanwhile, I would learn to write.

The idea as to how I might learn to write was suggested to me by being in Durgin and Bailey's shipyard in Baltimore and frequently seeing the ship carpenters, after hewing and getting a piece of timber ready for use, write on the timber the name of that part of the ship for which it was intended. When a piece of timber was intended for the larboard side, it would be marked thus—"L." When a piece was for the starboard side, it would be marked thus—"S." A piece for the larboard side forward, would be marked thus—"L.F." When a piece was for starboard side forward, it would be marked thus—"S.F." For larboard aft, it would be marked thus—"L.A." For starboard aft, it would be marked thus—"S.A." I soon learned the names of these letters and for what they were intended when placed upon a piece of timber in the shipyard. I immediately commenced copying them and in a short time was able to make the four letters named. After that, when I met with any boy who I knew could write, I would tell him I could write as well as he. The next word would be, "I don't believe you. Let me see you try it." I would then make the letters which I had been so fortunate as to learn and ask him to beat that. In this way I got a good many lessons in writing, which it is quite possible I should never have gotten in any other way.

During this time, my copybook was the board fence, brick wall, and pavement; my pen and ink was a lump of chalk. With these, I learned mainly how to write. I then commenced and continued copying the letters in Webster's Spelling Book until I could make them all without looking on the book. By this time, my little Master Thomas had gone to school and learned how to write and had written over a number of copybooks. These had been brought home and shown to some of our near neighbors and then laid aside. My mistress used to go to class meeting at the Wilk Street meetinghouse every Monday afternoon and leave me to take care of the house. When left thus, I used to spend the time in writing in the spaces left in Master Thomas's copybook, copying what he had written. I continued to do this until I could write a hand very similar to that of Master Thomas. Thus, after a long, tedious effort for years, I finally succeeded in learning how to write.

■ ■ ■ ■

Editor's Note: During the Civil War, Douglass assisted in the recruiting of freed enslaved men for the 54th and 55th Massachusetts Regiments and consistently argued for the emancipation of those enslaved. After the war, he was active in securing and protecting the rights of the freed slaves. In his later years, at different times, he was secretary of the Santo Domingo Commission, a marshal and recorder of deeds of the District of Columbia, and United States Minister to Haiti. His other autobiographical works are *My Bondage and My Freedom* and *The Life and Times of Frederick Douglass*, published in 1855 and 1881 respectively.

Questions for Discussion and Reflection

1. What strikes you about Douglass' passion to learn to read and write? How important is reading and writing in today's online culture? Explain your answer.
2. Does writing increase your personal power? Why? How? Give some examples from your own life.
3. Name some issues in the world today that are as important as the abolition of slavery. Who is doing something about them? Be specific. What might you do to help?

The Escape

by Sojourner Truth

Sojourner Truth (1797-1883), was born into slavery as Isabella Baumfree. She was the first African-American woman to win a court case when she reclaimed her son from the man who sold him back into slavery after his emancipation. One of the most important documents of slavery ever written, *Narrative of Sojourner Truth: A Northern Slave*, is the eloquent autobiography of a woman who became a pioneer in the struggles for racial and sexual equality. The spiritual, inspiring narrative bears witness to Sojourner Truth's thirty years as an enslaved woman in upstate New York. This excerpt is taken from the sections titled "Slaveholder's Promises" and "Her Escape." It is written in the third person.

After emancipation had been decreed by the State, some years before the time fixed for its consummation, Isabella's master told her if she would do well, and be faithful, he would give her "free papers" one year before she was legally free by statute. In the year 1826, she had a badly diseased hand, which greatly diminished her usefulness; and on the arrival of July 4, 1827, the time specified for her receiving her "free papers," she claimed the fulfillment of her master's promise; but he refused granting it, on account (as he alleged) of the loss he had sustained by her hand. She pleaded that she had worked all the time and done many things she was not wholly able to do, although she knew she had been less useful than formerly; but her master remained inflexible. Her very faithfulness probably operated against her now, and he found it less easy than he thought to give up the profits of his faithful "Bell," who had so long done him efficient service.

But Isabella inwardly determined that she would remain quietly with him only until she had spun his wool—about one hundred pounds—and then she would leave him, taking the rest of the time to herself. "Ah!" she says, with emphasis that cannot be written, "the slaveholders are TERRIBLE for promising to give you this or that, or such and such a privilege, if you will do thus and so; and when the time of fulfillment comes and one claims the promise they, forsooth, recollect nothing of the kind: and you are, like as not, taunted with being a LIAR or, at best, the slave is accused of not having performed his or her part or condition of the contract."

"Oh!" said Isabella, "I have felt as if I could not live through the operation sometimes. Just think of us—so eager for our pleasures, and just foolish enough to keep feeding and feeding ourselves up with the idea that we should get what had been thus fairly promised; and when we think it is almost in our hands, find ourselves flatly denied! Just think—how could we bear it?

■ ■ ■ ■

Why, there was a Charles Brodhead, who promised his slave Ned that when harvesting was over he might go and see his wife, who lived some twenty or thirty miles off. So Ned worked early and late, and as soon as the harvest was all in he claimed the promised boon. His master said he had merely told him he "would see if he could go, when the harvest was over; but now he saw that he could not go." But Ned, who still claimed a positive promise on which he had fully depended, went on cleaning his shoes. His master asked him if he intended going, and on his replying "yes," took up a sled-stick that lay near him and gave his master such a blow on the head as broke his skull, killing him dead on the spot. The poor colored people all felt struck down by the blow. Ah, and well they might! Yet it was but one of a long series of bloody, and other most effectual blows, struck against their liberty and their lives.

■ ■ ■ ■

But to return from our digression. Isabella, the subject of this narrative was to have been free July 4, 1827, but she continued with her master till the wool was spun and the heaviest of the "fall's work" closed up, when she concluded to take her freedom into her own hands and seek her fortune in some other place.

The question in Isabella's mind, and one not easily solved, now was, "How can I get away?" So, as was her usual custom, she "told God she was afraid to go in the night and in the day everybody would see her." At length, the thought came to her that she could leave just before the day dawned and get out of the neighborhood where she was known before the people were much astir. "Yes," said she fervently, "that's a good thought! Thank you, God, for that thought!"

So, receiving it as coming direct from God, she acted upon it; and one fine morning, a little before day-break, she might have been seen stepping stealthily away from the rear of Master Dumont's house, her infant on one arm and her wardrobe on the other—the bulk and weight of which, probably, she never found so convenient as on the present occasion, a cotton handkerchief containing both her clothes and her provisions.

As she gained the summit of a high hill, a considerable distance from her master's, the sun offended her by coming forth in all his pristine splendor. She thought it never was so light before; indeed, she thought it much too light. She stopped to look about her and ascertain if her pursuers were yet in sight. No one appeared and, for the first time, the question came up for settlement: "Where, and to whom, shall I go?

In all her thoughts of getting away, she had not once asked herself whither she should direct her steps. She sat down, fed her infant, and again turning her thoughts to God, her only help, she prayed him to direct her to some safe asylum. And soon it occurred to her that there was a man living somewhere in the direction she had been pursuing by the name of Levi Rowe, whom she had known and who, she thought, would be likely to befriend her. She accordingly pursued her way to his house, where she found him ready to entertain and assist her, though he was then on his deathbed.

He bade her partake of the hospitalities of his house, said he knew of two good places where she might get in, and requested his wife to show her where they were to be found. As soon as she came in sight of the first house, she recollected having seen it and its inhabitants before and instantly exclaimed, "That's the place for me; I shall stop there." She went there

22

and found the good people of the house, Mr. and Mrs. Van Wagener, absent; but she was kindly received and hospitably entertained by their excellent mother, till the return of her children. When they arrived, she made her case known to them. They listened to her story, assuring her they never turned the needy away, and willingly gave her employment.

■ ■ ■ ■

She had not been there long before her old master, Mr. Dumont, appeared as she had anticipated; for when she took French leave of him she resolved not to go too far from him and not put him to as much trouble in looking her up—for the latter he was sure to do—as he had done with Tom and Jack when they ran away from him a short time before. This was very considerate in Isabella, to say the least, and a proof that "like begets like." Dumont had often considered her feelings, though not always, and she was equally considerate.

When her master saw her, he said, "Well, Bell, so you've run away from me."

"No, I did not run away," she said. "I walked away by day-light, because you had promised me a year of my time."

His reply was, "You must go back with me."

But her decisive answer was, "No, I won't go back with you."

He said, "Well, I shall take the child."

This also was stoutly negated by Isabella.

Mr. Isaac S. Van Wagener then interposed, saying he had never been in the practice of buying and selling slaves and did not believe in slavery; but rather than have Isabella taken back by force he would buy her services for the balance of the year—for which her former master charged twenty dollars and five in addition for the child. The sum was paid, and Dumont departed; but not till he had heard Mr. Van Wagener tell Isabella not to call him master—adding, "there is but one master; and he who is your master is my master."

Isabella inquired what she should call him, and he answered, "Call me Isaac Van Wagener, and my wife is Maria Van Wagener." Isabella could not understand this and thought it a mighty change, as it most truly was, to go from a master whose word was law to simple Isaac S. Van Wagener, who was master to no one....

Editor's Note: *Narrative of Sojourner Truth* is a partial autobiography of the woman who became a pioneer in the struggles for racial and sexual equality. With an eloquence that resonates more than a century after its original publication in 1850, the narrative bears witness to Sojourner Truth's thirty years of bondage in upstate New York and to the mystical revelations that turned her into a passionate and indefatigable abolitionist.

Questions for Discussion and Reflection

1. How do powerless people exercise power? Give examples from Sojourner Truth's story above.

2. Have you ever been in a powerless situation? How did you react? Have you ever tried to help a powerless person? Tell the story of what happened.

3. What is the power of knowing your own family history and that of your people? What happens when it is hidden from you or destroyed in some way? Give examples from history.

Why Shouldn't a Woman Be a Reformer?

by Lucretia Mott

Lucretia Mott (1793-1880) was a Quaker minister, an abolitionist, a suffragette, and a women's-rights advocate. Along with Elizabeth Cady Stanton, she initiated the Seneca Falls Women's rights Convention in 1848, where she helped write the "Declaration of Sentiments." This is an excerpt from a speech Mott delivered at the 5th National Women's Rights Convention in Philadelphia on October 18, 1854.

have no prepared address to deliver to you, being unaccustomed to speak in that way; but I felt a wish to offer some views for your consideration, though in a desultory manner, which may lead to such reflection and discussion as will present the subject in a true light.

Why should not a woman seek to be a reformer? If she is to shrink from being such an iconoclast as shall "break the image of man's lower worship," as so long held up to view; if she is to fear to exercise her reason, and her noblest powers, lest she should be thought to "attempt to act like a man" and not "acknowledge his supremacy;" if she is to be satisfied with the narrow sphere assigned her by man, nor aspire to a higher, lest she should transcend the bounds of female delicacy; truly it is a mournful prospect for women. We would admit all the difference that our great and beneficent Creator has made, in the relation of man and woman, nor would we seek to disturb this relation; but we deny that the present position of woman in her true sphere of usefulness; nor will she attain to this sphere, until the disabilities and disadvantages—religious, civil, and social—that impede her progress are removed out of her way. These restrictions have enervated her mind and paralyzed her powers. While man assumes that the present is the original state designed for woman, that the existing "differences are not arbitrary nor the result of accident" but grounded in nature, she will not make the necessary effort to obtain her just rights, lest it should subject her to the kind of scorn and contemptuous manner in which she has been spoken of....

The question is often asked, "What does woman want, more than she [already] enjoys? What is she seeking to obtain? Of what rights is she deprived? What privileges are withheld from her?"

I answer: She asks nothing as favor but as right; she wants to be acknowledged a moral, responsible being. She is seeking not to be governed by laws in the making of which she has no voice. She is deprived of almost every right in civil society and is a cipher in the nation, except in the right of presenting a petition. In religious society her disabilities have greatly retarded her progress. Her exclusion from the pulpit or ministry, her duties marked out for her by her equal brother man subject to creeds, rules, and disciplines made for her by him, is unworthy her true dignity....

▓ ▓ ▓ ▓

An article in one of the daily papers lately presented the condition of needle-women in England. There might be a presentation of this class in our own country that would make the heart bleed. Public attention should be turned to this subject in order that avenues of more profitable employment may be opened to women, equally with men, may follow with respectability and success. Their talents and energies should be called forth and their powers brought into the highest exercise. The efforts of women in France are sometimes pointed to in ridicule and sarcasm, but depend upon it, the opening of profitable employment to women in that country is doing much for the enfranchisement of the sex. In England and America, it is not an uncommon thing for a wife to take up the business of her deceased husband and carry it on with success.

Our respected British Consul stated to me a circumstance that occurred some years ago of an editor of a political paper having died in England; it was proposed to his wife, an able writer, to take the editorial chair. She accepted. The patronage of the paper was greatly increased, and she a short time later retired from her labors with a handsome fortune. In that country, however, the opportunities are by no means general for woman's elevation.

In visiting the public school in London a few years since, I noticed that the boys were employed in linear drawing and instructed upon the blackboard in the higher branches of arithmetic and mathematics while the girls, after a short exercise in the mere elements of arithmetic, were seated during the bright hours of the morning stitching wristbands. I asked why there should be this difference made; why the girls too should not have the blackboard? The answer was that that they would not probably fill any station in society requiring such knowledge....

■ ■ ■ ■

Women's property has been taxed equally with that of men to sustain colleges endowed by the States; but women have not been permitted to enter those high seminaries of learning. Within a few year, however, some colleges have been instituted where young women are admitted upon nearly equal terms with young men; and numbers are availing themselves of their long-denied rights. This is among the signs of the times, indicative of an advance for women. The book of knowledge is not opened to her in vain. Already is she aiming to occupy important posts of honor and profit in our country. We have three female editors in our State and some in other States of the Union. Numbers [of women] are entering the medical profession; one received a diploma last year; others are preparing for a like result.

Let women then go on, not asking favors but claiming as right the removal of all hindrances to her elevation in the scale of being; let her receive encouragement for the proper cultivation of all her power so that she may enter profitably into the active business of life; employing her physical being by proper exercise and observance of the laws of health. Let her not be ambitious to display a fair hand to promenade the fashionable streets of our city but rather, coveting earnestly the best gives, let her strive to occupy such walks in society as will befit her true dignity in all the relations of life.

No fear that she will then transcend the proper limits of female delicacy. True modesty will be as fully preserved in acting out those important vocations as in the nursery or at the fireside ministering to man's self-indulgence. Then in the marriage union the independence of the husband and wife will be equal, their dependence mutual, and their obligations reciprocal.

In conclusion, let me say [to all women] with Nathaniel P. Willis: "Credit not the old-fashioned absurdity that woman's is a secondary lot, ministering to the necessities of her lord and master! It is a higher destiny I would award you. If your immortality is as complete and your gift of mind as capable as a man's of increase and elevation, I would put no wisdom of mine against God's evident allotment. I would charge you to water the undying bud and give it healthy culture and open its beauty to the sun; and then you may hope that when your life is bound up with another you will go on equally in in a fellowship that shall pervade every earthly interest."

■ ■ ■ ■

Editor's Note: Lucretia Mott and her husband were leaders in the Abolitionist movement, and she and other white and Black women founded the Philadelphia Female Anti-Slavery Society. Integrated from its founding, the organization opposed both slavery and racism, and developed close ties to Philadelphia's Black community. In 1850, she published the pamphlet *Discourse on Women* on the restrictions on women in Europe and the United States. In 1983, Lucretia Mott was inducted into the National Woman's Hall of Fame. The U.S. Treasury Department announced in 2016 that an image of Mott will appear on the back of a newly designed $10 bill, along with Sojourner Truth, Susan B. Anthony, Elizabeth Cady Stanton, Alice Paul, and the 1913 Woman Suffrage Procession. Designs for new $5, $10, and $20 bills were to be unveiled in 2020 in conjunction with the 100th anniversary of American women winning the right to vote via the Nineteenth Amendment in 1920.

Questions for Discussion and Reflection

1. Have you every been an "iconoclast" about anything? Describe what happened if you did. Explain why you never have, if you have not.
2. What is the role of writing, public speaking, assemblies, marches, and demonstrations in demanding societal change? Have you ever engaged in this kind of activity? Tell a story about why and what happened.
3. Are issues of powerlessness connected? Explain your answer. Give some examples.

The New Colossus

by Emma Lazarus

Emma Lazarus (1849-1887) was born in New York City to a wealthy sugar re-
fining family of Portuguese Sephardic Jewish descent whose roots extended to
the colonial days of New York City. In addition to writing poetry, including this
famous poem on the Statue of Liberty, Lazarus was also involved in charitable
work for refugees. At Ward's Island, she worked as an aide for Jewish immigrants
who had been detained by Castle Garden immigration officials. She was deeply
moved by the plight of the Russian Jews she met there, and these experiences
influenced her writing. Lazarus died in New York City on November 19, 1887, most
likely from Hodgkin's lymphoma, and was buried in New York City at Congregation Shearith Israel's Beth Olom Cemetery in Cypress Hills, Queens.

Not like the brazen giant of Greek fame,

With conquering limbs astride from land to land;

Here at our sea-washed, sunset gates shall stand

A mighty woman with a torch, whose flame

Is the imprisoned lightning, and her name

Mother of Exiles. From her beacon-hand

Glows world-wide welcome; her mild eyes command

The air-bridged harbor that twin cities frame.

"Keep, ancient lands, your storied pomp!" cries she

With silent lips. "Give me your tired, your poor,

Your huddled masses yearning to breathe free,

The wretched refuse of your teeming shore.

Send these, the homeless, tempest-tost to me,

I lift my lamp beside the golden door!"

■ ■ ■ ■

Editor's Note: In 1883, William Maxwell Evarts and author Constance Cary Harrison asked Emma Lazarus to compose a sonnet for the "Art Loan Fund Exhibition in Aid of the Bartholdi Pedestal Fund for the Statue of Liberty"—an art and literary auction to raise funds for the Statue's pedestal run by the American Committee for the Statue of Liberty. In turn, Lazarus, inspired by her own Sephardic Jewish heritage, her experiences working with refugees on Ward's Island, and the plight of the immigrant, wrote "The New Colossus" on November 2, 1883. After the auction, the sonnet appeared in Joseph Pulitzer's *New York World* as well as *The New York Times*. After its initial popularity, however, the sonnet slowly faded from public memory. It was not until 1901, years after Lazarus's death, that Georgina Schuyler, a friend of hers, found a book containing the sonnet in a bookshop and organized a civic effort to resurrect the lost work. Her efforts paid off, and in 1903 words from the sonnet were inscribed on a plaque and placed on the inner wall of the pedestal of the Statue of Liberty. Today, the plaque is on display inside the Statue's pedestal and an exact replica of the plaque can be found inside the Statue of Liberty Museum.

Questions for Discussion and Reflection

1. What are the power of symbols—statues, flags, plaques, even words on a page—for building power? Name one symbol which has moved you or that you used to motivate others. Tell the story of what happened.

2. Do poets and writers and other artists exercise power? In what ways? Explain your answer with examples.

3. Why is immigration about power? On both sides.

A Word to Tramps

by Lucy Gonzáles Parsons

Lucy (Lucia) Eldine Gonzáles Parsons (1851?-1942) specifically denied that she was a child of an enslaved person of African descent, claiming that she was born in Texas and her parents were Mexican and Native American, although her personal ethnic heritage is in considerable historical dispute. She described herself as a "Spanish-Indian maiden" to explain her dark complexion. On her death certificate her parents' names were listed as Pedro Díaz and Marites González, both born in Mexico. In 1871, she married Albert Parsons, whose *Waco Spectator* fought the Ku Klux Klan and demanded social and political equality for Black Americans. The white supremacy forces in Texas considered the couple dangerous and their marriage illegal and soon drove them from the state. This essay was published in *The Alarm*, vol. 1, no. 1, on October 4, 1884.

A word to the 30,000 now tramping the streets of this great city, with hands in pockets, gazing listlessly about you at the evidences of wealth and pleasure of which you own no part, not sufficient even to purchase yourself a bit of food with which to appease the pangs of hunger now gnawing at your vitals. It is with you and the hundreds of thousands of others similarly situated in this great land of plenty that I wish to have a word.

Have you not worked hard all your life since you were old enough for your labor to be of use in the production of wealth? Have you not toiled long, hard, and laboriously in producing wealth? And in all those years of drudgery, do you not know you have produced thousand upon thousands of dollars' worth of wealth, which you did not then, do not now, and—unless you act—never will, own any part in?

Do you not know when you were harnessed to a machine, and that machine harnessed to steam, and thus you toiled your ten, twelve, and sixteen hours in the twenty-four, that during this time in all these years you received only enough of your labor product to furnish yourself the bare, coarse necessaries of life and that when you wished to purchase anything for yourself and family it always had to be of the cheapest quality? If you wanted to go anywhere you had to wait until Sunday, so little did you receive for your unremitting toil that you dare not stop for a moment, as it were? And do you not know that with all your squeezing, pinching, and economizing, you never were enabled to keep but a few days ahead of the wolves of want? And that at last when the caprice of your employer saw fit to create an artificial famine by limiting production, that the fires in the furnace were extinguished, the iron horse to which you had been harnessed was stilled, the factory door locked up, you turned upon the highway a tramp, with hunger in your stomach and rags upon your back?

Yet your employer told you that it was over-production which made him close up. Who cared for the bitter tears and heart-pangs of your loving wife and helpless children, when you bid them a loving "God bless you!" and turned upon the tramper's road to seek employment elsewhere? I say, who cared for those heartaches and pains? You were only a "tramp" now—

to be execrated and denounced as a "worthless tramp and a vagrant" by that very class who had been engaged all those years in robbing you and yours.

■ ■ ■ ■

Then can you not see that the "good boss" or the "bad boss" cuts no figure whatever; that you are the common prey of both; and that their mission is simply robbery? Can you not see that it is the industrial system and not the "boss" that must be changed? Now, when all these bright summer and autumn days are going by, and you have no employment, and consequently can save up nothing, and when the winter's blast sweeps down from the north, and all the earth is wrapped in a shroud of ice, hearken not to the voice of the hypocrite who will tell you that it was ordained of God that "the poor ye have always!" or to the arrogant robber who will say to you that you "drank up all your wages last summer when you had work, and this is the reason why you have nothing now, and the workhouse or the woodyard is too good for you, and that you ought to be shot."

And shoot you they will, if you present your petitions in too emphatic a manner. So hearken not to them, but [listen]! Next winter, when the cold blasts are creeping through the rents in your seedy garments; when the frost is biting your feet through the holes in your worn-out shoes; and when all wretchedness seems to have centered in and upon you; when misery has marked you for her own and life has become a burden and existence a mockery; when you have walked the streets by day and slept upon hard boards by night and at last determined by your own hand to take your life—for you would rather go out into utter nothingness than to longer endure an existence which has become such a burden so perchance you determine to dash yourself into the cold embrace of the lake rather than longer suffer thus—halt before you commit this last tragic act in the drama of your simple existence. Stop!

■ ■ ■ ■

Is there nothing you can do to insure those whom you are about to orphan against a like fate? The waves will only dash over you in mockery of your rash act. But stroll you down the avenues of the rich and look through the magnificent plate windows into their voluptuous homes, and here you will discover the very identical robbers who have despoiled you and yours. Then let your tragedy be enacted here! Awaken them from their wanton sports at your expense. Send forth your petition and let them read it by the red glare of destruction. Thus when you cast "one long, lingering look behind," you can be assured that you have spoken to these robbers in the only language which they have ever been able to understand; for they have never yet deigned to notice any petition from their slaves that they were not compelled to read by the red glare bursting from the cannons' mouths or that was not handed to them upon the point of the sword.

You need no organization when you make up your mind to present this kind of petition. In fact, an organization would be a detriment to you; but each of you hungry tramps who read these lines avail yourselves of those little methods of warfare which science has placed in the hands of the poor man, and you will become a power in this or any other land. Learn the use of explosives!

■ ■ ■ ■

Editor's Note: When Lucy and Albert Parsons reached Chicago in 1873, they began a family and threw themselves into two new militant movements—one to build strong industrial unions and the other to agitate for socialism. Lucy concentrated on organizing working women and Albert became a famous radical organizer and speaker, one of the few important union leaders in Chicago who was not an immigrant. In 1886, the couple and their two children stepped onto Michigan Avenue to lead 80,000 working people in the world's first May Day parade and a demand for the eight-hour day. A protest rally called by Albert and others a few days after May Day became known as the Haymarket Riot when seven Chicago policemen died in a bomb blast. No evidence has ever been found pointing to those who made or detonated the bomb, but Albert Parsons and seven immigrant union leaders were arrested. Albert was one of four protestors who were eventually executed. When Lucy led the campaign to win a new trial, one Chicago official called her "more dangerous than a thousand rioters." Though Lucy had justified direct action against those who used violence against workers in the essay above, she later suggested very different strategies, including the formation of labor unions, organizing demonstrations around poverty and unemployment, urging women to fight for equality, and calling for the use of nonviolence resistance—telling workers they shouldn't "strike and go out and starve, but strike and remain in and take possession of the necessary property of production." Lucy Parsons continued to give fiery speeches in Chicago's Bughouse Square into her eighties, where she inspired a young Studs Terkel. She died on March 7, 1942, in a house fire in the Avondale neighborhood of Chicago. She is buried near her husband, Albert, at Waldheim Cemetery (now Forest Home Cemetery), near the Haymarket Martyrs' Monument in Forest Park, Illinois.

Questions for Discussion and Reflection

1. Is there ever a time when violence is acceptable or effective in protesting injustice? Explain your answer.
2. What is the role of petitions, marches, and demonstrations by the powerless? What are the alternatives for promoting justice? Give examples from your own life.
3. What is the role of rhetoric—both written and spoken—in organizing for power?

War with the Politicians

by Ohiyesa

Charles Alexander Eastman (1858-1939), whose Native American name is Ohiyesa (which means "The Winner"), was the son of a full-blooded Santee Sioux father. His mother, who died shortly after Ohiyesa's birth, was the granddaughter of a Sioux chief who married a U.S. army officer. Ohiyesa was raised in what is now Minnesota until 1862, when he became separated from his father, three brothers, and a sister and then lived a nomadic life under the care of an uncle and grandmother. At age 11, his father reappeared and had taken the last name of his wife's father, Eastman. He had adopted the culture and religion of the white settlers around Flandreau in the Dakota Territory. Ohiyesa took the name Charles Eastman and eventually graduated from Dartmouth College and received a degree in medicine from Boston College. His first medical position was as Government Physician for the Sioux at the Pine Ridge reservation in what is now South Dakota. This essay is excerpted from chapter VIII of his book, *From the Deep Woods to Civilization.*

have tried to make it clear that there was no "Indian outbreak" in 1890-91 and that such trouble as we had may justly be charged to the dishonest politicians, who through unfit appointees first robbed the Indians, then bullied them, and finally in a panic called for troops to suppress them. From my first days at Pine Ridge, certain Indians and white people had taken every occasion to whisper into my reluctant ears the tale of wrongs, real or fancied, committed by responsible officials on the reservation, or by their connivance. To me these stones were unbelievable, from the point of view of common decency. I held that a great government such as ours would never condone or permit any such practices while administering large trust funds and standing in the relation of guardian to a race made helpless by lack of education and of legal safeguards. At that time, I had not dreamed what American politics really is, and I had the most exalted admiration for our noted public men. Accordingly, I dismissed these reports as mere gossip or the inventions of mischief-makers.

In March of 1891, I was invited to address the Congregational Club of Chicago, and on my arrival in the city I found to my surprise that the press still fostered the illusion of a general Indian uprising in the spring. It was reported that all the towns adjoining the Sioux reservations had organized and were regularly drilling a home guard for their protection. These alarmists seemed either ignorant or forgetful of the fact that there were only about thirty thousand Sioux altogether, or perhaps six thousand men of fighting age, more than half of whom had been civilized and Christianized for a generation and had just proved their loyalty and steadfastness through a trying time. Furthermore, the leaders of the late "hostiles" were even then in confinement in Fort Sheridan. When I was approached by the reporters, I reminded them of this and said that everything was quiet in the field, but if there were any danger from the ghost dancers, Chicago was in the most immediate peril!

Fortunately, we had in the office of Commissioner of Indian Affairs at that time a sincere man, and one who was deeply in sympathy with educational and missionary work, General Morgan of Indiana. He was a lover of fair play, and throughout my fight for justice he gave me all the support within his power....

■ ■ ■ ■

In spite of all that I had gone through, life was not yet a serious matter to me. I had faith in everyone, and accepted civilization and Christianity at their face value—a great mistake, as I was to learn later on. I had come back to my people not to minister to their physical needs alone but to be a missionary in every sense of the word, and as I was much struck with the loss of manliness and independence in these, the first "reservation Indians" I had ever known, I longed above all things to help them to regain their self-respect.

On June 18, 1891, I was married to Elaine Goodale in the Church of the Ascension, New York City.... After spending a few days with my wife's family, we returned to the West by way of Montreal. At Flandreau, South Dakota, my brother John had gathered all the family and the whole band of Flandreau Sioux to welcome us. There my father had brought me home from Canada, an absolute wild Indian, only eighteen years earlier! My honored father had been dead for some years, but my brothers had arranged to have a handsome memorial to him erected and unveiled at that time.

Our new home was building when we reached Pine Ridge, and my wife and I started life together in the old barracks while planning the fin-

43

ishing and furnishing of the new. It was ready for us early in the fall. I had gained permission to add an open fireplace and a few other homelike touches at my own expense. We had the chiefs and leading men to dine with us, and quite as often some of the humbler Indians and poor old women were our guests. In fact, we kept open house, and the people loved to come and talk with us in their own tongue. My wife accompanied me on many of my trips now that I had a carriage, and was always prepared with clean clothing, bandages, and nourishing food for my needy patients....

■ ■ ■ ■

Meanwhile, though the troops had been recalled, we were under military agents; there were several changes, and our relations were pleasant with them all. The time came for the small annual payment of treaty money, and a one-hundred-thousand-dollar payment for depredation claims was also to be made by a special disbursing agent. This payment was not made by check, as usual, but in cash, and I was asked to be one of the three witnesses. I told the special agent that, as I was almost constantly occupied, it would be impossible for me to witness the payment, which would take several days; but he assured me that if only one of the three were present at a time it would be sufficient and, understanding my duties to be only nominal, I consented.

I was in the office from time to time while the payment was going on and saw the people sign their names, generally by mark, on the roll which had been prepared, opposite the amount which each person was supposed to receive; then a clerk at another desk handed that person in turn a hand-ful of silver and bills, and he or she passed out [the door] as quickly as possible. The money was not counted out to the person, and he or she was given no chance to count it until he got outside. Even then, many could not count it and did not clearly understand how much it ought to be, while the traders and others were close at hand to get all or part of it without delay.

Before I knew it, I was approached by one and another who declared that they had not received the full amount, and I found that in numerous cases reliable persons had counted the cash as soon as the payees came out of the office. A very able white teacher, a college graduate, counted for several old people who were proteges of hers; an influential native minister did the same, and so did several others; all reported that the amount was short from ten to fifteen per cent. When anyone brought a shortage to the attention of the disbursing agent or his clerk, he was curtly told that he had made a mistake or lost some of the money.

The complaints grew louder, and other suspicious circumstances were reported. Within a few days it was declared that an investigation would be ordered. The agent who had made the payment and immediately left the agency, being informed of the situation, came back and tried to procure affidavits to show that it had been an honest payment. He urged me to sign, as one of the original witnesses, arguing that I had already committed myself. I refused. I said, "After all, I did not see the full amount paid to each claimant. As the payment was conducted, it was impossible for me to do so. I trusted you, therefore I allowed you to use my name, but I don't care to sign again."

The regular agent in charge of our Indians at the time was, as I have said, an army officer, with military ideas of discipline. Like myself, he had been in the field much of the time while the payment was going on but had officially vouched for its correctness and signed all the papers, and he took his stand upon this. He remonstrated with me for my position in the matter and did his best to avoid an investigation; but I was convinced that a gross fraud had been committed and, in my inexperience, I believed that it had only to be exposed to be corrected.

I determined to do all in my power to secure justice for those poor, helpless people, even though it must appear that I was careless in signing the original papers. I added my protest to that of others, and the department sent out a Quaker, an inspector whose record was excellent and who went about the work in a direct and straightforward way. He engaged a reliable interpreter and called in witnesses on both sides. At the end of a fortnight, he reported that about ten thousand dollars had been dishonestly withheld from the Indians. A few of the better educated and more influential, especially mixed bloods, had been paid in full, while the old and ignorant had lost as high as fifteen or twenty per cent of their money. Evidence in support of this decision was sent to Washington.

After a short interval, I learned with astonishment that the report of this trusted inspector had not been accepted by the Secretary of the Interior, who had ordered a second investigation to supersede the first. Naturally, the second investigation was a farce and quickly ended in "whitewashing" the special payment. The next step was to punish those who had testified for the Indians or tried to bring about an honest investigation in the face of official opposition. Of these, I had been perhaps the most active and outspoken.

■ ■ ■ ■

The usual method of disciplining agency Indians in such a case is to deprive them of various privileges, possibly of rations also, and sometimes to imprison them on trivial pretexts. White men with Indian wives, and missionaries, may be ordered off the reservation as "disturbers of the peace," while with Government employees, some grounds are usually found for their dismissal from the service.

I was promptly charged with "insubordination" and other things, but my good friend, General Morgan, then Commissioner, declined to entertain the charges and I, on my part, kept up the fight at Washington through influential friends and made every effort to prove my case or, rather, the case of the people, for I had at no time any personal interest in the payment. The local authorities followed the usual tactics and undertook to force a resignation by making my position at Pine Ridge intolerable. An Indian agent has almost autocratic power, and the conditions of life on an agency are such as to make every resident largely dependent upon his good will. We soon found ourselves hampered in our work and harassed by every imaginable annoyance. My requisitions were overlooked or "forgotten," and it became difficult to secure the necessaries of life. I would receive a curt written order to proceed without delay to some remote point to visit a certain alleged patient; then, before I had covered the distance, would be overtaken by a mounted policeman with arbitrary orders to return at once to the agency. On driving in rapidly and reporting to the agent's office for details of the supposed emergency, I might be rebuked for overdriving the horses and charged with neglect of some chronic case about which I had either never been informed or to which it had been physically impossible for me to give regular attention.

This sort of thing went on for several months, and I was finally summoned to Washington for a personal conference. I think I may safely say that my story was believed by Senators Dawes and Hoar, and by Commissioner Morgan also. I saw the Secretary of the Interior and the President, but they were non-committal. On my return, the same inspector who had whitewashed the payment was directed to investigate the "strained relations" between the agent and myself; and my wife, who had meantime published several very frank letters in influential Eastern papers, was made a party in the case.

I will not dwell upon the farcical nature of this "investigation." The inspector was almost openly against us from the start, and the upshot of the affair was that I was shortly offered a transfer. The agent could not be dislodged, and my position had become impossible. The superintendent of the boarding school, a clergyman, and one or two others who had fought on our side were also forced to leave. We had many other warm sympathizers who could not speak out without risking their livelihood.

My wife and I declined to accept the compromise, being utterly disillusioned and disgusted with these revelations of government mismanagement in the field and realizing the helplessness of the best-equipped

Indians to secure a fair deal for their people. Later experience, both my own and that of others, has confirmed me in this view. Had it not been for strong friends in the East and on the press, and the unusual boldness and disregard of personal considerations with which we had conducted the fight, I could not have lasted a month. All other means failing, these people will not hesitate to manufacture evidence against a man's or a woman's personal reputation in order to attain their ends.

It was a great disappointment to us both to give up our plans of work and our first home, to which we had devoted much loving thought and most of our little means; but it seemed to us then the only thing to do. We had not the heart to begin the same thing over again elsewhere. I resigned my position in the Indian service and removed with my family to the city of St. Paul, where I proposed to enter upon the independent practice of medicine.

■ ■ ■ ■

Editor's Note: Ohiyesa was the first Native American born-and-raised medical doctor (he served at Wounded Knee on the day following the massacre there). He was also helped found the Boy Scouts of America, based partly on his knowledge of Native American life. At the 1933 World Fair, he was presented with a special medal honoring his achievements as a Native American. He wrote eleven books, including *Indian Boyhood, The Soul of the Indian, Indian Child Life, The Indian Today,* and *From the Deep Woods to Civilization.* Ohiyesa is controversial to this day because he adopted essential elements of the dominant culture while retaining his deep appreciation of Native American beliefs and practices. In his Foreword to *From the Deep Woods to Civilization* he wrote: "It is clearly impossible to tell the whole story, but much that cannot be told may be read 'between the lines.' The broad outlines, the salient features of an uncommon experience are here set forth in the hope that they may strengthen for some readers the conception of our common humanity."

Questions for Discussion and Reflection

1. What are some of the unique issues organizers and community leaders face in working across cultural lines (including their own)? Have you experienced any of these issues yourself? If so, tell about them.

2. Name some of the dangers oppressed people must be aware of in working with government or social service providers. Give some examples from your own life or from history.

3. Is it ever the right decision to give up and move on from a situation in which you are powerless? Debate the pros and cons, based on your own experience.

The March of the Mill Children

by Mother Jones

Mary Harris "Mother" Jones (1837-1930), was born in Cork, Ireland, and became a prominent American labor and community organizer who helped coordinate major strikes and co-founded the Industrial Workers of the World. In 1871, she began working as an organizer for the Knights of Labor and the United Mine Workers union. She was a very effective speaker, punctuating her speeches with stories, audience participation, humor, and dramatic stunts. In 1903, upset about the lax enforcement of the child labor laws in the Pennsylvania mines and silk mills, she organized a Children's March from Philadelphia to the home of the then president, Theodore Roosevelt, in Oyster Bay, New York.

In the spring of 1903, I went to Kensington, Pennsylvania, where seventy-five thousand textile workers were on strike. Of this number, at least ten thousand were little children. The workers were striking for more pay and shorter hours. Every day little children came into Union Headquarters, some with their hands off, some with the thumb missing, some with their fingers off at the knuckle. They were stooped things, round shouldered and skinny. Many of them were not over ten years of age, the state law prohibited their working before they were twelve years of age.

The law was poorly enforced, and the mothers of these children often swore falsely as to their children's age. In a single block in Kensington, fourteen women, mothers of twenty-two children all under twelve, explained it was a question of starvation or perjury. That the fathers had been killed or maimed at the mines.

I asked the newspaper men why they didn't publish the facts about child labor in Pennsylvania. They said they couldn't because the mill owners had stock in the papers. "Well, I've got stock in these little children." Said I, "And I'll arrange a little publicity."

We assembled a number of boys and girls one morning in Independence Park and from there we arranged to parade with banners to the courthouse where we would hold a meeting. A great crowd gathered in the public square in front of the city hall. I put the little boys with their fingers off and hands crushed and maimed on a platform. I held up their mutilated hands and showed them to the crowd and made the statement that Philadelphia's mansions were built on the broken bones, the quivering hearts, and the drooping heads of these children. That their little lives went out to make wealth for others. That neither state nor city officials paid any attention to these wrongs. That they did not care that these children were to be the future citizens of the nation.

The officials of the city hall were standing the open windows. I held the little ones of the mills high up above the heads of the crowd and pointed to their puny arms and legs and hollow chests. They were light to lift. I called upon the millionaire manufactures to cease their moral murders, and I cried to the officials in the open windows opposite, "Someday the workers will take possession of your city hall and, when we do, no child will be sacrificed on the altar of profit."

The officials quickly closed the windows, as they had closed their eyes and hearts.

■ ■ ■ ■

The reporters quoted my statement that Philadelphia mansions were built on the broken bones and quivering hearts of children. The Philadelphia papers and the New York papers got into a squabble with each other over the question. The universities discussed it. Preachers began talking. That was what I wanted. Public attention on the subject of child labor.

The matter quieted down for a while and I concluded the people needed stirring up again. The Liberty Bell that a century ago rang out for freedom against tyranny was touring the country, and crowds were coming to see it everywhere. That gave me an idea. These little children were striking for some of the freedom that childhood ought to have, and I decided that the children and I would go on a tour.

I asked some of the parents if they would let me have their little boys and girls for a week or ten days, promising to bring them back safe and sound. They consented. A man named Sweeny was marshal for our "army." A few men and women went with me to help with the children. They were on strike, and I thought they might as well have a little recreation. The children carried knapsacks on their backs which was a knife and fork, a tin cup, and a plate. We took along a wash boiler in which to cook the food on the road. One little fellow had a drum, and another had a fife. That was our band. We carried banners that said, "We want more schools and less hospitals." "We want time to play." "Prosperity is here. Where is ours?"

We started from Philadelphia where we held a great mass meeting. I then decided to go with the children to see President [Theodore] Roosevelt to ask him to have Congress pass a law prohibiting the exploitation of childhood. I thought that President Roosevelt might see these mill children and compare them with his own little ones, who were spending the summer on the seashore at Oyster Bay. I thought too, out of politeness, we might call on [J.P.] Morgan in Wall Street, who owned the mines where many of these children's fathers worked.

The children were very happy, having plenty to eat, taking baths in the brooks and rivers every day. I thought: When the strike is over and they go back to the mills, they will never have another holiday like this. All along the line of march, the farmers drove out to meet us with wagon loads of fruit and vegetables. Their wives brought the children clothes and money. The interurban trainmen would stop their trains and give us free rides.

Marshal Sweeny and I would go ahead to the towns and arrange sleeping quarters for the children and secure meeting halls. As we marched on, it grew terribly hot. There was no rain, and the roads were heavy with dust. From time to time we had to send some of the children back to their homes. They were too weak to stand the march.

We were on the outskirts of New Trenton, New Jersey, cooking our lunch in the wash boiler, when the conductor on the interurban [rail] car stopped and told us the police were coming down to notify us that we could not enter the town. There were mills in the town and the mill owners didn't like our coming. I said, "All right, the police will be just in time for lunch." Sure enough, the police came, and we invited them to dine with us. They looked at the little gathering of children with their tin plates and cups around the wash boiler. They just smiled and spoke kindly to the children and said nothing at all about not going into the city.

We went in, held our meeting, and it was the wives of the police who took the little children and cared for them that night, sending them back in the morning with a nice lunch rolled up in paper napkins.

Everywhere we had meetings; showing up with living children, the horrors of child labor. At one town the mayor said we could not hold a meeting because he did not have sufficient police protection. "These little children have never known any sort of protection, your honor," I said, "and they are used to going without it." He let us have our meeting. One night in Princeton, New Jersey, we slept in the big cool barn on Grover Cleveland's great estate. The heat became intense. There was much suffering in our ranks, for our little ones were not robust. The proprietor of the leading hotel sent for me. "Mother," he said, "order what you want and all you want for your army, and there's nothing to pay."

I called on the mayor of Princeton and asked for permission to speak opposite the campus of the university. I said I wanted to speak on higher education. The mayor gave me permission. A great crowd gathered, professors and students and the people; and I told them that the rich robbed these little children of any education of the lowest order that they might send their sons and daughters to places of higher education. That they used the hands and feet of little children that they might buy automobiles for their wives and police dogs for their daughters to talk French to. I said the mill owners take babies almost from the cradle. And I showed those professors children in our army who could scarcely read or write because they were working ten hours a day in the silk mills of Pennsylvania.

"Here's a textbook on economics," I said pointing to a little chap, James Ashworth, who was ten years old and was stooped over like an old man from carrying bundles of yarn that weighed seventy-five pounds. "He gets three dollars a week, and his sister who is fourteen gets six dollars. They work in a carpet factory ten hours a day while the children of the rich are getting their higher education."

That night we camped on the banks of Stony Brook, where years and years before the ragged Revolutionary Army camped, Washington's brave soldiers that made their fight for freedom. From Jersey City we marched to Hoboken. I sent a committee over to New York [City] Chief of Police Ebstein, asking for permission to march up Fourth Avenue to Madison Square, where I wanted to hold a meeting. The chief refused and forbade our entrance to the city.

■ ■ ■ ■

I went over myself to New York and saw Mayor Seth Low. The mayor was most courteous, but he said he would have to support the police commissioner. I asked him what the reason was for refusing us entrance to the city and he said that we were not citizens of New York.

"Oh, I think we will clear that up, Mr. Mayor," I said. "Permit me to call your attention to an incident which took place in this nation just a year ago. A piece of rotten royalty came over here from Germany, called Prince Henry. The Congress of the United States voted $45,000 to fill that fellow's stomach three weeks and to entertain him. His highness was getting $4,000,000 dividends out of the blood of the workers in this country. Was he a citizen of this land?"

"And it was reported, Mr. Mayor, that you and all the officials of New York and the University Club entertained that chap." And I repeated, "Was he a citizen of New York?"

"And it was reported, Mr. Mayor, that you and all the officials of New York and the University Club entertained that chap." And I repeated, "Was he a citizen of New York?"

"No, Mother," said the mayor, "he was not."

"And a Chinaman called Lee Woo was also entertained by the officials of New York. Was he a citizen of New York?"

"No, Mother, he was not."

"Did they ever create any wealth for our nation!"

"No, Mother, they did not," said he.

"Well, Mr. Mayor, these are the little citizens of the nation and they also produce its wealth. Aren't we entitled to enter your city!"

"Just wait" says he, and he called the commissioner of police over to his office. Well, finally they decided to let the army come in. We marched up Fourth Avenue to Madison Square, and police officers, captains, sergeants, roundsmen, and reserves from three precincts accompanied us. But the police would not let us hold a meeting in Madison Square. They insisted that the meeting be held in Twentieth Street.

I pointed out to the captain that the single-taxers were allowed to hold meetings in the square. "Yes," he said, "but they won't have twenty people and you might have twenty thousand." We marched to Twentieth Street. I told an immense crowd of the horrors of child labor in the mills around the anthracite region, and I showed them some of the children. I showed them Eddie Dunphy, a little fellow of twelve, whose job it was to sit all day on a high stool, handing the right thread to another worker. Eleven hours a day he sat on the high stool with dangerous machinery all about him. All day long, winter and summer, spring and fall, for three dollars a week. And then I showed them Gussie Rangnew, a little girl from whom all the childhood had gone. Her face was like an old woman's. Gussie packed stockings in a factory, eleven hours a day for a few cents a day.

We raised a lot of money for the strikers and hundreds of friends offered their homes to the little ones while we were in the city. The next day we went to Coney Island at the invitation of Mr. Bostick, who owned the wild animal show. The children had a wonderful day such as they never had in all their lives. After the exhibition of the trained animals, Mr. Bostick let me speak to the audience. There was a backdrop to the tiny stage of the Roman Coliseum, with the audience painted in and two Roman emperors down in front with their thumbs down. Right in front of the emperors were the empty iron cages of the animals. I put my little children in the cages, and they clung to the iron bars while I talked.

I told the crowd that the scene was typical of the aristocracy of employers with their thumb down to the little ones of the mills and factories and people sitting dumbly by:

+ We want President Roosevelt to hear the wail of the children who never have a chance to go to school but work eleven and twelve hours a day in the textile mills of Pennsylvania; who weave the carpets that he and you walk upon and the lace curtains in your windows and the clothes of the people. Fifty years ago, there was a cry against slavery and people gave up their lives to stop the selling of black children on the block. Today the white child is sold for two dollars a week to the manufacturers. Fifty years ago, the black babies were sold C.O.D. Today the white baby is sold on the installment plan.

+ In Georgia where children work day and night in the cotton mills they have just passed a bill to protect songbirds. What about little children from whom all song is gone?

+ I shall ask the president in the name of the aching hearts of these little ones that he emancipate them from slavery. I will tell the president that the prosperity he boasts of is the prosperity of the rich wrung from the poor and the helpless.

+ The trouble is that no one in Washington cares. I saw our legislators in one hour pass three bills for the relief of the railways, but when labor cries for aid for the children they will not listen.

+ I asked a man in prison once how he happened to be there, and he said he had stolen a pair of shoes. I told him that if he had stolen a railroad, he would be a United States Senator!

+ We are told that every American boy has the chance of being president. I tell you that these little boys in the iron cages would sell their chance any day for good square meals and a chance to play. These little toilers whom I have taken from the mills—deformed, dwarfed in body and soul, with nothing but toil before them—have never heard that they have a chance, the chance of every American male citizen, to become the president.

"You see those monkeys in those cages over there." I pointed to a side cage. "The professors are trying to teach them to talk. The monkeys are too wise for they fear that the manufacturers would buy them for slaves in their factories."

I saw a stylishly dressed young man down in the front of the audience. Several times he grinned. I stopped speaking and, pointing to him, I said, "Stop your smiling, young man! Leave this place! Go home and beg the mother who bore you in pain, as the mothers of these little children bore them, go home and beg her to give you brains and a heart."

He rose and slunk out, followed by the eyes of the children in the cage. The people stone still, and out in the rear a lion roared.

■ ■ ■ ■

The next day we left Coney Island for Manhattan Beach to visit Senator Platt, who had made an appointment to see me at nine o'clock in the morning. The children got stuck in the sand banks and I had a time cleaning the sand off the littlest ones. So we started to walk on the railroad track. I was told it was private property and we had to get off. Finally a saloon keeper showed us a short cut into the sacred grounds of the hotel and suddenly our army appeared in the lobby. The little fellows played "Hail, hail, the gang's all here" on their fifes and drums and Senator Platt, when he saw the little army, ran away through the back door.

I asked the manager if he would give children breakfast and charge it up to Senator, as we had an invitation to breakfast that morning with him. He gave us a private room and gave those children such a breakfast as they had never had in all their lives. I had breakfast too, and a reporter from of the Hearst papers, and I charged it all to Senator Platt.

We marched down to Oyster Bay, but the president refused to see us and would not answer my letters. But our march had done its work. We had drawn the attention of the nation to the crime of child labor. And while the strike of the textile workers in Kensington was lost and the children driven back to work, not long afterward the Pennsylvania legislature passed a child labor law that sent thousands of children home from the mills and kept thousands of others from entering the factory until they were fourteen years of age.

■ ■ ■ ■

Editor's note: This story is taken from *The Autobiography of Mother Jones*, written in 1925. In his Introduction to the book, Clarence Darrow wrote: "This little book is a story of a woman of action fired by a fine zeal. She defied calumny. She was not awed by guns or jails. She kept on her way regardless of friends and foes. She had but one love to which she was always true, and that was her cause. People of this type are bound to have conflicts within and without the ranks."

Questions for Discussion and Reflection

1. How or from whom might you learn to tell stories like Mother Jones? What are key elements in a good story? How important are the details and the characters? Why?

2. What is the role of street theater and public demonstrations in organizing? Give examples you have observed or participated in and tell when they worked and when they did not.

3. What is the role of your own passion and anger in organizing? Is it important to show/control them? Why or why not? How might you do so?

No Bibble-Babbling Mobs
of Scoundrels

by John L. Lewis

John Lllewllyn Lewis (1880-1969) was an American leader of organized labor who served as president of the United Mine Workers of America and was the founding president of the Committee (later Congress) of Industrial Organizations (CIO). This is an excerpt from his speech "Labor and the Nation," delivered on September 3, 1937, in Washington, DC.

In the steel industry, the corporations generally have accepted collective bargaining and negotiated wage agreements with the Committee for Industrial Organization. Eighty-five per cent of the industry is thus under contract [in 1937], and a peaceful relationship exists between the management and the workers. Written wage contracts have been negotiated with 399 steel companies covering 510,000 workers. One thousand thirty-one local lodges in 700 communities have been organized.

Five of the corporations in the steel industry elected to resist collective bargaining and undertook to destroy the steel workers' union. These companies filled their plants with industrial spies, assembled depots of guns and gas bombs, established barricades, controlled their communities with armed thugs, leased the police power of cities, and mobilized the military power of a state to guard them against the intrusion of collective bargaining within their plants.

During the strike [of 1937], eighteen steel workers were either shot to death or had their brains clubbed out by police or armed thugs in the pay of the steel companies. In Chicago, Mayor Kelly's police force was successful in killing ten strikers before they could escape the fury of the police, shooting eight of them in the back. One hundred sixty strikers were maimed and injured by police clubs, riot guns, and gas bombs, and were hospitalized. Hundreds of strikers were arrested, jailed, treated with brutality while incarcerated, and harassed by succeeding litigation. None but strikers were murdered, gassed, injured, jailed, or maltreated. No one had to die except the workers who were standing for the right guaranteed them by the Congress and written in the law.

The infamous Governor Davey of Ohio, successful in the last election because of his reiterated promises of fair treatment to labor, used the military power of the Commonwealth on the side of the Republican Steel Company and the Youngstown Sheet and Tube Company. Nearly half of the staggering military expenditure incident to the crushing of this strike in Ohio was borne by the federal government through the allocation of financial aid to the military establishment of the state.

The steel workers have now buried their dead, while the widows weep and watch their orphaned children become objects of public charity. The murder of these unarmed men has never been publicly rebuked by any authoritative officer of the state or federal government. Some of them, in extenuation, plead lack of jurisdiction, but murder as a crime against the moral code can always be rebuked without regard to the niceties of legalistic jurisdiction by those who profess to be the keepers of the public conscience.

Shortly after Kelly's police force in Chicago had indulged in their bloody orgy, Kelly came to Washington looking for political patronage. That patronage was forthcoming, and Kelly must believe that the killing of the strikers is no liability in partisan politics.

Meanwhile, the steel puppet Davey is still Governor of Ohio, but not for long, I think—not for long. The people of Ohio may be relied upon to mete our political justice to one who has betrayed his state, outraged the public conscience, and besmirched the public honor.

While the workers of the steel industry were going through blood and gas in defense of their rights and their homes and their families, elsewhere on the far-flung CIO front the hosts of labor were advancing and intelligent and permanent progress was being made. In scores of industries, plant after plant and company after company were negotiating sensible working agreements.

The men in the steel industry who sacrificed their all were nor merely aiding their fellows at home but were adding strength to the cause of their comrades in all industry. Labor was marching toward the goal of industrial democracy and contributing constructively toward a more rational arrangement of our domestic economy.

■ ■ ■ ■

Labor does not seek industrial strife. It wants peace, but a peace with justice. In the long struggle for labor's rights it has been patient and forbearing. Sabotage and destructive syndicalism have had no part in the American labor movement. Workers have kept faith in American institutions. Most of the conflicts, which have occurred have been when labor's right to live has been challenged and denied.

If there is to be peace in our industrial life, let employers recognize their obligation to their employees—at least to the degree set forth in existing statutes. Ordinary problems affecting wages, hours, and working conditions, in most instances, will quickly respond to negotiation in the council room.

The United States Chamber of Commerce, the National Association of Manufacturers, and similar groups representing industry and financial interests are rendering a disservice to the American people in their attempts to frustrate the organization of labor and in their refusal to accept collective bargaining as one of our economic institutions.

These groups are encouraging a systematic organization of vigilante groups to fight unionization under the sham pretext of local interests. They equip these vigilantes with tin hats, wooden clubs, gas masks, and lethal weapons and train them in the arts of brutality and oppression. They bring in snoops, finks, hatchet gangs, and Chowderhead Cohens to infest their plants and disturb the communities.

Fascist organizations have been launched and financed under the shabby pretext that the CIO movement is communistic. The real breeders of discontent and alien doctrines of government and philosophies subversive of good citizenship are such as these who take the law into their own hands. No tin-hat brigade of goose-stepping vigilantes or bibble-babbling mob of blackguarding and corporation-paid scoundrels will prevent the onward march of labor or divert its purpose to play its natural and rational part in the development of the economic, political, and social life of our nation.

Unionization, as opposed to communism, presupposes the relation of employment; it is based upon the wage system; and it recognizes fully and unreservedly the institution of private property and the right to investment profit. It is upon the fuller development of collective bargaining, the wider expansion of the labor movement, and the increased influence of labor in our national councils that the perpetuity of our democratic institutions must largely depend.

The organized workers of America, free in their industrial life, conscious partners in production, secure in their homes and enjoying a decent standard of living, will prove the finest bulwark against the intrusion of alien doctrines of government. Do those who have hatched this foolish cry of communism in the CIO fear the increased influence of labor in our democracy? Do they fear its influence will be cast on the side of shorter hours, a better system of distributed employment, better homes for the under-privileged, social security for the aged, a fairer distribution of the national income?

Certainly the workers that are being organized want a voice in the determination of these objectives of social justice. Certainly labor wants a fairer share in the national income. Assuredly labor wants a larger participation in increased productive efficiency. Obviously the population is entitled to participate in the fruits of the genius of our men of achievement in the field of the material sciences.

Labor has suffered, just as our farm population has suffered, from a viciously unequal distribution of the national income. In the exploitation of both classes of workers has been the source of panic and depression, and upon the economic welfare of both rests the best assurance of a sound and permanent prosperity.... Under the banner of the Committee for Industrial Organization American labor is on the march. Its objectives today are those it had in the beginning: to strive for the unionization of our unorganized millions of workers and for the acceptance of collective bargaining as a recognized American institution.

It seeks peace with the industrial world. It seeks cooperation and mutuality of effort with the agricultural population. It would avoid strikes. It would have its rights determined under the law by the peaceful negotiations and contract relationships that are supposed to characterize American commercial life. Until an aroused public opinion demands that employers accept that rule, labor has no recourse but to [either] surrender its rights or struggle for their realization with its own economic power.

■ ■ ■ ■

The objectives of this movement are not political in a partisan sense. Yet it is true that a political party which seeks the support of labor and makes pledges of good faith to labor must, in equity and good conscience, keep that faith and redeem those pledges.

The spectacle of august and dignified members of Congress, servants of the people and agents of the republic, skulking. in hallways and closets, hiding their faces in a party caucus to prevent a quorum from acting upon a labor measure, is one that emphasizes the perfidy of politicians and blasts the confidence of labor's millions in politicians' promises and statesmen's vows.

Labor next year cannot avoid the necessity of a political assay of the work and deeds of its so-called friends and its political beneficiaries. It must determine who are its friends in the arena of politics as elsewhere. It feels that its cause is just and that its friends should not view its struggle with neutral detachment or intone constant criticism of its activities.

Those who chant their praises of democracy but who lose no chance to drive their knives into labor's defenseless back must feel the weight of labor's woe even as its open adversaries must ever feel the thrust of labor's power.

Labor, like Israel, has many sorrows. Its women weep for their fallen and they lament for the future of the children of the race. It ill behooves one who has supped at labor's table and who has been sheltered in labor's house to curse with equal fervor and fine impartiality both labor and its adversaries when they become locked in deadly embrace.

I repeat that labor seeks peace and guarantees its own loyalty, but the voice of labor, insistent upon its rights, should not be annoying to the ears of justice or offensive to the conscience of the American people.

■ ■ ■ ■

Editor's Note: John L. Lewis was the subject of a fine biography by Saul Alinsky, the founder of the Industrial Areas Foundation (IAF). From the earliest days of the IAF with the Back of the Yards Community Council right up to today, unions have been involved with various IAF projects. Four current organizers with IAF—Lina Jamoul, Jonathan Lange, Ben Gordon, and Amy Vruno—are doing extensive work with organized labor.

Questions for Discussion and Reflection

1. Do you know much labor history? Why or why not? What are the main differences between the situation today and in the 1930s?

2. Why does organizing for power often come under violent attack? Should unions and community organizations fight back? How? Make a list of acceptable responses. Be specific.

3. What is the role of polarizing, personalizing, humor, and name-calling in organizing? Does "Bibble-Babbling Mobs of Scoundrels" cross a line? Explain your response.

Within the Limits of the Possible

by Stoyan Pribichevich

Stoyan Pribichevich (1905-1976) was an immigrant who became a journalist in the United States. Like many immigrants, he was highly educated but forced by economic necessity to do manual labor when he first arrived. In 1938, he wrote the article "In an American Factory" for *Harper's Magazine*, from which this essay is excerpted. Pribichevich was born in a district of the old Austro-Hungarian empire that became part of Yugoslavia after World War I. He graduated from the University of Belgrade. His father, Svetozar Pribićević, who died in 1936, was Yugoslav Minister of the Interior until he was exiled for not collaborating with King Alexander's dictatorship.

I came to America in 1934 as a political exile who could hardly speak English. In 1932, I had become involved in Yugoslav university-students' riots and in printing pamphlets against King Alexander's dictatorship. I was twenty-seven years of age then, a doctor of political science and a practicing lawyer in Belgrade. Before the political police could seize me, I managed to cross the Yugoslav frontier disguised as a peasant. I went to Paris, where I spent two years helping my father—a former member of the Yugoslav cabinet and also an exile—to write a book on democracy. I quarreled with the painters of Montparnasse on art, played the violin, and argued with my exiled countrymen in cafes clouded with tobacco smoke about the perfect democratic society. Then I thought I would visit a relative of mine in New York. I signed under oath a long, printed paper in English declaring that I was not a bomb thrower, lunatic, or venereal patient, and landed in Manhattan....

Finally I secured work. Despite my four languages and legal training, it was the job of a worker in an Ohio machine shop. It happened this way. Three and a half years ago I met a manufacturer from Cleveland at a party in New York. He teased me, saying that as a newcomer to America I should learn about American life by spending a few months as a worker in his shops. I did not see him again. When in 1936 I was unable to find a job in New York and found myself penniless, I wrote to him and asked whether he remembered me and his invitation. He replied that he did and renewed his offer. I packed my things and went. Instead of a few months, I spent a whole year in his shop....

■ ■ ■ ■

The so-called "turret lathe" was manufactured in this shop. This is a machine that in its turn makes tools and machine parts. You can fabricate almost anything with it, from automobile parts to bullets.

The factory itself was spotless. I had seen orderly European shops, but they had not gleamed with such beautiful cleanliness. I was assigned to the second shift. Through underground passages I was led to the Assembly, another huge room where the finished parts of turret lathe machines were put together, tested, and taken apart for shipment. The workers cast curious glances at the newcomer. They were amused at my clumsy attempts to punch the clock and showed me a vacant locker along the left wall where I changed clothes. Then, at four o-clock [in the morning], the note of the factory bell sounded in my ears and our shift started off like a regiment toward the machines in the center. Holding our toolboxes in our hands, we waited in line for the foreman to assign us our jobs....

The factory reminded me of a European dictatorial state, where bureaucrats plan and order and citizens work and obey. The board of the Company was the government, and the workers were the people, ruled through a centralized hierarchy of officials and controlled by a mechanized system of registration, bookkeeping, time cards, and punch clocks. Like citizens of authoritarian states, we did our individual assignments without knowing their purpose or the general plan of work. I met a worker whose specialty was to assemble gear boxes to the turret lathe machines who had no idea what the machines were for. The foreman was our supreme visible authority. With his superiors we could not communicate. And the president, with his board members and directors, sat high above us like an invisible, unapproachable god. Watchmen were stationed inside and outside the building to let nobody in or out except on a special permit. We even had our numbers. Mine was 1941....

■ ■ ■ ■

I often hear about the unemployment of people over forty. But in this machine shop, wherever skill or experience was needed most the workers were over forty. And even physically many of them had more resistance than the younger ones. I did not really mind being ignorant of a mechanic's work. I could always ask for help or advice. But unfortunately I belong to that class of persons who become panicky every time they have to hammer a nail or open a stubborn lock. Every worker knew, for instance, how to sharpen a drill on the automatic stone wheel. But in my hands the thing invariably went crooked, and I left part of my skin on the whirling grinder.

Stamping numbers on a machine part, I would first hit gently; the number would not come out; then I would gather myself for a terrific whack which, of course, would land right on my knuckles. And the holes I drilled were always cock-eyed. Irritated and impatient, I tried to overcome my subconscious fear of mechanical things by the use of physical force and, naturally, ruined both my work and my hands. It took me a long time to realize that a mechanic's ability resides in a careful deliberation and calculation of movements rather than in brute strength. I began to observe that my fellow-workers used their hands with caution, sized up every load before lifting it, took care to place their fingers in the right places, and then pushed or pulled with just the required physical energy. When their efforts were unsuccessful, they repeated them slowly over and over again. It was a superb lesson in self-control and patience. Like a fine racehorse, a machine wants to be treated firmly, but with kindness and intelligence....

Whenever I got stuck and called for help, unable to find the cause of trouble, my neighbor would shout over the noise: "Find out! Think!" Then he would come closer, look the machine over, and adjust something at the far opposite end that had made my bar in front fit badly. It was this power of quick mechanical diagnosis that my legally, abstractly trained mind could not grasp. But no worker or instructor ever troubled to give me a theoretical explanation of a job. They would say: "Watch me," then pull a lever, push a button, turn a wheel, and stand back for me to repeat their movements. They would tell me how, but never why....

■ ■ ■ ■

After a full year spent in the factory, I returned to New York. Looking back upon my year-long experience in this American shop, I am fully aware that it does not give a general picture of the American industrial life. One can arrive at a just evaluation of it only by comparing it with industrial conditions elsewhere, here and abroad. We were paid an average rate of 84 cents an hour. We worked 40 hours a week, in clean, healthy surroundings. We were given time and a half for overtime. We had time for rest, amusements, and cultural activities. We had two weeks' vacation with pay. We were treated fairly as human beings and as workers. The foremen were willing to make exceptions in emergencies and to help out in trouble. Not seldom they would give us time-saving jobs (the so-called "good jobs") when we were behind on our time cards. But the people whose character left the deepest impression on me were the workers. Humaneness and sympathy were concealed under their brusque ways and manners. On their faces, which sometimes reminded me of those of the peasants in my old country, lines of dishonesty or wickedness were rarely to be found. Many of them came from distant, forlorn corners of the United States or from

75

far-off, backward countries; they grew into the soil of a new community, excelled at work, and managed to give their children better care than they had enjoyed. When I think how tremendously handicapped they were by lack of means as well as of background and education, I wonder if perhaps they are not more able people than I. They were of simple taste and reasonable sane attitude toward life. No fanaticism colored their discontent. And their ambitions were undistorted by megalomaniac wishes to make "a career" or do "great things."

Their objectives in life were within the limits of the possible. Again and again I feel compelled to reflect upon the question that one young married worker once put to me: "What are you living for?

■ ■ ■ ■

Editor's Note: Stoyan Pribichevich had a distinguished career in journalism. He was an associate editor of *Fortune* magazine and a foreign correspondent for *Time* and *Life* magazines during World War II. Pribichevich was believed to have been the only representative of the American press behind the German lines in Yugoslavia in 1944. In early May of that year he was flown into Yugoslavia, landed 10 miles behind the fighting front, and was taken immediately to Marshal Tito's mountain stronghold. He was the first American newsman to meet Tito face-to-face (they talked in Serbo-Croatian) and the first correspondent to talk directly with the partisans in their own language. He lived in Flushing, Queens, in New York City, and died at 71 years of age. His book *Macedonia: Its People and History* is still available.

Questions for Discussion and Reflection

1. Name some life experiences you have had outside your comfort zone. How did your assumptions, prejudices, and stereotypes—about things like class, education, work, ethnicity, family—hinder you?

2. What is your own extended family's "migration" story? Tell part of it in some detail.

3. What do you think the author meant when he wrote that for the workers in the factory the "objectives of life were within the limits of the possible"? How does this statement inform, challenge, or inspire your own approach to power?

"Don't Get Mad, Get Smart"

by Pauli Murray

Pauli Murray (1911-1985) was a poet, memoirist, lawyer, organizer, early civil rights and feminist leader, and one of the first women ordained to the priesthood in the Episcopal Church. This excerpt is taken from her book, *Song in a Weary Heart: Memoir of an American Pilgrimage.*

The events of my final days as a (college) student in Washington climaxed six years of intense personal involvement in the struggle against segregation that had begun in 1938 with my application for admission to the University of North Carolina. If there were moments of deep despair in those years, there was also the sustaining knowledge that the quest for human dignity is part of a continuous movement through time and history linked to a higher force. Years later Dr. Martin Luther King, Jr., expressed the same concept when he said that in the struggle for justice one has "cosmic companionship." Pitting my intelligence against the ludicrous authorities who enforced an irrational set of arrangements and, above all, learning to harness my emotions to an innovative power instead of exploding in a fury of destructive waste were challenges I could respond to. Somewhere along the way I adopted the slogan, "Don't get mad, get smart."

The tension between my urge toward kamikaze defiance of Jim Crow and the more demanding discipline of plodding research—which often seemed to lead nowhere—kept me striving continually to achieve some kind of balance. In the process I discovered that joining others in the effort to overturn an entrenched system of injustice is often like running a relay. There were times when I didn't even know the outcome of the race, other times when it was my privilege to break the ribbon at the finish line, and still others when I share an overwhelming sense of accomplishment and exhilaration even though my contribution had been made early in the contest, not at its culmination....

■ ■ ■ ■

I had entered law school preoccupied with the racial struggle and single-mindedly bent upon become a civil rights attorney, but I graduated an unabashed feminist as well. Ironically, my effort to become a more proficient advocate in the first struggle led directly into the second through an unanticipated chain of events which began in the late fall of my senior year.

One day Dean (William) Hastie (of Howard University) called me into his office to discuss what I planned to do after graduation. To my utter surprise, he spoke of the possibility of my returning to teach at the law school after a year of graduate study, and with that possibility in mind he recommended that I apply for a Rosenwald fellowship. For a number of reasons, "graduate study" meant to me "graduate study at Harvard University." At least half of the Howard Law School faculty had studied at Harvard, both Hastie and Leon Ransom held doctorates from its law school, and it had become a tradition of Howard to groom an exceptionally promising law graduate for a future faculty position by sending him to Harvard "to put on the gloss" of a prestigious graduate degree in law. My greatest rival in the preceding class, Francisco Carniero, who had graduated with top honors and as Chief Justice of the Court of peers, was now completing his year of graduate law there. We had run neck and neck in courses we took together, he topping my by a couple of points in one and I topping him in another.

Naively unaware of Harvard's policy toward women, I was stunned when my schoolmates began kidding me. "Murray," someone said, "don't you know they're not going to let you into Harvard?" Harvard, it became clear, did not admit women to its law school.

Then my hopes were raised by a rumor which circulated around campus that Harvard was opening up to women students. Accordingly, when filling out my application to the Rosenwald Fund, I wrote in the space provided for choice of law school: "I should like to obtain my Master's degree at Harvard University, in the event they have removed their bar against women students. If not, then I should like to work at Yale University or at any other University which has advance study in the field of labor law." I also wrote to the secretary of Harvard Law School, requesting confirmation or denial of the rumor I had heard. The answer was prompt. On January 5, 1944, the secretary's office wrote back: "Harvard Law School… is not open to women for registration."

The verdict was disappointing, of course, but with all the other preoccupations of my senior year, the matter probably would have rested there if I had not won the Rosenwald fellowship or at least if the names of the award winners had not been published nationwide. The announcement, made in late spring, listed me among fifteen white Southerners and twenty-two Negroes (including such notables as E. Franklin Frazier, Adelaide Cromwell Hill, Chester Himes, Rayford W. Logan, Dorothy Porter, and Margaret Walker) who received awards "for creative talent or distinguished scholarship." Mine was the only award in the field of law, and all the news stories reported that I was to do graduate study in labor law at Harvard University.

I was embarrassed to receive congratulatory messages from a number of people who were either unaware of Harvard's restrictive policy or assumed I had broken the barrier. At the same time, some of the men at Howard stepped up their banter, not without a touch of malicious glee. Until then I had been able to lick my wounds in private, but the public disclosure of my dilemma mortified me and presented a challenge I could not pass over lightly. If my schoolmates expected me to dissolve into tears under their stinging gibes, they were disappointed. I simply sat down and wrote a letter of application to Harvard Law School, which was duly processed, and I received a written request for my college transcript and a photograph....

■ ■ ■ ■

Editor's note: After a long fight, the faculty at the Harvard University Law School voted 7-7 not to admit Pauli Murray, but she went on to a distinguished career in law. Harvard finally admitted women to its law school in 1950.

Questions for Discussion or Reflection

1. What does it mean for an organizer to have patience? How does an organizer deal with losing?
2. What is the personal side of powerlessness? How do you cope with it?
3. How does an organizer build enough power to take on a Harvard University and win?

The Student Voice

by Student Nonviolent Coordinating Committee

The Student Non-Violent Coordinating Committee (SNCC) was formed in 1960. It published the first edition of its newsletter "The Student Voice" in June of that year. Here are three articles from that newsletter that capture the passion for justice and the commitment to non-violence that were hallmarks of the civil rights movement of the 1960s. The first article is titled "Atlanta Story" and was written by H. Julian Bond and Melvin A. McCaw. Bond also contributed a short poem titled simply "#1." Rev. J.M. Lawson, Jr., presented the "Statement of Purpose" for the organization, and Dr. Martin Luther King, Jr., contributed a list of seven rules "To Win Racial Justice."

Special report: Atlanta Story

Students from Clark, Morehouse, Morris Brown, Spelman Colleges; the Blayton School of Accounting, Atlanta University; and the Interdenominational Theological Center have come together in a united effort to break the shackles of immorality, archaic traditions, and complacency in an energetic struggle for human rights.

On Wednesday, March 9th, students from six of the institutions published an "Appeal for Human Rights" in three of Atlanta's leading newspapers. The "Appeal for Human Rights" is an expression of the students' dissatisfaction with the treatment of Negroes in Atlanta and Georgia in particular, and discrimination and segregation wherever they may exist. The students of the Atlanta University Center hoped that an appeal of this nature would be successful in provoking the consciences of the people of Atlanta, Georgia; the nation; and the world to refrain from the immoral practices of refusing to grant to some those guaranteed rights which are due every member of the human race.

Tuesday, March 15th, prompted by the same spirit which produced the "Appeal for Human Rights," while requesting service in nine different eating establishments housed in publicly supported buildings, seventy-seven students were arrested in seven of the restaurants. The two establishments where no arrests were made were located in federal buildings. One of the students, a minor, has been banned from Georgia.

On April 15th, five of the six signers of the "Appeal for Human Rights" and two students who were not originally arrested for their request for service were also indicted. The eighty-three students are now awaiting adjudication for violation of Georgia laws. They face possible maximum sentences and fines of forty years in jail and twenty-seven thousand dollars per person.

At this time, students have initiated a program of "selective buying" aimed at large food store chains in an effort to secure equal job opportunities.

On May 17th, in observance of the sixth anniversary of the Supreme Court decision regarding desegregation of public schools, three thousand students from the Atlanta University Center began a peaceful march to the

Capitol of the State of Georgia. They were defiantly met by one hundred armed state troopers, sporting three-foot cudgels, tear gas bombs, and fire hoses. Upon orders from the chief of the Atlanta Police Department, the students were re-routed.

The Committee on the Appeal for Human Rights is constantly seeking opportunities to negotiate with governmental and private business officials to help secure equal rights through understanding.

The struggle for human rights is a constant fight, and one which the students do not plan to relinquish until full equality is won for *all*.

■ ■ ■ ■

#1
I too, hear America singing
But from where I stand
I can only hear Little Richard
And Fats Domino.
But sometimes,
I hear Ray Charles
Drowning in his own tears
or Bird
Relaxing at Camarillo
or Horace Silver doodling,
Then I don't mind standing
a little longer.

85

■ ■ ■ ■

SNCC Statement of Purpose

Carrying out the mandate of the Raleigh Conference to write a statement of purpose for the movement, the Temporary Student Nonviolent Coordinating Committee submits for careful consideration the following draft. We urge all local state or regional groups to examine it closely. Each member of our movement must work diligently to understand the depths of nonviolence.

We affirm the philosophical or religious ideal of nonviolence as the foundation of our purpose, the pre-supposition of our faith, and the manner of our action. Nonviolence, as it grows from Judaic-Christian traditions, seeks a social order of justice permeated by love. Integration of human endeavor represents the crucial first step towards such a society.

Through nonviolence, courage displaces fear; love transforms hate. Acceptance dissipates prejudice; hope ends despair. Peace dominates war; faith reconciles doubt. Mutual regards cancel enmity. Justice for all overthrows injustice. The redemptive community supersedes systems of gross social immorality.

Love is the central motif of nonviolence. Love is the force by which God binds human beings to the divine and humans to humans. Such love goes to the extreme; it remains loving and forgiving even in the midst of hostility. It matches the capacity of evil to inflict suffering with an even more enduring capacity to absorb evil, all the while persisting in love.

By appealing to conscience and standing on the moral nature of human existence, nonviolence nurtures the atmosphere in which reconciliation and justice become actual possibilities.

■ ■ ■ ■

To Win Racial Justice

1. Use active non-violent resistance to evil.
2. Never seek to defeat or humiliate your opponent, but to win his or her friendship and understanding.
3. The nonviolent resister seeks to defeat the forces of evil, not the persons who happen to be doing evil.
4. Avoid external physical violence but also internal violence spirit. (Hating the opponent.)
5. Accept suffering without retaliation.
6. Have confidence that the universe is on the side of justice.
7. Recognize that the center of non-violence is the love of God operating in the human heart.

■ ■ ■ ■

Editor's Note: In addition to the Student Nonviolent Coordinating Committee (SNCC), other key organizations in the civil rights organizing efforts of the 1960s-1970s included the National Association for the Advancement of Colored People (NAACP), the Southern Christian Leadership Conference (SCLC), the Congress of Racial Equality (CORE), and many others. Some key black leaders and organizers of the civil rights movement, in order of their year of birth, include the following: A. Philip Randolph, Roy Wilkens, Ella Baker, Thurgood Marshall, Pauli Murray, Bayard Rustin, Rosa Parks, Fannie Lou Hamer, James Farmer, Joseph Lowery, Charles Evers, Medger Evers, Whitney Young, Jr., Malcolm X, Ralph Abernathy, Hosea Williams, Coretta Scott King, James Forman, James Lawson, Martin Luther King, Jr., Dorothy Cotton, Andrew Young, James Meredith, Roy Innis, Bob Moses, Barbara Jordan, John Lewis, Stokely Carmichael, Jesse Jackson, Jr., Al Sharpton.

Questions for Discussion and Reflection

1. Is nonviolence an integral part of successful organizing? Explain your answer. Give examples.

2. How many of the black organizers and leaders in the editor's note do you know? What others would you add to the list? Why? Start a list of key leaders and organizers of other races and ethnic groups in the United States.

3. What is the role of young people in organizing? How can they learn the history, the elements, and the practice of power in society? Be specific.

Much Bigger Than a Hamburger or a Coke

by Ella Baker

Ella J. Baker (1903-1986) was born in Norfolk, Virginia, and raised in Littleton, North Carolina. While serving as Executive Secretary for the Southern Christian Leadership Conference (SCLC), she helped organize the founding conference of Student Nonviolent Coordinating Committee (SNCC) held at Shaw University in Raleigh, North Carolina, during the Easter weekend of 1960. Baker is said to have persuaded Martin Luther King to put up the $800 needed to hold the conference. Speaking to the conference, Baker told the students that their struggle was "much bigger than a hamburger or even a giant-sized coke," a reference to the sit-ins at lunch counters and restaurants they were participating in. In presenting this bigger picture and encouraging young activists to form their own organization, she displayed a talent she had been employing for more than two decades: assisting people to empower themselves. The students decided to form their own organization, separate from the other civil rights groups. With the formation of SNCC, Baker encouraged the students to organize from the bottom up. In the summer of 1960, she urged civil rights organizer Bob Moses to meet local NAACP leader Amzie Moore in Cleveland, Mississippi, and out of this meeting emerged SNCC's first voter registration project and eventually the Mississippi Freedom Democratic Party (MFDP). Four years later, Baker was the coordinator of the Washington, D.C., office of the MFDP and wrote the letter below to delegates from other states to the 1964 Democratic National Convention being held in Atlantic City, New Jersey, that August. It is a good example of the power of "persuasive writing" many leaders and organizers exhibit.

July 20, 1964

Dear Convention Delegate,

Three mothers' sons who sought to secure political democracy for the people of Mississippi probably lie covered beneath the murky swamps near Philadelphia, a small town in that state.

If they have paid with their lives for believing in the right of the governed to have a voice in the election of those who govern them, all Democrats who can register and vote with freedom are now challenged as never before. The long and systematic denial of the Negro's right to vote in Mississippi, and the flagrant disloyalty of the "regular" Mississippi Democratic Party to the principles of the National Democratic Party demand that new channels be created through which all the people of Mississippi can be represented in the 1964 Democratic National Convention. To do less at this historic moment would be a disgrace.

The Freedom Democratic Party parallels the structure and the proceedings of the existing Democratic party, with the notable exceptions that it is open to all citizens and has declared its loyalty to the announced principles and platforms of the National Democratic Party. A delegation from the Freedom Party will seek to be seated at the Atlantic City Convention. This challenge has received support from the following states either through state conventions or executive committees: California, Michigan, New York, Minnesota, Oregon, Wisconsin, Massachusetts, and the District of Columbia.

We urge that your entire delegation use the full weight of its prestige and voting strength to see that the challenge raised by the Mississippi Freedom Democratic Party receives a full and open hearing before the Credentials Committee of the Convention and, if the Credentials Committee fails to seat the Freedom Democratic Party, that your delegation call for a minority report and a roll-call vote to permit the Mississippi issue to be discussed on the floor of the Convention.

The people of Mississippi depend on you for help. We look forward to your support at the convention in Atlantic City.

Yours sincerely,

Ella J. Baker

Coordinator, Washington Office

Mississippi Freedom Democratic Party

■ ■ ■ ■

Editor's Note: The Mississippi Freedom Democratic Party (MFDP) left the 1964 Democratic Convention rather than be compromised by accepting the two observer seats offered them. President Lyndon Johnson tried unsuccessfully to prevent the MFDP leader Fannie Lou Hamer from making a speech on the floor of the convention, and Hammer said of the proposed compromise, "We didn't come all this way for no two seats, 'cause all of us is tired." After people in the United States heard Hamer's speech, different segments of the U.S. population were outraged and began calling into the White House seeking justice for Black people in the South. The next year President Johnson persuaded Congress to pass the Voting Rights Act of 1965, which authorized the federal government to oversee elections at the state and local level and enforce practices that would support legitimate voter registration and voting in areas with an historic under-representation of certain parts of the population. According to her biographers, Ella Baker's belief was that organizing people meant they could lead themselves. After all, who else was better qualified to articulate their needs? She often said, "strong people don't need strong leaders." But Baker was well-known for her talent in making things happen.

Questions for Discussion and Reflection

1. What should the relationship between institutionally based relational organizing and electoral politics? Give examples from your own experience or history or the current political situation.

2. What is the difference between a tactic and a strategy? How did Ella Baker describe both in this one short letter?

3. Persuasive speaking and writing is one more tool in a leader's or an organizer's toolbox. Give an example of a speaker or writer who has changed your mind about something. How could you learn to speak or write like that?

We Cannot Be Patient

by John R. Lewis

John Robert Lewis (1940-2020) was the youngest person to speak at the Civil Rights March on Washington in August 28, 1963. He was one of the original "Freedom Riders," a chair of the Student Non-Violent Coordinating Committee (SNCC), and one of the main organizers and leaders of the protest at the Edmund Pettus Bridge in Selma, Alabama, on March 7, 1965, known as "Bloody Sunday," where Lewis was so badly beaten by the police that his skull was fractured. Less than three weeks later, President Lyndon B. Johnson introduced the Voting Rights Act, and Congress passed it the same year. The removal of discriminatory restrictions such as poll taxes and literacy tests allowed Blacks in the South meaningful access to the vote for the first time since Reconstruction. In just two years, the percentage of Black people registered to vote in the jurisdictions the act covered increased from less than one-third to more than fifty percent. Black voter participation allowed meaningful access to democracy. The year the law was enacted, there were six Black members of Congress. After the 2018 election, there were fifty-two. According to Paul Butler, the author of *Chokehold: Policing Black Men*, "The march's leaders censored the speech John Lewis wanted to give, arguing that it was too radical. The event leaders forced Lewis to tone down provocations, including this call to action: 'We will march through the South, through the heart of Dixie, the way Sherman did. We shall pursue our own scorched earth policy and burn Jim Crow to the ground—nonviolently. We shall fragment the South into a thousand pieces and put them back together in the image of democracy.' They made him change that to: 'We will march through the South...with the spirit of love and with the spirit of dignity we have shown here today.' But the words Lewis didn't speak are the ones America needs to hear right now."

We march today for jobs and freedom, but we have nothing to be proud of. For hundreds and thousands of our brothers and sisters are not here. For they are receiving starvation wages, or no wages at all. While we stand here, there are sharecroppers in the Delta of Mississippi who are out in the fields working for less than three dollars a day, twelve hours a day. While we stand here there are students in jail on trumped-up charges. Our brother James Farmer, along with many others, is also in jail. We come here today with a great sense of misgiving.

It is true that we support the administration's civil rights bill. We support it with great reservations, however. Unless Title III is put in this bill, there is nothing to protect the young children and old women who must face police dogs and fire hoses in the South while they engage in peaceful demonstrations. In its present form, this bill will not protect the citizens of Danville, Virginia, who must live in constant fear of a police state. It will not protect the hundreds and thousands of people that have been arrested on trumped charges. What about the three young men, SNCC field secretaries in Americus, Georgia, who face the death penalty for engaging in peaceful protest?

As it stands now, the voting section of this bill will not help the thousands of Black people who want to vote. It will not help the citizens of

Mississippi, of Alabama and Georgia, who are qualified to vote, but lack a sixth-grade education. "One man, one vote" is the African cry. It is ours too. It must be ours!

We must have legislation that will protect the Mississippi sharecropper who is put off of his farm because he dares to register to vote. We need a bill that will provide for the homeless and starving people of this nation. We need a bill that will ensure the equality of a maid who earns five dollars a week in a home of a family whose total income is $100,000 a year. We must have a good Federal Employment Practices Committee bill.

■ ■ ■ ■

My friends, let us not forget that we are involved in a serious social revolution. By and large, American politics is dominated by politicians who build their careers on immoral compromises and ally themselves with open forms of political, economic, and social exploitation. There are exceptions, of course. We salute those. But what political leader can stand up and say, "My party is the party of principles"? For the party of Kennedy is also the party of Eastland. The party of Javits is also the party of Goldwater. Where is our party? Where is the political party that will make it unnecessary to march on Washington?

Where is the political party that will make it unnecessary to march in the streets of Birmingham? Where is the political party that will protect the citizens of Albany, Georgia? Do you know that in Albany, Georgia, nine of our leaders have been indicted, not by the Dixiecrats, but by the federal government for peaceful protest? But what did the federal government do when Albany's deputy sheriff beat Attorney C.B. King and left him half-dead? What did the federal government do when local police officials kicked and assaulted the pregnant wife of Slater King, and she lost her baby?

To those who have said, "Be patient and wait," we have long said that we cannot be patient. We do not want our freedom gradually, but we want to be free now! We are tired. We are tired of being beaten by policemen. We are tired of seeing our people locked up in jail over and over again. And then you holler, "Be patient." How long can we be patient? We want our freedom and we want it now. We do not want to go to jail. But we will go to jail if this is the price we must pay for love, brotherhood, and true peace.

■ ■ ■ ■

I appeal to all of you to get into this great revolution that is sweeping this nation. Get in and stay in the streets of every city, every village and hamlet of this nation until true freedom comes, until the revolution of 1776 is complete. We must get in this revolution and complete the revolution. For in the Delta in Mississippi, in southwest Georgia, in the Black Belt of Alabama, in Harlem, in Chicago, Detroit, Philadelphia, and all over this nation, the Black masses are on the march for jobs and freedom.

They're talking about slow down and stop. We will not stop. All of the forces of Eastland, Barnett, Wallace, and Thurmond will not stop this revolution. If we do not get meaningful legislation out of this Congress, the time will come when we will not confine our marching to Washington. We will march through the South; through the streets of Jackson, through the streets of Danville, through the streets of Cambridge, through the streets of Birmingham. But we will march with the spirit of love and with the spirit of dignity that we have shown here today. By the force of our demands, our determination, and our numbers, we shall splinter the segregated South into a thousand pieces and put them together in the image of God and democracy. We must say: "Wake up America! Wake up!" For we cannot stop, and we will not and cannot be patient.

■ ■ ■ ■

Editor's Note: In remarks taken from his interview with Krista Tippett on March 28, 2013, for the On Being Project, John Lewis reflected on his life-long commitment to non-violence: "First of all, you have to grow. It's just not something that is natural. You have to be taught the way of peace, the way of love, the way of nonviolence. And in the religious sense, in the moral sense, you can say that in the bosom of every human being there is a spark of the divine. So you don't have a right as a human to abuse that spark of the divine in your fellow human being. We, from time to time, would discuss that if you see someone attacking you, beating you, spitting on you, you have to think that person, you know, years ago was an innocent child, an innocent little baby. And so what happened? Did something go wrong? Did the environment or someone teach that person to hate, to abuse others? So you try to appeal to the goodness of every human being and you don't give up. You never give up on anyone." (The complete recording and transcript of this remarkable interview is available at onbeing.org/programs/john-lewis-love-in-action/#transcript.)

Questions for Discussion and Reflection

1. Do organizers and leaders have to be patient? Explain your answer with examples.

2. How would you react if the leaders of your organization asked you to change some of your prepared comments for an important event? Why?

3. What are some of the implications of adopting non-violence and love as a lifelong strategy for working for justice and equality? How do you feel about those implications for your own leadership and organizing?

PART TWO

Foundations of Organizing

Foundations of Organizing

This section is mostly about a kind of organizing called "community" or "citizens" or "organization of organizations." Even more specifically, it focuses on the kind of organizing that has been practiced since 1940 by the Industrial Areas Foundation (IAF). There are literally thousands of individuals and networks that do community organizing work. You can get a master's degree from many universities in it, and many people have written books about it.

Five things distinguish IAF organizing: it is fiercely non-partisan; it is institutionally based (that is, you can only join through a member institution or organization, not as an individual); it seeks "relational power" instead of "dominant" power; it is committed to the training and development of leaders; and it is uncompromising in demanding of itself an openness to radical diversity in its membership.

Part Two contains twenty-one essays or stories from founders, past and current supervisors and lead organizers, and longtime volunteer leaders and friends of the IAF, including: Saul Alinsky; Cesar Chavez; Michael Gecan; Zeik Saidman; Tom Mosgaller; Ernesto Cortes, Jr.; Arnie Graf; Kathleen O'Toole; Lionel Edmonds; Jeff Krehbiel; several articles on Christine Stephens by Ernesto Cortes, Jr., Elizabeth Valdez, Anna Eng, Lady Carlson, Krysten King, Josephine Lopez Paul, and Pearl Ceasar; Ed Chambers; Dick Harmon; Ronnie Crudup; and Martin Trimble.

■ ■ ■ ■

Reveille for Radicals

by Saul D. Alinsky

Saul Alinsky (1909-1972) founded the Industrial Areas Foundation (IAF) in 1940 with board members that included Catholic Bishop Bernard Shields of Chicago. His first "People's Organization" was the Back of the Yards Community Council on Chicago's south side in 1939, which he organized with Joe Megan under the motto, "We the people will work out our own destiny." Alinsky went on to organize through the 1950s and 1960s in Chicago, Kansas City, upstate New York, and other locations. He was a supporter of and mentor to Fred Ross, Dolores Huerta, and Cesar Chavez of the United Farmworkers; a friend of Msgrs. John Egan and George Higgins of Chicago; and a biographer of John L. Lewis, the founder of the Congress of Industrial Organizations (CIO). He died of a heart attack on the streets of Carmel, California, at the age of 63.

The history of America is the story of America's Radicals. It is a saga of revolution, battle, words on paper setting hearts on fire, ferment and turmoil; it is the story of every rallying cry of the American people. It is the story of the American Revolution, of the public schools, of the battle for free land, of emancipation, of the unceasing struggle for the ever-increasing liberation of humankind.

The humanitarian idealism of the *Declaration of Independence* has always echoed as a battle-dry in the hearts of those who dream of an America

107

dedicated to democratic ends. I cannot be long ignored or repudiated, for sooner or later it returns to plague the council of practical politics. It is constantly breaking out in fresh revolt. Without its freshening influence, our political history would have been much more sordid and materialistic....

■ ■ ■ ■

The fundamental issue that will resolve the fate of democracy is whether or not we really believe in democracy. Democracy as a way of life has been intellectually accepted but emotionally rejected. The democratic way of life is predicated upon faith in the masses of humankind, yet few of the leaders of democracy really possess faith in the people. If anything, our democratic way of life is permeated by people's fear of other people. The powerful few fear the many, and the many distrust one another. Personal opportunism and greedy exploitation link the precinct captain, the mayor, the governor, and the Congress into one cynical family. It is difficult to find the faintest flicker of faith in others whether one scours the Democrats from the southern racist poll taxers to their northern corrupt city machines or scrutinizes the decayed reactionaries of the Republicans. On the contrary, it will be found that with few exceptions all these leaders, regardless of their party labels or affiliations, share in common a deep fear and suspicion of the masses of people. Let the masses remain inert, unthinking; do not disturb them, do not arouse them, do not get them moving—for if you do you are an agitator, a troublemaker, a Red! You are un-American. You are a Radical.

The past, the glorious past with all of its comfortable familiarity, was rooted in a general surrender of everyday democratic rights and responsibilities of the people. It was founded on masses of people who were and still are denied the opportunity to participate; who are frustrated at every turn, and who have been mute for so long that they have lost their voices. Only at rare intervals did this quiet, peaceful, seemingly dead foundation stir and move. These upheavals were the revolutions of people fighting for the opportunity to play a part in their world, for a chance to belong, to live like human beings.

These masses of people were and are the substance of society. If they continue inarticulate, apathetic, disinterested, forlorn, and alone in their abysmal anonymity, then democracy is ended. Substance determines structure, and the form of economy and politics will be and always has been a reflection of either the active desires of a democratically minded citizenry or the passive torpor of a people whose innate dignity and strength have atrophied from disuse and who will follow slave-like after a dictator. It is irony worthy of the gods that here in the greatest democracy on earth is found the least concern of the prime element of democracy—citizens who shoulder obligations and stand up for their rights. A people's democracy is a dynamic expression of a living, participating, informed, active, and free people. It is a way of life that belongs to the people, that draws its very lifeblood from popular participation. Democracy is alive, and like any other living thing it either flourishes and grows or withers and dies. There is no in-between. It is freedom and life or dictatorship and death....

■ ■ ■ ■

This, then, is the job ahead. It is the job of building broad, deep, People's Organizations, which are all-inclusive of both the people and their many organizations. It is the job of uniting, through a common interest which far transcends individual differences, all the institutions and agencies representative of the people. It is the job of building a People's Organization so that people will have faith in themselves and in their brothers and sisters. It is the job of educating our people so that they will be informed to the point of being able to exercise an intelligent critical choice as to what is true and what is false. It is the job of instilling confidence in people so they are sure they can destroy the evils which afflict them and their neighbors—whether unemployment, war, or anything else. Organizing is the greatest job one could have—the actual opportunity of creating and building a world of decency, dignity, peace, security, happiness; a world worth of human beings and worthy of the name of civilization. This is the job ahead.

The building of these People's Organizations and the achievement of popular participation cannot and will not be done by denouncing the present deplorable condition of democracy. It will not be done by wailing self-recriminations or the constant issue of books saying, "Americans, awake!" It can be done only by setting ourselves to the dirty, monotonous, heart-breaking job of building People's Organizations. It can be done only by possessing the infinite patience and faith to hang on as parts of the organization disintegrate; to build, add on, and continue to build....

■ ■ ■ ■

Let it sound, then. Let it come—strident, ringing, and heart-stir-ring…. Let it sound again boldly—shattering the death-like silence of de-cay. Let it reach every corner of America, and let its echoes go beyond and shake the hearts of dictators everywhere…. Sound it now. Whether it be the hoarse voice, the bell, the written word, or the trumpet, let it come. Sound it clear and unwavering: REVEILLE FOR RADICALS!

■ ■ ■ ■

Editor's Note: Saul Alinsky wrote two seminal books on community orga-nizing, *Reveille for Radicals* in 1945 and *Rules for Radicals* in 1971, which are still in print and quoted often today on both the left and the right.

Questions for Discussion and Reflection

1. Compare and contrast the situation of democracy in America as Alinsky described it above in 1945 with the state of democracy in America today. What strikes you? Be specific.
2. Describe any experience you have with a "People's Organization." How did it make you feel? What did you accomplish with it?
3. Define the word "radical." Would you accept that label for yourself? If not, what others might you use? If yes, explain why.

Getting Started in Organizing

by Cesar Chavez

Cesario Estrada Chavez (1927-1993) was a labor and civil rights leader, a farm-worker, a proponent of non-violent social change, and environmental and con-sumer-rights advocate. He served in the U.S. Navy in the western Pacific in the aftermath of World War II. He worked with Fred Ross and Saul Alinsky in the Community Service Organization (CSO), which he left in 1962 to organize what became the United Farm Workers of America (UFWA) union, a member of the AFL-CIO.

t really started for me in 1950 in San Jose, California, when I was working on an Apricot Farm. We figured that Fred Ross was just another social worker doing a study of farm conditions, and I kept refusing to meet with him. But he was persistent. Finally, I got together some of the rough element in San Jose. We were going to have a little reception for him to teach the gringo a little bit of how we felt. There were about thirty of us in the house, young guys mostly. I was supposed to give them a signal—change my cigarette from my right had to my left—and then we were going to give him a lot of hell. But he started talking and the more he talked, the more wide-eyed I became and the less inclined I was to give the signal. A couple of guys who were pretty drunk at the time still wanted to give the gringo the business, but we got rid of them. This fellow was making a lot of sense, and I wanted to hear what he had to say.

Fred Ross was an organizer for the Community Service Organization (CSO), which was working with Mexican Americans in the cities. I
became immediately really involved. Before long I was heading a voter registration drive. All the time, I was observing the things Fred did, secretly,
because I wanted to lean how to organize, to see how it was done. I was
impressed with his patience and understanding of people. I thought this
was a tool, one of the greatest things he had....

After six months of working every night in San Jose, Fred assigned me
to take over the CSO chapter in Decoto. It was a tough spot to fill. I would
suggest something, and people would say, "No, let's wait till Fred gets back,"
or "Fred wouldn't do it that way." This is pretty much a pattern with people,
I discovered whether I was put in Fred's position, or later, when someone
else was put in my position. After the Decoto assignment, I was sent to
start a new chapter of the CSO in Oakland. Fred came to a place in San
Jose called the Hole-in-the-Wall and we talked for half an hour over coffee. He was in a rush to leave, but I wanted to keep him talking; I was that
scared of my assignment.

▓ ▓ ▓ ▓

Those were hard times in Oakland. First of all, it was a big city and
I'd get lost every time I went anywhere. Then I arranged a series of house
meetings. I would get to the meeting early and drive back and forth past
the house, too nervous to go in and face the people. Finally, I would force

113

myself to go inside and sit in a corner. I was quite thin then, and young, and most of the people were middle-aged. Someone would say, "Where's the organizer?" And I would pipe up, "Here I am!" Then they would say in Spanish—these were very poor people and we hardly spoke anything but Spanish—"Ha! This *kid?*" Most of them said they were interested, but the hardest part was to get them to start pushing themselves on their own initiative.

The idea was to set up a meeting and then get each attending person to call his or her own house meeting, inviting new people—a sort of chain letter effect. After a house meeting, I would lie awake going over the whole thing, playing the tape back, trying to see why people laughed at one point, or why they were for one thing and against another. I was also learning to read and write, those late evening. I had left school in the 7th grade after attending sixty-seven different schools, and my reading wasn't the best.

At our first organizing meeting we had 368 people. I'll never forget it because it was very important to me. You eat your heart out; the meeting is called for seven o'clock and you start to worry about four. You wait. Will they show up? Then the first one arrives. By seven there are only twenty people; you have everything in order; you have to look calm. But little by little they filter in and at a certain point you know it will be a success....

■ ■ ■ ■

For more than ten years I worked for the CSO. As the organization grew, we found ourselves meeting in fancier and fancier motels and holding expensive conventions. Doctors, lawyers, and politicians began joining. They would get elected to some office in the organization and then, for all practical purposes, leave. Intent on using the CSO for their own purposes, these "leaders," many of them, lacked the urgency we had to have. When I became general director, I began to press for a program to organize farm workers into a union, an idea most of the leadership opposed. So I started a revolt within the CSO. I refused to sit at the head table at meeting, refused to wear a suit and tie, and finally I even refused to shave and cut my hair. It used to embarrass some of the professionals.

At every meeting, I got up and gave my standard speech: We shouldn't meet in fancy motels, we were getting away from the people, farm workers had to be organized. But nothing happened. In March of 1962, I resigned and came to Delano to begin organizing the Valley on my own.

■ ■ ■ ■

Editor's Note: Cesar Chavez went on to organize the National Farm Workers Association, which later became the United Farm Workers of America (UFWA). Many books, biographies, critical studies, and documentaries have been produced on hits life and work, but he did not write much himself. This excerpt is taken from the fine collection of his speeches, *An Organizer's Tale*, edited and with an Introduction by Ilan Stavans. Chavez is quoted there saying, "If this spirit grows from within the farm labor movement, one day we can use the force that we have to help correct a lot if things that are wrong in this society. But that is for the future. Before you can run, you have to learn to walk."

Questions for Discussion and Reflection

1. Do you have a mentor? Have you mentored others? Make a list of them and recall one story about the power of mentoring you experienced.
2. What is/was the hardest part (for you) of getting started in organizing? What is/was blocking you? How do/did you overcome those blocks?
3. Have you ever organized a house meeting or a small action? If so, how did you feel before it began? What happened and how did you feel afterwards? If you have never organized anything, think about and share why.

Black and White in Chicago

by Michael Gecan

Mike Gecan (born 1949) has spent his entire adult life organizing, initially as a high-school volunteer for the Contract Buyers League in Chicago and later with the Industrial Areas Foundation (IAF). He was the lead organizer of East Brooklyn Churches (EBC) in New York City throughout the 1980s when that institutionally-based organization conceived and executed The Nehemiah Plan that rebuilt the East New York community with over 6000 new, owner-occupied homes. Gecan became a co-executive director of the national Industrial Areas Foundation after the retirement of Ed Chambers and oversaw the development of the Metro IAF in the states east of the Mississippi River and oversees. He is now working on new organizing initiatives in several states.

I recalled a morning in 1965. It was February 1, a Monday, and my family and I woke up to front page news about two guys I knew well. We lived on the corner of Springfield and Ferdinand in the West Garfield Park neighborhood of Chicago. At the time, it was tough, blue-collar, and white. Across the street, a few years before, the Del Vecchio family had bought a home—444 North Springfield. The family was a unique in one way. The mother was a single parent, divorced or separated from her husband. George Del Vecchio was about my age at the time—sixteen. When he moved into the area, he decided that he would establish himself as the

117

toughest guy around. He needed to prove himself against the person who held that title at the time—Mike Stepkowicz. George waited in a gangway one afternoon for Stepkowicz to walk by. Then he walked out, cold-cocked him, and beat him half to death. From then on, George was the one who called the shots. One of his closest friends was another tough fellow—Joey Varchetto. Varchetto was the center fielder on our baseball team. We played our league games at Kells Field on Chicago Avenue and Homan. In the middle of the last season, as we struggled as a .500 team, Joey called a players-only meeting. He said: "No more losing. The next guy makes us lose, I'm going to kill." We never doubted that Joey meant this literally. My teammates and I played as if our lives depended on it. We went undefeated the rest of the way!

Both George and Joey were already using drugs—barbiturates, also called "goof balls" or "pep pills." George also had a rifle, which he showed off to us one afternoon in his basement. He also pulled a sheet from a closet, smeared with blood. "My father's blood," he said. "Wish I'd killed the bastard." We didn't know if the story was true, but not one of us thought to challenge him.

One Sunday night, George and Joey and a third guy, Eugene Waswill, got high and went out to find more money for more pills with a handgun we didn't know they had. They spotted a man, Fred A. Christiansen, taking a walk near his home a few miles north of our neighborhood. They shot him, but Christiansen, wounded, cried for help. Then Del Vecchio fired five more bullets into him, killing him for the $11 they found in his wallet. Because Del Vecchio and Varchetto were just sixteen, they were tried as juveniles. They served time and were released at age twenty-one. Del Vecchio killed again—this time the six-year old son of his girlfriend—and was executed by the State of Illinois. Varchetto was gunned down by a rival gangster some years later. I don't know what happened to Waswill.

■ ■ ■ ■

So already, in 1965, I experienced personally one stark chapter in what would unfold over time as the story of urban decline: guns, gangs, drugs, family breakdown, and violent deaths. And in the next year or so, the second chapter would unfold. It featured the massive double exodus: the first of African American families out of slum conditions and into white working-class blocks; the second the frightened flight of those white families into nearby neighborhoods or expanding suburbs. I was right in the middle of that in Chicago.

Two summers after the Christiansen murder, my family began getting calls from real estate brokers. They phoned incessantly, deep in the night at times, sometimes in the middle of the night, with this message: "They're coming; your house is losing value every day; move now or lose everything, or stay and get knifed by one of them." The these unscrupulous "realtors" spoke whatever language the person at the other end of the line spoke—a Croatian broker calling those of us like me who were Croatians, an Italian calling Italians, a Pole calling Poles. The sound of that summer was of deep rumble and shifting gears of moving trucks. Day after day, trucks rolled down Springfield, Avers, Harding, and across Ferdinand, Ohio, Huron, taking the belongings of our neighbors out and delivering the furniture of our new Black neighbors in. Some of our neighbors, embarrassed to be seen fleeing, literally had the truck come in the middle of the night.

By the end of the summer, the section of our parish area, Our Lady of the Angels, that had been 99.5% white (one Black family had lived in isolation but relative peace at the end of our block) was now 99.5% black (my family remained only because my Croatian immigrant grandmother, not five-foot-tall but tough as nails, refused to leave). The terms for this money-making scheme—"panic peddling" or "block busting"—were familiar to every on-the-edge blue collar ethnic family in any big city in the United States. This drama had victims and villains and rhythms. For some, the victims were the hardworking white families that felt threatened and forced to run losing whatever equity they had built up in their homes, losing life-long relationships, re-starting in another neighborhood. And the villains, to us, were the Black families that brought crime and decay with them, like so many extra pieces of luggage. But as I learned not that much later in my life, the victims were also the Black families who were desperate to get out of rat infested apartments in the ghetto, eager to own a home of their own and see their kids play in a fenced backyard and attend a decent school. And they were victimized by those who left and refused to welcome them into our neighborhoods and churches and schools.

The real villains, of course, were the well-organized team of real estate operators, landlords, mortgage brokers, and local machine politicians (who cried crocodile tears as neighborhood after neighborhood were destroyed and re-segregated while they raked in cash and favors from the crowd that drove and profited from the process).

This housing dynamic distilled the relentless erosion of one of the prime foundations of working class life—an affordable home, slowly gaining equity, in a stable neighborhood—into a racial psychodrama of black versus white and white versus black. And it masked another pattern of slow and undramatic unraveling that had already begun to weaken neighborhoods like the one I lived in as a kid....

■ ■ ■ ■

George Del Vecchio's mother, terrified by her bully son's temper and tantrums, saw trouble coming and had tried to find him a psychiatric treatment facility. But she couldn't bring herself to put him in a youth home that had earned its poor reputation, and she simply decided to hope and pray that he "would grow out of his condition."

While we could see and hear the moving trucks, observe the handguns and avoid the gunfire, swallow or flee the pills and other drugs displayed by pushers, track the blocks shifting from all-white to all-black in the course of a single summer, we at least had institutions, however flawed, that were "ours" that we could turn to or not turn to back when I was young. But the history of the slow and steady erosion of one set of institutions in our country and the slow and steady growth of another set of very different institutions has been largely hidden or ignored or denied.

Editor's Note: Mike Gecan was a ten-year-old fourth-grade student caught in the devastating fire at Our Lady of the Angels Catholic School on December 1, 1958. He has written several books and many articles on organizing, including *Going Public: An Organizer's Guide to Citizen Action* and *People's Institutions in Decline: Causes, Consequences, Cures.*

Questions for Discussion and Reflection

1. Did you have an experience of personal injustice or powerlessness when you were growing up? Tell the story in as much detail as possible.

2. List the people's institutions you belong to (e.g., religious, community, civic, labor, business, ethnic). List the relative health of each institution: "dying," "in trouble," "acceptable," "healthy," "vibrant." Explain your answers and what you might do to help build them up if you wanted to.

3. How have you seen racism influence people's perceptions of public policies? Have you tried to do something about it? What happened or might happen when or if you did?

A Career in Organizing

by A. Zeik Saidman

A. Zeik Saidman (born 1946) has done organizing his entire adult life as a community organizer, union organizer, mayoral political aide, and public facilitator. He worked in El Paso and Fort Worth, Texas; Chicago, Illinois; and Denver, Colorado. He is a leader through his synagogue in Coloradans for the Common Good, an affiliate of the Industrial Areas Foundation (IAF). Saidman also produced the Denver premiere of the play, *Red Hot Patriot: The Kick-Ass Wit of Molly Ivins*, about a Texas journalist and supporter of community organizing who was twice nominated for a Pulitzer Prize.

I n the midst of a busy career, few of us have the luxury of time to think about what makes us get up every morning and why we do what we do. Only later, reflecting on more than 50 years in the trenches as an organizer in a variety of capacities, did I arrive at the realization that I was driven all along by my idealism and the cultural milieu in which my generation came of age believing that we really could change the world.

One of the lessons drilled into to me at the Industrial Areas Foundation (IAF) was an understanding of the tension that exists between "the world as it is" and "the world as you would like it to be." This lesson has been incorporated into speeches by both Barack and Michelle Obama. Idealism tempered by the political reality of knowing when you can win is the art of successful work in the public arena and was a continuing theme over my career. I was drawn to be an advocate for the disadvantaged and the underdogs of our society, whether I was working as a community organizer, union organizer, a mayoral aide, or university-related public facilitator.

Perhaps this commitment was shaped by my childhood experiences when we were the only Jewish family in a small town in rural Pennsylvania and I learned to readily identify with the feeling of being the outsider. I also read Holocaust literature growing up, and the dismay and rage I felt about what the Nazis did to those who they considered inferior peoples (gays, Slavs, Gypsies, Jews) gave me the cold anger and determination to fight for the have-nots. The fights were never easy, and we didn't win them all; but in thinking about what kept me going from the time I was an innocent man in his early twenties until I had become a worldly old hand in his early seventies, I have to admit a big part was the excitement of political battle.

The grassroots organizations I was involved with ran actions against powerful institutions and formidable public figures. Our leaders were on TV. Issues we championed were in the media. When we would win on a demand, I felt I truly was changing the world. The work was never boring. There was a limited shelf life for the issues, so it was intellectually stimulating to immerse myself in something important, mobilize local leaders to confront the problem, and then move on to the next challenge. Furthermore, principles that were important to me such as fairness, equity, equality, and justice were the focus of our efforts. I never felt that I was compromising my ideals. Along the way, I forged deep public relationships with many everyday folks. I also particularly enjoyed the ethics, humor, and intellect of the clergy from the different faith traditions that I met when building congregational-based citizens organizations. At the same time, my work was aligned with my own faith tradition. The concept of *Tikkun Olam*—healing of the world—is a central tenet of Judaism. The Talmud teaches "to save one life is to save the world." I felt my work resonated with those tenets of faith. Finally, though I focused on my own education and development early on, as I matured personally and professionally I discovered real satisfaction in seeing people grow and develop as leaders. Often, years after we had worked together, I would learn that I had changed ordinary people's lives in ways I never realized.

■ ■ ■ ■

When I arrived in the Windy City in December of 1969, Judge Julius Hoffman was presiding over the circus known as the "Chicago Seven" trial. I was awed by the skyscrapers and the energy of the city that Carl Sandburg called the "hog butcher for the world." The IAF was founded by Saul Alinsky, the fountainhead of all community organizing. Saul was in his late fifties when I came to Chicago, and he died suddenly in 1972.

I first heard Alinsky speak in a small room to would-be community organizers. I was impressed by his depth and remember he seemed low-key and old, since I was a brash twenty-three-year-old. Saul didn't come across as the radical, rabble-rouser portrayed by the media. His demeanor seemed more that of a philosopher. Over the next five years I worked in various projects out of Chicago with the support of the IAF. The most memorable were helping to create the Campaign Against Pollution (CAP) and acting as an advisor to the Menominee Native Americans' DRUMS organization. CAP came into existence because the air on the South Side of Chicago was so polluted with emissions from the Commonwealth Edison power plants that it rained sulfuric acid. Paint on the cars parked in these neighborhoods faded.

The IAF lead organizer, Pete Martinez, supervised a cadre of young organizers in a grassroots fight against Com Ed. Using the Catholic parishes as a base of power, we focused on the company's annual stockholder meeting. My assignment was to recruit sympathetic students from local colleges and universities to attend. We billed it as the People's Stockholders meeting. It was an era of guerilla theater, and Studs Terkel, a writer and nationally known radio host, agreed to be the master of ceremonies for our meeting. We had a group of older women from one of the Catholic parishes who performed a "can-can" dance. We collected stock proxies and tried to get our allies inside Com Ed's stockholders meeting. CAP turned out a couple thousand supporters to the action.

Keeping the pressure on after this event, Mayor Richard J. Daley (the original) told representatives from Com Ed to meet with CAP. Daley didn't like this kind of antics in his city. It was the beginning of cleaning up the power plants. (Later, CAP went on to beat Daley in a fight over the building of the so-called "Crosstown Expressway" through the heart of many of the most stable ethnic neighborhoods in Chicago.)

■ ■ ■ ■

The Native American Menominee reservation was in far northeastern Wisconsin, but a large number of the Menominees lived in Chicago's Uptown area. I was hired by a foundation to be an advisor to DRUMS (Determination of Rights and Unity for Menominee Stockholders), an organization formed by activist members of the tribe. It was led by the charismatic Jim White. (His Native American name was Washinawatok.)

The Bureau of Indian Affairs had decided that the Menominees were a successful tribe, in part because they were running a profitable lumber mill. The reservation's land had been divided and each member of the tribe had been given shares that were held by the First Wisconsin Trust Company, a large local bank. Unscrupulous realtors and their cohorts tried to get vulnerable (impoverished and sometimes alcoholic) members of the tribe to sign over their stocks to them. Real estate interests wanted the stock options so they could get title to the land and build vacation homes along the Wolf River. One of the Alinsky-style tactics we employed targeted the First Wisconsin's flagship bank in Milwaukee. We had members of the tribe open savings accounts with pennies, disrupting the bank's business. As part of that action, Lloyd Poweless, the tribe's medicine man, put a curse on the bank's upper management. He entered the main lobby holding the skin of a dead weasel aloft. Lloyd delivered an oath containing language like "Let your woman go barren and your children not prosper." Embarrassed and shocked, the First Wisconsin Trust reconsidered its role as a trustee for the Menominees.

■ ■ ■ ■

Editor's Note: Zeik Saidman lives in Denver with his wife, Alana Smart, who is an organizer as well. He wrote the book *Mixing It Up in the Public Arena* about his career in public life, from which this essay is adapted.

Questions for Discussion and Reflection

1. What were your first experiences in public life? How have they shaped what you do now? Be specific.
2. Should organizers work with ethnic or racial groups of which they are not members? If so, why, how, and when? What should the organizers and the leaders in this situation think about?
3. What is the relationship between art and organizing? Should artists be seeking to build power with other institutions in their communities? How would this work?

Learning from the Elderly in Philly

by Tom Mosgaller

Tom Mosgaller (born 1946) organized with the Industrial Areas Foundation from 1972-1985 and 2012-2016 in Chicago, Philadelphia, Central Pennsylvania, and Wisconsin. He also served as Organizational Development Director for three mayors of the city of Madison, Wisconsin, and is past president and ethics officer of the American Society for Quality (ASQ), with 85,000 members worldwide. He spent six years as Director of Systems Change at the University of Wisconsin School of Engineering.

recently got off a plane in Philadelphia and caught the center city train line to Reading Terminal. It was a route I had become familiar with as a consultant working with the city's behavioral health system. As the conductor came down the aisle to punch my ticket, he looked at me and said, "Pardon me, sir. You look like you might be a senior citizen." I nodded and he explained that I would get half off my fare. I asked if he knew why seniors got a discount, and he said he didn't, but then he told he told me there had been a reduced fare for the elderly for at least thirty-five years— as long as he'd been working for the transit system.

I was immediately transported back to 1972 when I had joined an organizing effort in Philly that fought for the reduced fare for the elderly. Never would I have thought that almost fifty years later I would benefit personally from one of my youthful organizing campaigns so many years earlier. It triggered a whole set of memories about that amazing time and place, but more importantly fond memories of the wonderful leaders I had the privilege of working and learning from back then.

■ ■ ■ ■

As a rural farm boy from Wisconsin who had grown up on a struggling dairy farm without indoor plumbing or running water, I had seen my dad join other farmers in the 1960s in dumping their milk to get fair prices for farmers. And as a high school Catholic seminarian searching for something meaningful to do in the world, I had looked for something big (but perhaps not so big that I had to take a vow of celibacy to pursue it).

College for me was just a way to get off the farm, and the sports I played there were a wonderful escape; but people my age were marching against the Vietnam War, scornful of military inductees, and often looking for ways to get out of the draft or out of the country. Nothing in my limited world made any of these options attractive, and I didn't stumble across anything that suggested I could change the world I wanted to escape.

Then along came the draft and, somewhat miraculously, I spent two years as a military police sergeant with the 10th Mountain Division on the German border. When I got out, I was ready for anything. I returned from my military service in the winter of 1972 trying to navigate civilian life in the midst of an antiwar movement. A friend told me about a feature article he had read in *Playboy* magazine, of all places, about a guy named

Saul Alinsky and something called the Industrial Areas Foundation (IAF) in Chicago. I was immediately intrigued by the idea of a career working with people who didn't pull punches, were willing to talk about power and change, and more importantly were getting things done.

■ ■ ■ ■

I set up a meeting with the two organizers who were leading the day-to-day operations of IAF, Ed Chambers and Dick Harmon. When I drove to downtown Chicago from rural Wisconsin for the meeting, however, I was greeted with the news that Saul Alinsky had died the day before. I expected them to send me back home, but they didn't. Throughout the interview process, it was evident that the two were shaken by the loss of the IAF's founder and their mentor, but neither Chambers nor Harmon ever mentioned him to me again. Weird, I thought to myself, but understandable given their desire to stay focused on keeping the legacy of Alinsky alive.

After a mere ten days of training, I was assigned to work on an organizing campaign to stop Mayor Richard M. Daley's proposed Crosstown Expressway from cutting through the heart of Chicago's near Westside neighborhoods. The emersion into the deep end of Chicago politics in a battle with the original Daley machine was an eye-opening experience and whetted my appetite for organizing.

Before I could even get settled into Chicago, though, Chambers approached me and asked if I would go to Philadelphia. There was a fledgling organizing effort called the Council on Community Organizations

(COCO) that was looking for an organizer. Without much thought I packed my bag, got in my little Chevy Vega, and headed to Philly, with my only grounding being my brief stint in Chicago. Strange, I thought back then, but I was convinced I was invincible and knew all I needed to know.

When I got to Philly the religious and civic leaders of COCO offered me a trial period, a small stipend, gas money, and a place to stay. That is where my organizing journey really began. I was twenty-four years old. I knew no one, had not grown up in big cities, and was told my mission was to organize senior citizens. Undaunted by this reality, I accepted the challenge and began doing relational meetings with union retirees, elderly in their churches, and older residents of neighborhoods across the city to find out what they cared about.

The first action campaign the elderly had taken on under the name of the Action Group for the Elderly (AGE) was getting free checking for the elderly from First Pennsylvania Bank. This initial victory led to other financial institutions in the region to offer free checking as a way to make it safer for elderly to use checking rather than carrying cash, reducing their fear of being robbed and physically harmed, especially at the beginning of the month when social security checks came in the mail. This gave AGE leaders the will to take on the next big organizing opportunity.

■ ■ ■ ■

Mayor Frank Rizzo, the former police commissioner, was known for his tough-cop demeanor. He had pledged that if he was elected mayor he would lead the charge for lowering the transit fare for the elderly. AGE had made a mental note of his campaign pledge and was determined to hold him to his public promise.

That same spring, the Southeast Pennsylvania Transit Authority, known as SEPTA, scheduled a public hearing to see how deep the support was for a reduced fare for the elderly. AGE was brand new, with only one victory under its belt, a small leadership team, and no real experience taking on a big issue like getting the transit fares reduced for an entire region and class of people. But the leaders decided to do it anyway.

Eight AGE leaders went to the SEPTA hearing carrying a single 3'-by-4' sign stating their position supporting reducing fares for the elderly from 35 to 15 cents a ride. Flyers with the same message were handed out to everyone in the packed hearing room, and the overflow crowd that had shown up were standing two-deep along the walls and down the hallway. The hearing examiners were surprised by the large turnout, and when AGE leaders raised the sign and asked how many in attendance were in favor of AGE's request for a 15-cent fare, everyone raised their AGE flyers (even though they were not AGE members) and waved them in support. The AGE leaders made one request, that the SEPTA hearing officers reschedule the meeting so all the elderly standing could have seats and a proper opportunity to voice their opinion about the fare reduction. The hearing officers agreed, and a new hearing was scheduled for a month later in a better room that could accommodate all the people. Everyone cheered!

AGE leaders continued to press for a speedy resolution of the fare demand and spent the month mobilizing. They had only eight people at the original hearing but pledged to have 600 at the rescheduled hearing.

When the SEPTA hearing was held in June, over 750 elderly from across the region packed the large ballroom at the Ben Franklin Hotel in downtown Philly. Milton Shapp, Pennsylvania's newly elected reformist governor, surprised everyone by announcing at the hearing that he would champion the proposal for a 15-cent fare and use the state lottery (established in the 1960s) to fund it. The elderly were ecstatic and rose to applaud the governor for taking the lead.

One of the leaders of AGE, however, knew that Mayor Rizzo had ambitions to become governor and called the mayor's office in city hall just down the street from the Ben Franklin Hotel to tip off the mayor that Shapp had announced his support for the 15-cent fare. Within minutes Rizzo bounded off the elevator at the Ben Franklin, clapped his hands loudly, and announced to everyone within ear shot that he was going into the hearing to propose the fare be reduced to 10 cents! Rizzo and his entourage headed up the center aisle where Frank Bradley, who was leading the AGE delegation intercepted the mayor. Bradley, a sturdy 5'10" stood toe to toe in front of Rizzo, who was an imposing 6'2", and the AGE leader would not budge. Bradley looked Rizzo in the eye and said, "Mayor, all of us seniors here are ready to get on board the fare reduction train. All you have to do is blow the whistle and we will work with you to get the SEPTA commission votes to make it happen. What do you say Mr. Mayor?" The room was silent, the media was filming, and Bradly and Rizzo locked eyes. Suddenly, Rizzo said loudly, "Then let's get this training moving!" The ballroom broke into wild applause, and the headline the next day highlighted the role AGE played in getting the mayor and governor to compete for the support of the elderly. Soon after the hearing the SEPTA board voted to approve the recommendation reducing the fare for the elderly in the five-county region to ten cents.

■ ■ ■ ■

This victory solidified the power of the elderly of Philadelphia as an organized force to be reckoned with and launched a series of other actions leading to reducing water and gas rates, better security for the elderly living in public housing, and the retrofitting of city buses by lowering the steps and installing grab bars to make it easier to enter and exit safely. A 10-million-dollar block grant was secured to support senior citizen meal programs.

In February of 1973, the newly constituted Action Alliance of Senior Citizens of Greater Philadelphia held its founding convention. Over 1,600 delegates representing 123 senior-citizen organizations packed the hall. Both Mayor Rizzo and Governor Shapp were invited as keynoters. Shapp announced that he would lead the effort to use lottery funds to provide free fare for the elderly across the entire state of Pennsylvania. (Frank Bradley, the International Electrical Workers (IEW) leader, was elected President of the Action Alliance; Mike Tyson of the Steelworkers was elected First VP; Lillian Holliday, an African American church leader, was elected Second VP; and Doris Selig, representing the Jewish Community Centers, was elected Secretary-Treasurer.)

Following the founding convention, the Action Alliance held the governor to his promise of free fares across the state for the elderly, and at the second convention in 1974, 250 senior-citizen organizations packed the Philadelphia Convention Center with over 2500 delegates. Local radio station KYW broadcast the event live on site all day.

The Action Alliance went on to champion senior causes for over twenty-five years and became a national model for the building of broad-based coalitions of the elderly and disabled.

Frank Rizzo moved on to a more complex political world, with increasingly racist policies and major controversies that marred his political reputation and undermined his quest to become governor. His endorsement of Richard Nixon in 1972 and change of political parties moved him to the national stage, but in an undesirable light. He died of a heart attack while running to return to the mayoralty in 1991. Milton Shapp ran unsuccessfully for the Democratic Party nomination for President of the United States in 1976 and eventually retired.

The Action Alliance maintained its independence through it all.

■ ■ ■ ■

Editor's Note: Tom Mosgaller continues to work on large systems change in the fields of education, healthcare, and agriculture. He has maintained his agrarian roots by raising grass-fed beef on his farm outside Madison, Wisconsin. Mosgaller and his wife, Donna, have two adult children and four grandchildren. They met in Philadelphia when Tom was organizing the Action Alliance of Senior Citizens. Mosgaller says, "While I went on to serve as organizer for other organizing efforts in central Pennsylvania, among farmers in my home state of Wisconsin, and most recently with teachers in Wisconsin after then governor Scott Walker pulled the trap door on unions, I will always look back with gratitude for the opportunity to cut my teeth in organizing with people who had organized during the depression, led their unions and churches during and after World War II, survived the red-baiting of the 1950s, and never took their foot off the pedal no matter what their age." One of Mosgaller's mentors was a Wisconsinite by the name of Ben Logan, who died a few years ago. Logan's book *The Land Remembers* opens with a phrase that Mosgaller used recently to deliver the eulogy for a farm family's daughter, a fifty-year-old fifth-grade teacher/farmer who died unexpectedly of cancer, leaving behind a whole lot of grief: "Once you have lived on the land, been a partner with its moods, secrets, and seasons, you cannot leave. The living land remembers, touching you in unguarded moments, saying, 'I am here. You are part of me.'"

Questions for Discussion and Reflection

1. What does the IAF mean when it tells leaders and organizers "Never do for people what they can do for themselves." Why is the this the "Iron Rule" of power?

2. Alinsky used to call playing one side off against the other "social jiu-jitsu." Do you have an example from your own life or from history of practicing social jiu-jitsu? Tell the story.

3. Why is it more powerful to organize with diversity than against it? How do groups get played off against one another? Why and how does relational organizing overcome divisions between people of different backgrounds, ages, beliefs, experience?

The Power of Public Conversation

by Ernesto Cortes, Jr.

Ernesto Cortes, Jr. (born 1943) was the founding lead organizer of Communities Organized for Public Services (COPS) in San Antonio in 1974, the longest-running current affiliate of the Industrial Areas Foundation (IAF). COPS and other IAF organizations in Texas have had a major impact on incorporating the Latino population into the political landscape in that state. Cortes became the co-executive director of the national Industrial Areas Foundation after the retirement of Ed Chambers and continues to oversee the development of the W/SW IAF in the states west of the Mississippi River. He has been awarded the H.J. Heinz Award for Public Policy and a "genius" award by the McArthur Foundation.

n this age of "political correctness," instead of engaging in conversation, debate, or argument, most of us engage in "station identification," in which we basically identify ourselves and our predetermined positions, then (at best) pause appropriately while some else speaks and we think about what we are going to say next. Or we avoid conversation completely, especially if we know it has the potential to expose tension and conflict, as political discussions often do. As a result, the real conversations of engagement—of listening, and particularly of listening to another person as someone with a different perspective, a different point of view, a different story or history—rarely takes place anymore.

Yet it is only through these kinds of conversations that we develop the capacity to think long-term, to consider something outside of our own experience, to reconsider our own experience, and to develop a larger vision of our neighborhood, our state, or our society. Unfortunately, most people don't develop the capacity to have deliberative conversations on their own. These still must be developed inside what we in the Industrial Areas Foundation (IAF) call "people's institutions," that is, institutions that people in them own and control.

■ ■ ■ ■

Recent decades have witnessed an erosion of the institutions Alexis de Tocqueville (in his seminal book *Democracy in America*) thought were so important to sustain our associative democracy: family, neighborhood organization, political party, congregation, labor union, and mutual aid society. One of the purposes of these mediating institutions had been to assist people in slowing down, navigating, and adjusting to change, be it economic, political, personal, or societal. It is particularly damaging that at the same time these institutions have been deteriorating the rate of change in modern society has increased dramatically. The weakening of these institutions has meant that massive technological and cultural changes, embedded in and concomitant with the globalizing forces transforming our world, have untethered what de Toqueville called our "Augustinian Souls," by which he meant the tension between our inclination toward self-absorbed narcissism and, at the same time, our tendency to overreach in an attempt to dominate, creating an internal migration into our own selves. For the wealthy, this is manifested in a culture of class narcissism; and for those not so wealthy, it becomes alienation, or Simone Weil's concept of *malheur*—a crushing of the spirit that occurs when life becomes so overwhelming that only the instincts for survival are relevant.

A counterweight to these forces is for organized mediating institutions to place an emphasis on practices focused on character development, *philia* (Aristotle's notion of political friendship), *phroenesis* (the practical wisdom which comes form *metis* or tacit knowledge), *praxis* (action that is aimed, calculated, and develops reflective thinking), and the justice that emerges when all parties with a stake in the question are involved in the deliberation. These qualities require the customs and habits of deliberation and negotiation necessary for the successful functioning of a free and open democratic society.

In my own experience, organizing cultivates those practices when we take time to teach people to have one-to-one relational meetings and reflect on them afterwards. The practices are further developed when the relational meetings lead to house meetings, whether they take place in a home or a school or a recreation center of a church or synagogue or mosque or temple. These small group meetings are about telling stories and developing narratives, but also about inquiring into the deep concerns affecting people's daily lives. The quality of schools, the absence of safe playground equipment, flooding, low wages, lack of healthcare—these types of issues are all too often a part of the daily lives of low- and moderate-income families. These small-group conversations, properly directed and aimed, then lead to research actions to explore the dynamics, dimensions, and complexities of an issue in order to prepare for public action.

■ ■ ■ ■

Through this process we learn to engage people who come from other contexts—business leaders, bureaucrats, union allies, and so forth. Properly conducted, these conversations help people get inside one another's moral universe through sharing their stories and experiences and, by so doing, begin to develop political friendships (*philia*). Another way of thinking about it is that the organizing process is about putting a relational concept of self-interest in tension with being concerned for others. It enables people to understand that sustaining and developing their own self-interest requires them to be concerned with the self-interest of others. This doesn't happen naturally, but only through the institutions that develop the relational context in which people begin to understand, for example, that for their children to do well in school requires a public education system that enables other people's children to succeed as well. Or, as Benjamin Franklin so prosaically put it: "If we don't hang together, we all hang separately."

An example of this kind of transformation occurred in the early 1980s when the Texas Industrial Areas Foundation Network was organizing to support a new public education finance and accountability system known as House Bill 72. One of the biggest stumbling blocks for our network was the issue of funding for bilingual education. Members of some of the more middle-class Anglo congregations involved in the network thought bilingual education was a strategy that kept Latino students from learning English and becoming "more American." It was only through conversations and engagement (e.g., twenty-seven house meetings in just one congregation alone) with those who had experiences different from their own that a common understanding emerged. This is just one illustration of how the organizing process can overcome obstacles to creating one of the prerequisites that Aristotle though was necessary for the common good—the connection of our "politicalness" to our humanity.

■ ■ ■ ■

REVEILLE FOR A NEW GENERATION

Editor's Note: Ernie Cortes is the executive director of the SW/W Industrial Areas Foundation. His work is the subject of the book *Cold Anger: A Story of Faith and Politics* by Mary Beth Rogers, with a Foreword by Bill Moyers.

Questions for Discussion and Reflection

1. List the differences between a public and a private conversation. Which are more effect for organizing? Why?

2. What is the connection between our "politicalness" and our humanity? Give some concrete examples from your own life.

3. Name ways others shut down conversation with you. Be specific. Now name the ways you shut down conversations with others.

Rebuilding BUILD

by Arnie Graf

Arnie Graf (born 1943) was an organizer for Communities Organized for Public Service (COPS) in San Antonio, Texas; Baltimoreans United In Leadership
Development (BUILD) in Baltimore, Maryland; Washington Interfaith Network
(WIN) in the District of Columbia; and several other organizations. He also
served as a co-executive director of the Industrial Areas Foundation (IAF) from
2010-2012. This essay is expanded in a new book of stories, *Lessons Learned*,
about his organizing career by Graf that was published by ACTA Publications
in 2020.

W hen he had recruited me to take the job as the lead organizer
in Baltimore in 1980, Ed Chambers, then executive director
of the IAF at the time told me that, although Baltimoreans
United in Leadership Development (BUILD) was floundering, he had
three reasons to believe in its possibilities. Their names were Monsignor
Clare O'Dwyer, Rev. Wendell Phillips, and Rev. Vernon Dobson.

Unfortunately for me, when I began my work in September of 1980,
Msgr. O'Dwyer had just announced his retirement. So much for the first
leg of my BUILD leadership stool!

My first meeting with Rev. Phillips, on the other hand, was unfor-
gettable. I did not know what to expect, since I had not met him during

my interviews with the leaders in March 1980. When I called him for a one-to-one, he told me to meet him on the front porch of his home. As I sat waiting for him, I heard a loud roar from a huge motorcycle coming down the street. The man driving the bike pulled into the driveway next to the porch where I was sitting. He was a very large black man with long hair, wearing a torn tee shirt and torn shorts. He got off his motorbike and yelled, "Are you Arnie Graf?" He came onto the porch, offered me a drink, and then began talking. I quickly realized what a smart, engaging, humorous man I was with. Rev. Phillips had striking blue eyes, a huge stomach, an infectious laugh. and an engaging mind. He had founded the first African American United Church of Christ congregation in Baltimore.

After asking me about my background and past experiences, he told me of his long engagement with the Black civil rights struggles in Baltimore. Later, as I got to know his congregation, I met some of his wonderful leaders. Some of them became part of the initial corps of leaders who reorganized BUILD. I often visited the pastor in his office, and on his desk was a big sign that said, "Baby Blue." I stopped by there for support, advice, laughter, and intellectual stimulation. He was a unique person who showed me a lot of love. Rev. Phillips had strong doubts about BUILD's viability, but he promised that now I was on the job he would take a wait-and-see approach rather than leave the organization.

My next visit was to the third leg of the stool, Rev. Vernon Dobson, the pastor of Union Baptist Church. In Rev. Dobson, I eventually found a mentor, pastor, teacher, colleague, and dear friend. His nickname in the community was "father," because people from all walks of life came to him for assistance and advice. The constant stream of people who came to his office ranged from addicts and homeless people to city council members, congresspeople, and senators. He was a lion of a man. His voice boomed. His anger and his humor were both dramatic and contagious—a unique combination. I instinctively knew I had to connect to Rev. Dobson in a special way as Msgr. O'Dwyer had retired and Rev. Phillips was, at best, very skeptical about BUILD's future.

But as unusual as my meeting with Rev. Phillips was, my first meeting with Rev. Dobson left me feeling confused and defeated. As I drove up to Union Baptist Church for my scheduled meeting with Rev. Dobson, I saw a group of African American men arguing loudly. As I got out of my car, I observed Rev. Dobson in the middle of the group, talking louder than anyone else. As I stood there taking in the scene, a white man in a pick-up truck parked behind me. The man got out of his truck and walked into the screaming group and at the top of his lungs yelled, "Is Shorty Red here?" The group got quiet and stared at the man.

Rev. Dobson yelled at the man, "What do you want with him?" The man said that he wanted to buy more of the bricks that Shorty was selling him for 25 cents per brick. Just at that moment, a short man with red hair took off down the street like a bat out of hell. After a couple of seconds, the entire group, with Rev. Dobson in the lead, took off after Shorty. Rev. Dobson was yelling, "Shorty, if I catch you, I am going to kill you!"

I soon learned that "Shorty Red" was one of the many people that Rev. Dobson looked after. It seemed that Shorty—instead of helping Rev. Dobson's crew build a coffee house on the corner of Dolphin and Lanvale as a place where people from the community could gather in a safe and comfortable place—was selling the bricks at night to this white guy for a quarter a brick!

And here I was, the new lead organizer of BUILD, an organization of only ten congregations that was $32,000 in debt, standing across the street from Union Baptist Church, watching the third leg of the stool running down the street threatening a man's life.

I got into my car and sat there feeling confused, lost, and hopeless.

After a while, I started to drive aimlessly around the neighborhood. At some point I began to take in the scenery: hundreds of abandoned homes, trash strewn everywhere, broken glass-filled vacant lots, men standing on corners with vacant eyes, young women crossing the streets with baby carriages, children laughing and playing, police and ambulance sirens blasting constantly, elderly people sitting on their stoops talking with one another, and teenagers playing basketball in schoolyards—just as I had done in my twenties in New York City.

The next day, I arose ready to work—albeit unsure of what to do with such a weak organization in such a distressed city.

■ ■ ■ ■

Over the next weeks, I met with over 250 people individually for thirty-to-sixty minutes each. The people I met with lived all over the city. They were an economically diverse group: some middle-class, some working class, and some low income. Most were leaders or at least active in their congregation, school, or neighborhood in one way or the other. I met Vivian Washington, the woman who founded the Pacquin School, the first public high school for pregnant teenagers. I met successful doctors, lawyers, dentists, and accountants. I met Wendell Wright, a lover of classical music who raised scholarship money for Black artists to pursue their careers. I met numerous teachers, principals, and adults who ran athletic and social clubs for youth and teenagers. I heard stirring choirs and powerful preaching. I met people who were true historians and story tellers.

I also met many struggling mothers and fathers who were too scarred to even want to believe that anything could change. While I saw some of the failings of religious institutions, I also saw the strength, grace, power and beauty of the Black church. In my meetings, I was listening for three things. First, I was listening for people's personal stories; second, I tried to find out if they had a following; and, third, I wanted to find out if any of them had an appetite to act publicly on the issues of concern they raised.

After every individual meeting I had, I wrote a brief summary on an index card briefly highlighting stories I heard, the problem areas people raised, and a notation of other organizations they belonged to and if they were willing to act on the areas of their concern. I also noted the names of other leaders they suggested I meet. While people raised education, youth concerns, crime, housing, and unemployment as issues of concern, underlying all of these issues were race and racism. Deciding on an issue to attack that would result in a meaningful victory was a difficult task, given BUILD's lack of power at the time.

As I listened to people, however, the lack of affordable housing often came up. I knew from my previous organizing experience in Milwaukee that local banks often "red-lined" African American neighborhoods. Redlining is the practice by banks of drawing red lines around neighborhoods where they would not make home mortgage or rehab loans. While no bank would admit to this practice, I knew we could get the records of every bank's lending practices through the Community Reinvestment Act (CRA). This Act was passed by Congress in the 1970s—a victory that our organization in Milwaukee was tangentially involved in at the time.

As I asked people who raised housing as an issue about the behavior of Baltimore's banks, many said it was extremely difficult, if not impossible, to get a mortgage or home improvement loan in the neighborhood where they lived.

I began to agitate around the behavior of Baltimore's banks toward the Black community, and I discovered that the banks, with their big presence downtown, stood out as a symbol of the resentment many people felt toward the white power establishment in the city. I received a visceral response from many leaders, especially when I told them that through the CRA we would be able to prove the banks' racist policies. While skeptical, a number of people volunteered to get the lending information on each bank and tabulate the data of mortgage loans by zip code for the year 1979. What we learned was that of the $426 million in mortgage loans granted by all of the major banks in Baltimore that year, only 1.6% of those loans were made to the zip codes that represented the Black neighborhoods in the city. Given that 60% of Baltimore's population was African American, this statistic even astounded leaders like Rev. Dobson.

■ ■ ■ ■

The first step BUILD needed to take was to organize as many people as possible to reveal our findings to a broad cross-section of people in a dramatic way. To do this, I met with the pastors and lay leaders that still belonged to BUILD. I also called all the people who had raised housing and racist bank behavior to me during my individual meetings. The leadership team asked people to come to Our Lady of Lourdes Roman Catholic Church to see the proof we had uncovered. Additionally, we worked hard to get the media there.

We brought a couple of leaders from each member congregation to plan the agenda and to select the spokespeople. I taught that night that an action is like a three-act drama. Before the play, we needed to work on the logistics and do a rehearsal. We asked the leaders to pledge how many people they committed to bring to Our Lady of Lourdes on the night of the action. Our goal was to fill the basement of the church with 225 people. After two rehearsals, we were as ready as we were going to be.

I did not sleep much the night before the action. I knew that if this action was a failure, we would most likely have to end our effort in Baltimore. About fifteen minutes before the action, the room was only half filled, but in the next fifteen minutes the rest of the room filled up. In fact, we had to set up more chairs to accommodate everyone. Putting out additional chairs is an organizer's delight. The leaders and I were feeling good. Even the media showed up and, very importantly, Rev. Dobson and Rev. Phillips came.

We had great visuals that showed the mortgage lending practice by every bank in the year 1979 by zip code. Fr. Eugene McKenna, SSJ, the pastor of Our Lady of Lourdes and a wonderful man, revealed the data for each bank in a very dramatic way. People booed spontaneously as the results of each bank was were revealed. The action ended with volunteers signing up to meet with various bank presidents.

The next morning, I sat in the BUILD office reading the press accounts of our action—waiting to hear from some of the bank presidents' response to BUILD's request to meet with them. After waiting by the phone over two hours, I knew no bank president had any intention of reacting to BUILD's request to meet. (The first issue for this organization, as always, was recognition. Without recognition, you do not exist.) The leaders were simultaneously deeply disappointed and incensed by being ignored. They called an emergency meeting to decide what to do next. I had met with the members of the planning team individually. Their responses ranged from, "I told you so" to a desire not to give up.

At the next meeting, I began with a training session on the ingredients of power. Boiled down to their essence, they are: organized people and organized money. I asked the leaders how much money they thought that their congregations, schools, Head Start Centers, and other institutions— as well as their individual members—had in a bank. At the next meeting, I took forty-five minutes to teach that money was an important source of power. We dedicated the next forty-five minutes to the description of a proposal: doing an anonymous survey in the member congregations to see where people and their congregations, organizations, and members banked and to ascertain how much money they had in their accounts.

Getting the congregations' budgets for their church, schools, and other organizations was the easy part; finding out where and how much money people had in their accounts, even though the survey was to be anonymous, was going to be the hard part. To obtain the various pastors' agreement to this idea, we held a clergy meeting to get their buy-in. Additionally, the lay leaders met with their pastors to ask them to take the lead on this idea, because without the pastors' leadership, this idea would never take place. With the pastors' agreements, BUILD held "Survey Sunday."

The leaders collected the surveys at the end of each Sunday service and then tabulated the results. To their surprise, the total that their members, congregations, and organizations had sitting in the banks that refused to meet with BUILD was $15 million. While objectively in a modern economy this is not a lot of money, it was certainly much more than the leaders had expected. The reality of controlling $15 million emboldened the leaders. The leaders next step was to call a meeting of the BUILD membership to review the results of the survey. This time there was no concern about the size of the turnout.

Phyllis Douglas, BUILD's president, and Fr. McKenna did an excellent job in walking through the results of the survey. To pour salt in the wound, we had learned from Vinnie Quayle, the director of St. Ambrose Housing, a well-respected nonprofit affordable housing organization, that there was a Maryland State law that guaranteed mortgage loans made by banks under a certain amount of money to qualified borrowers. This meant that banks willing to make loans to mostly African American city residents would not lose any money even if the borrower defaulted on the mortgage payments. This fact, plus having $15 million in the banks, emboldened the people to act if the bank presidents continued to refuse to meet with BUILD. The rest is a story for another time.

■ ■ ■ ■

Editor's Note: Arnie Graf is now retired and continues to mentor and support leaders and organizers. He lives in Maryland with his wife Lucile and has written a memoir, *Lessons Learned*, on his life as an organizer. He says: "The lessons I learned as a young and struggling teacher informed my work as an organizer over a period of 45 years with the Industrial Areas Foundation. I hope my book will effectively demonstrate the key universal lessons I have learned about power, self-interest, building real and enduring public relationships, training and developing leaders, and turning paralysis or random activity into effective action and lasting impact. Ultimately, I will consider myself to be a success if I can inspire new people to take up organizing as their life's work."

Questions for Discussion and Reflection

1. "All organizing is reorganizing." What does this organizing aphorism mean to you? Give an example or two from your own life.

2. Make a list of the qualities of a leader that organizers look for. How many of these qualities do you have? How and why would you want to learn and exhibit more of them?

3. "Power comes from organized people and organized money." Give examples of organized people, organized money, and organized people + money.

Two Stories and a Poem

by Kathleen O'Toole

Kathleen O'Toole (born 1952) began organizing 1975 and worked with the Industrial Areas Foundation (IAF) as an organizer, supervisor, and trainer between 1989-2013. She was part of the first cadre of [lay] women to become lead organizers in the IAF network and continues to mentor and consult with leaders and organizers. She organized in low-income communities in Wilmington, Delaware; New Orleans, Louisiana; Trenton, NJ; Baltimore, Maryland; and the suburbs of Washington, DC. Also a widely published poet, O'Toole says, "Poetry does matter—to me, and my poetry to others—when it interrogates faith in the face of failed and fractured human relationships, celebrates beauty and grace in tension with the questions of injustice framed for me in years of work in poor and vulnerable communities."

t is late 1976. The United States of America has just celebrated its bicentennial. I am twenty-four years old and a year into my first organizing job just thirty miles from Philadelphia in my hometown of Wilmington, Delaware—the site of the longest national guard occupation following the civil unrest that followed Martin Luther King's assassination in 1968, and (not coincidentally) the home of the DuPont corporate headquarters.

As a rookie organizer for Wilmington United Neighborhoods (WUN), an umbrella organization of religious and civic groups typical of the many community organizations, including Industrial Areas Foundation (IAF) affiliates in 1970s, I'm assigned to organize our fight against a blatant move by local power brokers to close two of three campuses of the Wilmington Medical Center (WMC) and build a brand new campus in the suburbs. We would later discover some hospital board minutes that revealed the decision to move had been made within a year of "the riots," noting that the Medical Center would likely have to leave "…some medical services…for the type of population that would be left in the city in the 1980s."

We had launched our campaign at an assembly of 800 church and neighborhood leaders and held candlelight vigils, town halls, and marches of 200-300 people for over a year. On this day, though, I'm with a small delegation of WUN leaders who had crashed a Medical Center press conference where the WMC representatives would reiterate that their "Plan Omega" would go forward and that it would be "unchanged" based on the community uproar. It was to be their "final offer." No "concessions" would be made.

I remember two things about that day. First, the *who-do-you-think-you-are-to question-us* dismissal of our leaders by the WMC President and Board Representative (who just happened to be a DuPont Senior VP), and in particular the latter's refusal to acknowledge or even look at Mrs. Lillian Oliver, an elder lay leader of Union Baptist Church, who'd marched in Selma and from whom I'd learned the stories of the National Guard occupation of Wilmington's Black neighborhoods in 1968.

Second, I remember the hot tears and rage I felt as I returned, feeling completely defeated, to the parking garage after the action, and the moment this good Irish Catholic kid from the suburbs thought to myself: "If I had a (fill in the blank), I'd blow something up." That day, I'd felt the powerlessness that was the daily bread of many of my Wilmington neighbors. What I had not learned (yet) was the difference between neighborhood organizing for protest and a more long-term, broad-based organizing for power.

■ ■ ■ ■

Pentecost Sunday, 1994, nearly two decades later, in my second year as lead organizer of Baltimoreans United in Leadership Development (BUILD), the IAF affiliate in Baltimore, 500 church leaders pack the sanctuary of Knox Presbyterian Church for an action in which BUILD leaders—along with Gerald McEntee, National President of the IAF-allied union the American Federation of Federal, State, County, and Municipal Employees (AFSCME), and Catholic Auxiliary Bishop John Ricard of the Archdiocese of Baltimore—will throw open the doors of the church to more than 100 low-wage workers and join them in founding Solidarity Sponsoring Committee (SSC), a new workers' association that would eventually become an AFSCME local. Together they would call for a "new social compact" in which service and contractual workers would share in the fruits of the city's publicly funded development by earning a "living family wage." An ordinance was working its way through Baltimore City Council that, when approved six months later, would become the nation's first living-wage bill, soon to be replicated in more than one hundred other jurisdictions.

The power I experienced on this day, bringing organized labor, newly organized workers, and organized religious institutions together was electrifying to a woman who had recently turned forty. I still remember the moment when the church leaders stood to cheer the procession of custodial workers, hotel housekeepers, and school bus drivers entering the sanctuary, whom our leaders and organizers had met on downtown street corners, at bus stops, around school buildings, over coffee at McDonalds, in church soup kitchens, and in house meetings for over a year, and whose names and stories and aspirations we now knew.

Then there were lots of loud "Amens" when Bishop Ricard, an otherwise mild-mannered member of the Catholic hierarchy and an African-American native of Louisiana, caught fire—embracing these worker-leaders as precious children of God, drawing on one-hundred years of Catholic social teaching to proclaim the right of these and all workers to organize and receive just compensation. The power of that moment, when the moral imagination of the religious teachings I had been taught since childhood was embodied by the political muscle of nearly fifty dues-paying congregations in BUILD who had organized their people—and their money—persistently and consistently in Baltimore for nearly twenty years, negotiating college scholarships, insuring jobs from the corporate sector for city high school graduates, and building hundreds of houses for homeowners of modest income on public land. Now they were aiming their power and alliances at the city's economic life.

BUILD did not win all we had aimed for in the Living Wage Campaign, namely tying living wage jobs as a condition to all public subsidies in the city. But the staged increases for all workers hired through city (and many state) contracts from the then $4.25/hour minimum wage to $6.60 (it's now, in 2020, over $12) immediately saw workers, like SSC leader Renee Brown and her husband, pay off predatory school loans, make home repairs, and invest in their neighborhoods. Hundreds of Baltimore Community College students who would have been forced to leave school under the Clinton "workfare" rules, were able to finish their degrees with prospects of better paying jobs, precisely because BUILD had the political clout (in an election year) to negotiate a pilot program called "School Counts" with Maryland Governor Parris Glendenning. And the IAF's "living wage" campaigns multiplied nationally.

■ ■ ■ ■

In addition to organizing, I have followed my other great passion in life, which is to write poetry. Here is a poem I wrote in 1993 about one of the many actions we had in Baltimore, this one related to policing in a low-income African American neighborhood. I wrote it while reflecting on Saul Alinsky's dictum: "The first issue is always recognition." This poem was first published in my first full-length poetry collection, *Meanwhile* (2011, David Roberts Books.)

Baltimore, 1993

The police commander shuffles his papers

never looking up, never looking into

the faces that look at him, who see

behind his aversion a trail of ancestors,

of authority's faces, always averted

when white sheets bled the night,

diverted as justice suited itself. Don't look

to these eyes to recognize your face

distant son of Ashanti, daughter of X.

The mirrored shades are in his head,

reflecting only the blind and empty light.

A break in the action. Down the rain-cleared

street, I enter a McDonald's, still on edge.

Beside me a man drags a worn duffle: all

his belongings, I guess, along with the clothes

on his back. He dumps his pockets out

onto the counter. Three packs of matches,

four quarters, some loose small change. Coffee,

he mutters. The youths behind the counter

exchange grins. Their eyes say it all.

His never look up, never look out

from the footage that must be reeling inside.

Before this night ends, I'll agitate the leaders
who noticed the commander's grunts and nods,
name the power gained with signed agreements
on official paper, even see recognition dawn
in a few faces. I know my dollar's worth of burger
won't begin to remedy the bag man's hunger,
yet that moment turned the youngsters' gaze
his way. On these streets epiphanies are dear.
Cost and consequence blur once I arrive
home to unbend my own face in the mirror.

▪ ▪ ▪ ▪

Editor's Note: Kathleen O'Toole has taught writing at Johns Hopkins University and the Maryland Institute College of Art and left her last full-time job at Catholic Relief Services in 2018. She has won many awards for poetry and published her work in many journals, anthologies, and magazines. O'Toole is the current Poet Laureate of Takoma Park, Maryland, and says that she continues to delight—and write—sailing the Chesapeake Bay and its tributaries with her husband (and best publicist) John Ruthrauff. She has taken vows as a Benedictine Oblate at Emmanuel Monastery in Baltimore. Her latest book of poems is titled *This Far* (Paraclete Press, 2019), of which poet Paul Mariani writes: "Kathleen O'Toole is not only a master of poetic form, but a seasoned pilgrim whom we can trust."

Questions for Discussion and Reflection

1. What do you think Saul Alinsky meant when he said that the "first issue" is always "recognition"? Give some examples from your own life. Be specific.

2. Why do organizers agitate leaders and vice versa? Is it a good thing or a bad thing? Explain your answer with a story or a poem, either one of your own or someone else's.

3. What does it feel like to win—or to lose—an issue that is vitally important to you and to your community? Why are epiphanies "dear"? What are the "costs and consequences" of them, and why do they "blur"?

Ice Breaker

by Pastor H. Lionel Edmonds

Pastor H. Lionel Edmonds is the Senior Minister of Mt. Lebanon Baptist Church in Washington, DC. In 1996, Pastor Edmonds became the co-founder of the Washington Interfaith Network (WIN), which has won major victories in the nation's capital such as the billion dollar Neighborhood Investment Fund (a fund that produced over two-hundred million dollars for affordable housing created by WIN congregations and ally institutions), the Project Labor Agreement (an agreement between the city and the building trades unions that has produced thousands of jobs for Washington residents entering the construction industry), and the one-hundred-million-dollar Youth Investment Fund (a fund that created after-school programming for District of Columbia public schools).

Life's universals can descend upon us while we are performing our daily responsibilities, even while clearing a block of ice inside a grocery store meat freezer.

I did not expect to learn a great universal of power while I held an ice pick and stared at a seemingly unmovable and insurmountable ten-foot block of ice in a particular grocery store in Washington, DC, in the summer of 1984. Yet what I learned that day has benefited my calling as a pastor and my work as a community leader and organizer for nearly four decades.

■ ■ ■ ■

In my early twenties, I was a college student with a young family, working at a local Safeway grocery store in Washington. I would work my morning shift at the store in Dupont Circle, then go over to the University of the District of Columbia for afternoon and evening classes. I had felt the call to enter the ministry a few years back and was academically preparing myself for pastoral work. But since few congregations at that time in the African American Church community employed ministers on their payroll outside of the pastor, with my young family to support I had to work to help make ends meet.

Not everyone in the grocery store viewed my ministry intentions with a graceful eye. My manager at the store was, in particular, quite obstinate. He seemed offended by my desire to earn an undergraduate degree, let alone my pursuit of a graduate divinity degree. I must confess that sometimes I would use some "Old Testament" language when I talked about him at home with my wife, in particular about the ways he would constantly put up hurdles to block my educational progress. For example, my boss had a habit of changing my work schedule at the last moment, thus making it almost impossible for me to attend my afternoon and evening classes. Oftentimes I wanted to quit that job, but in the back of my mind I could hear the voice of my wife telling me not to break the eleventh commandment: "Happy wife, happy life." Needless to say, I stuck things out at Safeway.

■ ■ ■ ■

One afternoon at work I was ready to clock out and go to class when my manager approached me. I knew what was about to come down. "Lionel," he said with a certain smirk on his face, "I need you to go downstairs into the meat freezer and clean it up before you leave today." I mumbled a couple of Old Testament words under my breath and proceeded downstairs to the meat freezer, my nemesis right behind me to enjoy the show. What I met when I opened the freezer door made me understand why he had that silly smile on his face. Before my eyes, standing like the iceberg that sank the Titanic, was a block of ice that was at least ten feet wide and ten feet high. "Here's an ice pick," my manager grinned. "You might need this. Don't forget, I need that block of ice removed completely before you leave today."

The anger and rage that was boiling in me like lava from an active volcano should have melted that block of ice by itself, but it didn't. Thoughts of quitting right then and there flooded my soul. I knew I would never be able to break up that iceberg in front of me in time to still make my classes. But then the eleventh commandment flashed in front of my mind's eye, and I simply stood there with that old wooden ice pick in my hand, staring at the gigantic block of ice that went from the freezer floor almost to the ceiling.

That's when the Spirit of God spoke to me. I was not within the fellowship of the House of God's house when the Spirit spoke, I was in a grocery store freezer; yet God has a way of revealing universal truths in strange and peculiar places: "Take what your opponent has given you, that ice pick in your hand, and hit the block of ice at its base."

I walked over to the iceberg and took a big swing at it, hitting the bottom of the ten-foot block with the sharp end of the ice pick. When I pulled the pick back, I noticed a crack had begun to be formed at the base of the ice.

"Hit it again," the Spirit said. I took another swing, placing the ice pick right where the crack had begun to take shape. This time the crack raced all the way up to the middle of the ice, like a sprinter running a race. I didn't have to hear the Divine again, for I immediately gave the iceberg a third whack, and this time the crack preceded all the way to the top—ten feet up—and I jumped back as the entire iceberg tumbled and fell like a stack of cards. The noise of the collapse caused the manager to come running back into the freezer. The astonished look on his face as he saw the pieces of ice lying of the freezer floor was one I will never forget. "Here's your pick, Boss," I said. "I'm going to class." And I strolled out of the freezer.

■ ■ ■ ■

What I learned that day was a lesson in power. The manager thought he possessed power over my Black body. He felt he could control my movements and mess with my life. But the universal lesson I learned that day is that power is not owned by the oppressor. Power belongs to those who possess the capacity to think in a creative and organized way and then to act with strength and precision.

I also learned that power needs a target to express itself, just as my power needed an ice block in a grocery store freezer. I learned that the Lord will send us the resources we need to accomplish the task—even using the resources of a bully, like my manager, who unknowingly gave me the ice pick that ultimately contributed to the fall of the obstacle he had created for me. I learned the principle of applied pressure: that no matter how large the obstacle, it can fall if you hit it correctly and sustain or repeat the hit.

I did finish undergraduate school and ultimately entered the Howard University School of Divinity. That's where I met Arnie Graf, an organizer with the Industrial Areas Foundation (IAF), who was teaching a workshop on community organizing that I attended. A few years later, Arnie asked if I would help him create an IAF affiliate in Washington, DC. We did, calling it the Washington Interfaith Network (WIN). We've been breaking icebergs in the system ever since.

■ ■ ■ ■

Editor's Note: Pastor Edmonds has gone on to write books and articles on spiritual formation, helped to establish over thirty million dollars of affordable housing at Mt. Lebanon Baptist Church, assisted in the creation of economic development programs and ministries for congregational growth throughout Washington, DC, and is now organizing with lead organizer Coleman Milling in building a new Metro Industrial Areas Foundation affiliate in Maryland called the Prince George's County Leadership Action Network.

Questions for Discussion and Reflection

1. Name a "block of ice" you had to confront in your life? What happened? What did you learn about power from the experience?

2. Do you believe in "the principle of applied pressure"? How does it work?

3. How do your religious and/or philosophical beliefs and training support your ability and willingness to take effective action? Be specific, with examples.

The Myth of Scarcity

by Jeffrey K. Krehbiel

Rev. Jeffrey K. Krehbiel (1959-2017) was a native of Ann Arbor, Michigan, and was ordained a minister in the Presbyterian Church (USA). He served as a pastor on the West Side of Manhattan, in inner-city Wilmington, Delaware, and at the Church of the Pilgrims in Washington, DC. Krehbiel believed the church is called to be a community of alternative values and practices that bears witness to the gospel in common life and also believed faith communities could challenge themselves to become agents of change, leading to his decades-long commitment to community organizing. In 1994, he co-founded the Wilmington Interfaith Network, and in Washington, DC, he served as co-chair of the Washington Interfaith Network—both affiliates of the Industrial Areas Foundation (IAF).

have a friend who calls himself a "community-organizing fundamentalist." By that he means that community organizing offers the best hope not only for the renewal of American democracy but also for the renewal of the church itself. This phrase speaks to me. I have been involved in community organizing for over twenty-five years and have come to know firsthand more than a dozen groups organized on a "broad-based" or "faith-based" model. Together, these organizations have fought to build thousands of units of affordable housing, reform troubled public schools, put police on the streets, and invest millions of dollars in city neighborhoods.

What I have learned from community organizing has helped me understand not only how any congregation or religious institution can effectively impact its local community but also how it can strengthen its own membership at the same time. This is the unique gift that I believe institutionally based community organizing offers to congregations of all faiths and denominations. Despite this truth, however, the basic vocabulary of community organizing—e.g., "power," "self-interest," "anger"—has always been troubling to many religious leaders. How often at a worship service, during the corporate prayer of confession, we are asked to disavow our preference for "the currency of power" and our "selfish ambition," while being exhorted to consider our own interests last? Jesus is understood by many church people to be a model of self-effacing humility and powerlessness, while community organizers and leaders exult in the virtue of self-interest and the necessity of anger and power. For many religious people, the vocabulary of faith and the vocabulary of organizing seem to be at odds, if not in outright contradiction.

Over the years, however, not only has my faith influenced the way I organize but organizing has influenced the way I read the Bible. If Karl Barth is right, that preaching is the art of holding the Bible in one hand and the newspaper in the other, then the interpretive task of the preacher involves bringing the experience of our daily lives to bear upon our reading of the Bible and vice versa. As I have done so, while engaged in the nitty-gritty work of organizing—conducting one-on-one individual meetings with members of my church and residents of the community, researching issues like code enforcement and tax increment financing, negotiating with public officials for affordable housing and community investment—I have discovered vistas in the Biblical text that I had not noticed before, and over time have come to see the task of organizing not only as compatible with my Christian faith, but deeply rooted in the Biblical narrative.

■ ■ ■ ■

I am aware that most organizing as done by the Industrial Areas Foundation does (and should) take place in an interfaith context. I know that those of other faith traditions do similar reflection from within their own faith tradition as I do from mine. I can say the same of the foundational texts of the other great religious and philosophical movements.

The Quaker writer Parker Palmer has suggested that the tension in our culture is between what biblical scholar Walter Brueggemann calls the "myth of scarcity and the liturgy of abundance." The myth of scarcity leads to isolation. The liturgy of abundance is celebrated in community. Jesus pushes his disciples into relationship. Their leadership is still critical; it is they who organize the crowd. But it is in relationship in the context of community that the resources flow. So it is in organizing: Leaders learn the art of the individual, one-to-one, relational meeting, leaving the safe confines of hearth and home to forge relationships across social divides. And, as happened to Moses' and Jesus' and Muhammad's disciples, out of community comes common action. Whereas in social outreach ministries, congregations often meet neighbors at the point of their need—through food pantries and soup kitchens and shelters—in organizing, relationships are formed at the point of strength. The Iron Rule of IAF organizing is "Never do for others what they can do for themselves." Organizers enter a community not to catalogue a litany of the community's deficits but to identify and train leaders. A fundamental assumption of organizing is that every community has, already within it, leaders capable of acting on their own behalf in relationship with others. The goal of organizing is to find and cultivate those leaders.

This is a lesson that leaders—in and out of their church, synagogue, mosque, temple, or secular organization—must learn and relearn, again and again. Many of us know the experience of feeling as if everything depended on us, and all of us have had moments at least when the needs of others feel like a burden. Leaders and managers in the corporate, government, and nonprofit worlds know the same experience. The myth of scarcity leads us to imagine that we are the only ones with leadership skills and to assume that the only options are to send people away with their needs unmet or to have them depend upon us alone. Perhaps in a misguided attempt to please those we serve, we clergy are often the worst violators of the Iron Rule of organizing. We are constantly doing for others what they are fully capable of doing for themselves. Social service agencies do the same thing—assume that the best thing we can do in the community outside our door is to identify a need and then meet it.

■ ■ ■ ■

Organizing requires a fundamental reorientation of our approach. The community around us has resources, not just needs, and our role in organizing for power is to help identify them. So when we organizers and leaders enter a community, we engage people in conversations about what matters most in their lives. What are their passions, their hopes, their dreams? What have been the experiences that shaped their values and character? What sort of future do they want for themselves and their families? How do they cope with the daily frustrations of life in their community? What actions have they taken in their lives to make change? How are they in relationship with those who live around them? Are they willing to work with others to forge a different sort of future? Are they in touch with their own reservoir of anger—memory and grief—so that they might take the necessary risks required to build the sort of relational power that can make real change happen?

Jesus tells a parable about prayer that features an annoying widow who pesters an unjust judge until he gives her what she wants. A literal translation of the Greek has the judge saying, "I will grant her justice so that she will stop battering me." And the punch line is, "When the Human One [the Son of Man] comes, will he find such faith on earth?" What sort of faith is Jesus talking about? Faith like the widow, who keeps on battering the judge until she gets what she wants. Faith like the Syrophoenician woman, who won't take no for an answer. Faith like Bartimaeus, who won't be silenced by Jesus' impatient disciples. Faith like the friends of the paralytic, who tore the roof right off the house.

Frederick Douglass famously said, "Power concedes nothing without a demand. It never did and it never will." In that sense, community organizing embodies Jesus' parable. The widow is wholly without power. A woman alone in a male-ordered culture, she had few individual rights of her own. In the Hebrew, Christian, and Muslim scriptures, the widow, along with the orphan and the sojourner, are singled out as categories of people who deserve particular care within the community of faith. That is because the system is stacked against them. The most likely cause for the woman's suit before the judge would have been the rights to her husband's estate. It was not uncommon for unscrupulous executors to leave the widow with nothing. It is not an exaggeration to say that this case may well have been an issue of life and death for her.

For the judge, on the other hand, it was just another routine matter. Though a person of status and power, he was just a cog in a system that was designed to maintain the privilege of those like him. His role was to dismiss the woman's complaint and strike a deal with her adversary. She might make a bit of a fuss, but that's how things were done, and no one would have expected a different outcome. Yet the widow refuses to play her assigned role. Unable to compete in the back-room negotiations that would have been available to her opponent, she takes her case public. In a culture in which she had no voice, she refuses to keep silent. She badgers the judge—and here the Greek has a certain amount of irony: The word used means to "give a black eye," a term related to boxing. In other words, the poor, beleaguered judge complains that the little old widow is beating him up!

The widow doesn't attack the judge's motives or credibility. She sim-

175

ply insists that he do the right thing. She badgers and batters him until he gives in. And he finally does, not because she was right, not because it is the just thing to do, not because he is worried about what God might think of his behavior, not because he is suddenly converted by the force of her argument. No. He relents because he is tired of her constant complaining and just wants her to go away.

In the arsenal of tools available to community organizations, persistence and public exposure are two of most potent weapons. Many are the times that public officials have caved to the demands of a community organization not because the organization was full of good people who cared about justice but simply because the officials wanted to be left alone. That has been one of the most important lessons I have learned in community organizing. I used to believe that ideas matter. Well, they do matter. But having a good idea isn't enough; being right isn't enough; being on the side of the poor and oppressed isn't enough. If you aren't willing to fight, you will quickly find that Frederick Douglass was right on target: Power concedes nothing without a demand; it never has, and it never will.

■ ■ ■ ■

Editor's Note: In 2010, Krehbiel authored *Reflecting with Scripture on Community Organizing*, from which this essay is adapted. He was an early advocate for LGBTQ inclusiveness in the church as pastor of More Light congregations since the earliest days of that interfaith movement and as Board Member of More Light Presbyterians.

Questions for Discussion and Reflection

1. What is a society like if it is based on scarcity instead of abundance? Which kind of society do you believe in? Why?
2. What does your religious faith or philosophical orientation teach about power? How does that teaching influence how you act? Be specific.
3. Do you agree with Pastor Krehbiel's interpretation of the parable of the widow? Why or why not? How does such an interpretation lead to organizing for power?

Relating to Muslims (et al.)

by Edward T. Chambers

Edward T. Chambers (1930-2015) was the long-time Executive Director of the Industrial Areas Foundation (IAF). He was the lead organizer in many of the IAF organizing efforts in the 1950s and 1960s, including The Woodlawn Organization in Chicago and FIGHT in Rochester, New York. He mentored an entire generation of organizers and community leaders in what he called "the skills of public life." Chambers was named the successor to IAF founder Saul Alinsky in 1972 and retired 38 years later in 2010.

I n the late 1990s, I was helping to organize a new citizens power organization in the city and suburbs of Chicago. It dawned on me that we had no involvement by the Muslim community, which had quietly grown into a considerable new force in the area. (In fact, there were more Muslims than Jews in Chicago, and Muslims were one of the fastest-growing groups in the metropolitan area.) The problem was that—like most Americans—I knew few Muslims and had even fewer real relationships. Fortunately, I had a skill to do something about it, and I did.

We were at the time only six months away from the founding convention of United Power for Action and Justice. The IAF organizers, the many leaders, and I had done thousands of one-to-ones with mainline and evangelical Protestants, liberal and conservative Catholics, conservative and reform Jews, labor unions, civic and neighborhood organizations, social service and health institutions, labor unions and business organizations, and just about every other group we could find. We had involved Latinos, African-Americans, Asian-Americans; middle-class and poor; north, west and south sides; city and suburban. We knew that the founding convention was going to be the most diverse group ever assembled in a political arena that functioned primarily on the "divide-and-conquer" philosophy of the old Mayor Daley machine, now run by his son and other protégés in typical Chicago fashion. But we had zero Muslims, and I was not willing to move forward without them.

Then I remembered one conversation I had much earlier with a gentle Muslim business leader named Talat Othman that had gone fairly well. So I checked with two other sources, and they confirmed that he was a key person in the Islamic community. I called Mr. Othman for a one-to-one meeting. He agreed, and I traveled to his suburban Chicago office to meet him. On the way, I decided to take a risk: I would fold three relational meetings into this one! By that I meant that I would go beyond what I would normally have done in a first or second relational meeting and discuss my organizational needs very frankly in the hope that they would meet his self-interests as well.

In our one-to-one relational meeting, Mr. Othman recognized my problem, but he also heard my values and my passion. And he saw, even if only faintly, the self-interest of the Muslim community in being part of this organizing effort from the very beginning. He told me, "Mr. Chambers, you would have to go to the southwest suburbs of Chicago and meet with the leaders of our mosques there." He knew that was where the Muslim organizational strength in the region was centered, and he gave me the names of leaders of six mosques. He said he would call them and tell them I would be calling and urge them to meet with me. He took a big risk in doing this, and I will always remember him for his courage and faith in me.

I went to work. I had a series of meetings with the leaders of those mosques, which led to a delegation of some 220 Muslims from five key mosques being present at the United Power for Action and Justice founding convention in the fall of 1997 at the University of Illinois in its Chicago Pavilion. There were 10,000 people at that convention, but none were more important than those 220 followers of Islam. In fact, I made sure that they were seated in some of the front rows of the convention.

Of course, this beginning led to other relational meetings with other Muslim-American leaders after the convention was over. That is why four years later, on September 11, 2001, United Power for Action and Justice was able to do something that no other organization in America was able to do.

Almost immediately after 9/11, the Muslim leaders inside United Power for Action and Justice began meeting with the non-Muslim leaders about how they could jointly respond in a significant way to the terrorist attack and the subsequent targeting of Muslim-Americans with hate crimes, discrimination, and prejudice. These leaders decided that what was needed more than anything else was a very large and very public meeting that would both introduce the growing Muslim-American community to their Chicagoland neighbors and also begin the process of developing real, mutually respectful, public relationships between Muslims and non-Muslims in the Chicago area.

The vision was large: We would organize some 4000 people—half followers of Islam and the other half everyone else—to meet on Sunday, November 18, 2001, at Chicago's Navy Pier—one of the largest and most prestigious public spaces in Chicago. The event was called simply "Chicagoans and Islam," and it was one of the most successful actions I have ever observed, because it was completely based on the idea of relational action.

Why did people show up? They came for several reasons. They came because they were scared—on both sides. Nothing like 9/11 had ever happened on such a large scale in American history, and no one knew what was going to happen next.

They came because they really did not know each other. Most of the non-Muslims at the meeting had never talked with a Muslim before, at least not about anything important. The Muslims came because they knew the history of immigrants in this country and specifically in Chicago, and they knew that immigrants had never really been welcomed. This would not only be an opportunity for them to introduce themselves to their new neighbors. It would also be a chance for their new neighbors to welcome them into the community.

And finally, both "sides" came because they were organized and had relationships with one another.

This meeting was not called by the governor or the mayor; the politicians could never have pulled it off. It was called by an organization that had spent the previous four-five years building relationships, face-to-face and one-to-one. This meeting was not merely announced in the media in the hope that people would just show up. (In fact, you had to have a ticket to get in!) It was organized through all the member institutions of United Power for Action and Justice, including our Muslim member institutions. People showed up on buses. Four thousand people pledged they would come, and over 3900 of them showed up. There were no "incidents," because everyone who was there was there for the same reason: to meet people they did not know or understand. Two thousand of them were Muslim, and two thousand were from every ethnic background and geographic community that makes up Chicagoland. Many of them were teenagers and young adults, encouraged to be there by their parents and clergy. The meeting was co-chaired by a Muslim businessman and a Catholic businessman. The highlight of the meeting came when a young Muslim woman and a young Christian woman conducted a short relational meeting on the stage in front of the entire crowd. There is a famous photo of the two of them hugging, which ran on the front page of the *Chicago Tribune* the next morning.

Immediately after the two young women finished, people were paired off in twos, one Muslim and one non-Muslim, to do a one-to-one relational meeting, right there on the floor of the convention hall. The sound and the energy of those 2000 relational meetings reverberated at Navy Pier and continues to do so throughout Chicagoland to this day.

▦ ▦ ▦ ▦

While the dominant culture tells us that smart phones, emails, texts, and Internet chat rooms and blogs have made face-to-face, person-to-person communication obsolete, organizers and leaders who regularly do the intense work of relational meetings understand that these disciplined conversations touch our depths in a unique and irreplaceable way, even if one never sees the other person again. In relational meetings, the "why" questions so often avoided by people have a space in which to surface: Why are things like they are; why am I doing what I do; why don't I spend more time on the things I say are most important to me?

A relational meeting isn't selling or pushing an issue or membership or task in an organization or congregation. Those conducting a series of one-to-ones must listen and share rather than offer solutions. What is the other person thinking and feeling? What makes this person tick? What's his or her number-one priority? Our basic tools are our eyes, ears, and feelings—as well as our instinct and intuition.

Short succinct questions are the best: "Why do you say that;" "what's that mean to you;" "why do you care;" "have you ever tried to do anything about it?" You must be prepared to interrupt with brief, tight questions like these, to then shut up and listen, and finally to share some equally important things about yourself. Even as you are talking or listening, you need to be alert for the next question. The art of relational meetings has to do with this in-and-out movement. We are looking for interests, talents, and connections across the spectrum of race, class, faith, and politics. A one-to-one is an entry point to public life.

In casual meetings, we take people as they present themselves. We don't push or probe. We don't dig. We don't challenge where a notion came from. A relational meeting is an entry point to public life. It is what I call a "mixing of human spirits" and it has a certain form and requires certain skills to practice. Those of us who become practiced in the art of the relational meeting have learned to use our whole selves—body and spirit, charms and personality, compassion and wit, humor and anger—in intense, focused, human encounters. When a good one-to-one occurs, two people connect in a way that transcends ordinary, everyday conversation. Both people have the opportunity to pause and reflect on their personal experience regarding the tension between the world-as-it-is and the world-as-it-should-be. At that moment, a new public relationship can be born, two human spirits can mix, and both people can gain the power to be truer to their best selves, to live more effectively and creatively, and to take action together for the common good.

■ ■ ■ ■

Editor's Note: Ed Chambers was diagnosed with Alzheimer's and retired in 2010 and spent his remaining years with his wife and family in Skibbereen, Ireland. Chambers is widely credited for leading the IAF to become the premier community organizing network in the U.S. and around the world. He wrote a book titled *Roots for Radicals: Organizing for Power, Action, and Justice* and several booklets on his organizing methods in the "Mulling about Acting in the World-As-It-Is" series. He was given an award for his "Friendship to the Muslim Community" by the Mosque Foundation of Bridgeview, Illinois.

Questions for Discussion and Reflection

1. Who are the new immigrants into your community? Are you getting to know them and them you? If not, why not, and how can you help make that happen?

2. Make a list of the differences between chance encounters and intentional meetings. What is the percentage of each that you or other leaders in your institution do in a typical month? What is preventing you from doing more public, focused, one-to-one relational meetings?

3. Do you really want to relate with people who are strangers or different from you? If not, why not? If yes, how can you organize to make sure it happens?

Two Nurse-Logs

by Dick Harmon

Richard (Dick) Harmon (born 1937) organized in Chicago, Buffalo, New York City, and the Pacific Northwest. He mentored and supervised organizers in multiple projects and was the associate director of the Industrial Areas Foundation (IAF) Training Institute from 1968-1976.

I n the Pacific Northwest, where my family has lived for over twenty years, there is, strange as it may sound, a powerful, daily action in our forests which may be useful to those of us who reflect on love, community, and power near the end of our lives.

It's called a *nurse-log*. It's as old as the forests, and it replicates by different names among all living species—even us mighty humans.

When a tree in the forest begins to decline from age or disease, it continues its purpose and lifework by seeding the soil with its leaves and letting just the right amount of sunlight through the canopy to help its smaller neighbors flourish.

As it becomes weaker, the nurse-log leans more, loses branches, and finally snaps and falls to the soil of the forest floor. Here, resting on the ground, dead and useless to some human eyes, it continues its work of sharing with and protecting its neighbors, intentionally—if you will—nursing new life, new generations, new power in the forest.

186

For around the fallen tree gathers all manner of organisms, from creepers and crawlers to birds and small animals to mosses and grass, bringing into being new soil, new seeds, new plants—including new trees, the literal children of the nurse-log—growing right out of its fallen trunk.

This is the tree's life-work—from its standing, to its lying down, to its merging with all the life it has birthed and mid-wived from its body. In what humans may call its death, a nurse-log literally nurtures new life into flourishing. The tree participates in the universal process of sacrifice, or mutual feeding—of life, death, and rebirth.

Story

I met Ed Chambers in the spring of 1961, but he and I worked closely together during two intense periods. First was in 1964-65, when he came in to bring order to The Woodlawn Organization (TWO) on the south side of Chicago in the community surrounding the University of Chicago, where I was organizing. In 1965, Ed left to start up the FIGHT organization in Rochester, and a year later I went to Buffalo to organize an IAF organization there we called BUILD. Ed and I talked sporadically over the next two years.

The second time we worked together day-to-day was from late 1968 to mid-1976. We both returned to Chicago to establish the Industrial Areas Foundation (IAF) Training Institute and create what has become IAF's network of affiliates. The Training Institute years were times of great intensity, passion, and creativity for both of us. We were an interesting pair (and then an interesting trio when Peter Martinez joined us), fiercely determined to nurture enough organizers and leaders to build a significant national network of nonpartisan, multi-cultural, multi-interest organizations.

We had to learn from our own organizing experience and our own imaginations how to teach power and organizing, through both workshops and new organizing efforts. Looking back, it was easy, because we were working with a lot of fine people who were hungry to learn, hungry to experience, hungry to build organizations capable of re-balancing the careening *polis* of that time. Through that early process, key organizers emerged for the follow-on generations of IAF teachers and organizers.

■ ■ ■ ■

But the intensity of those years and our work also revealed that both Ed and I were deeply imperfect people, and our deepest imperfections were amplified by the curse that we shared: addiction to alcohol.

In retrospect, I see Ed and I as brothers deeply acquainted with suffering—like all organizers and community leaders—bundles of paradoxes operating in the tension of freedom and control, great generosity and narrow self-interest, work and family, public and personal, compassion and cruelty, cooperation and competition, transparency and secrecy. In Ed and me, as in all good leaders and organizers, those paradoxes were enlarged, approaching larger-than-life status at times.

Our last face-to-face conversation was in mid-2007—a great,

wide-ranging three or four hours in the dog-eared IAF office, deep in Chicago's Loop, cluttered with books and files—two old veterans looking again at the state of organizing and discussing the books we liked and didn't like at the time.

It was familiar, like two old comfortable shoes.

But it was also clear that both of us were in decline, that aging and disease were doing their work. I told Ed I was getting ready to retire and suggested he might actually like retirement. His reply: "No, I can't think of anything else to do." He then advised me, "Death isn't so bad, Dick, just don't get old."

At that point, he asked me about my drinking and I told him I'd been lucky and had stayed sober since late 1981. He said he had stopped drinking as well. I didn't believe him, but I didn't challenge him either.

Then, for the first time in our nearly forty years of working together, Ed asked me about my earliest years. "What you've done in organizing, it came out of troubles in your childhood?"

"Yes," I said, surprised at the turn in the conversation, and I gave him a sketch of what happened to both sides of my family in the Great Depression—not too much to bore him, but more than I had ever shared with him.

I asked, "And you?" Ed nodded, but he gave me no stories about himself in return.

I know about armor and moats that protect us from our own interior tsunamis, wounds, and scars. So I understood Ed's silence. But I glimpsed the suffering of this vulnerable giant, who was at that moment deeply afraid of no longer being useful.

Ed's culture had not told him the story of the nurse-log, to help him know that organizers and community leaders also—when we lean, then fall, then lie down, can still be useful—albeit in new ways, because by returning the gift we've been given to the next generation of organizers and leaders we remain part of the creation process that underlies healthy organizing and community.

■ ■ ■ ■

Editor's Note: Dick Harmon is retired and lives in Portland, Oregon, with his wife, Carole. He continues to reflect and write, and to mentor young organizers and community leaders.

Questions for Discussion and Reflection

1. What is the proper role of organizers and community and institutional leaders as they grow older and retire? Give an example of one person who is doing it right. What specifically do they do, and how do they do it?

2. List things that can get in the way of working to build power. Which are temptations for you or others you know? How have you or they responded?

3. Do you think it is wise to admit to failings or weaknesses if you are trying to be powerful? Why or why not? Tell a story one way or the other.

Collaboration in Organizing

by Ernesto Cortes, Jr.

Ernesto Cortes, Jr., and Sister Christine Stephens, CDP, were two driving forces behind the development of the West/Southwest Industrial Areas Foundation (W/SW IAF), which covers IAF projects west of the Mississippi River and in some other countries. Here Cortes reflects on his collaboration with Stephens over forty-three years until her death in 2019. It is followed in this book by essays by six women organizers who were trained by and also collaborated with Sr. Christine.

first met Sister Christine Stephens in 1976 after making a presentation to a group of leaders about the possibilities of organizing in Houston. I was lead organizer with Communities Organized for Public Service (COPS) in San Antonio at the time, and after the session she came up to me and told me she was a Sister of Divine Providence and spent a lot of time in San Antonio. She said she was impressed with the impact of COPS in the neighborhoods around Our Lady of the Lake University. Trying to be succinct, pithy, and wise, I said to her, "Sister, it's just a matter of stringing together rosary beads." Afterwards, she told me, she thought, *You jerk! What do you think I do, sit around all day stringing together rosary beads?*

Sr. Christine could be tough, but she always had myself and her colleagues' back. Christine was a friend, colleague, mentor, agitator, and organizer. In fact, she was an organizer's organizer.

■ ■ ■ ■

One of Christine's most important qualities, as you'll read in the six essays that follow, was her sense of humor. She had enormous capacity for perspective and what George Orwell described as the "generous anger" of Charles Dickens. During an Industrial Areas Foundation (IAF) national training, Christine was listening to our IAF colleagues regale us with a caricature a trainee made of Christine (as the trainees were allowed to do only after the training was over). And Christine howled at the exaggerated accuracy and insightfulness of the trainee's description of her.

I once got in an argument with Christine about Davy Crockett and how he had tried to surrender and was found by the Mexican army under a mattress, quaking in fear, at the Battle of the Alamo. And she asked me, "How would *you* know, Ernie? There were no survivors of the Alamo!" I told her, "Christine, there were over 3,000 Mexicans who survived the Battle of the Alamo." When she realized her faux pas, she howled, laughing at herself with me and her colleagues.

■ ■ ■ ■

At Christine's funeral, I quoted a line from Macbeth that "nothing became her more in this life than the leaving of it." In retrospect, what I should have said was, "nothing became her more in this life than the *living* of it." Christine was always full of energy, imagination, and intellectual curiosity. When she became co-director of the IAF with myself, Arnie Graf, and Mike Gecan after the retirement of Ed Chambers, Mike told me that, of the four of us, the indispensable one was Christine. She had an incredible mastery of the finances of a broad-based organization. She understood what we teach about "hard" money, the money the leaders control, money that gave the leaders their independence and their ability to set their agenda. She understood its importance to ownership, dignity, and self-respect. She understood that hard money meant that the organization had a future. She understood the importance of the IAF contracts with affiliates, which bonded longtime organizers to the local organization they worked for at that time.

More than anyone else, Christine understood the importance of building infrastructure inside an organization and inside the member institutional units of the organization. Her total focus was the mentoring and development of leadership. She reveled in the transformation of leaders and would record their most eloquent speeches. I remember her making me listen (when I was supervising her while she was lead organizer of both COPS and Metro Alliance in San Antonio) to an extraordinary public speech by one leader, Vikki Luna. Christine celebrated Vikki's emergence as a leader. I also remember how Christine loved telling the story of Virginia Ramirez and how she developed the kind of anger we teach in the IAF that is not just private but public.

■ ■ ■ ■

Christine was the lead organizer at one time or another of almost every major IAF organization in Texas: The Metropolitan Organization in Houston, COPS and Metro Alliance in San Antonio, Valley Interfaith in the Rio Grande Valley, and Dallas Area Interfaith. She supervised the development of other organizations in Austin, West Texas, and El Paso. She particularly enjoyed working with people who were working class and people of color, treating them all with respect and dignity—even to the point of taking them on when they needed taking on. Christine could fight with leaders as strong as Rev. Gerald Britt in Dallas, Mrs. Lovalla Norman, and Juanita Mitchell in Houston, and Reverend Claude Black in San Antonio. She had a tenacity of purpose that helped someone like the indomitable former COPS/Metro leader Father Albert Benavidez become so respected and admired. But probably her shining example was the way in which she handled the fight in the *colonias*, as described in Elizabeth Valdez' essay that follows this one.

I remember a meeting with then Texas State Comptroller, Bob Bullock, and his staff. We were looking at the capacity of local people to pay for the infrastructure needed in the *colonias* in the Rio Grande Valley. Staff was saying we needed to aggressively go after people who were delinquent on their property taxes and Christine shot back, "Yeah, and make thousands of people homeless."

Well, as we were trying to figure out the financing, the water board staff and governor's staff focused on trying to make the financing work in the form of loans that the *colonia* residents would have to pay back. They originally wanted it to be an 80/20 deal: 80% loans and 20% grants. We wanted the opposite. Ultimately, we agreed on 60/40 in favor of the residents, until then Governor Bill Clements threatened to veto the bill unless we agreed to 40% grants and 60% loans. Sr. Christine was not in the room during that particular meeting, and when she saw the revised bill, she said, "No, this is wrong." She had carefully calculated what each *colonia* household would have to pay based on our formula of 60/40.

Christine marched down to the Legislative Council Office to have them retype the bill back to our 60% grants and 40% loans and then ran to the floor of the legislature and gave our version to the bill sponsor, who got it in time for it to pass with our 60% grants/40% loans provision intact.

■ ■ ■ ■

Christine was always there to help build the network. When Terri Brown, the lead organizer of Valley Interfaith died suddenly, Christine went back to being the lead organizer there until a full-time organizer could be found. She also helped build an infrastructure of Organizer Groups that she convened on a regular basis for training and development.

Christine used to say that her job in retirement was similar to the task of Aaron and Moses' brother-in-law, Hobab, in the book of Exodus. When Joshua waged battle with the Amalekites, he would have the army look up at Moses on the mountain. If Moses' arms were up, the army would prevail. If they fell out of tiredness, the Amalekites would prevail. And so, Aaron and his brother-in-law would hold up Moses' arms. Christine used to say her job was to help hold up my arms.

I think, in all honesty, Christine believed her job—her mission—was to defeat the Amalekites. *Amalekites* was a word the Hebrews used to describe any people who were brutal, oppressors of the poor and needy, and lacking in care for those who were strangers. Christine would stand up to modern Amalekites who are bullies and snobbish, who looked down on other people. She understood the "safe rule" in the Melian Dialogue from Thucydides' *The Peloponnesian War* better than anyone, particularly the notion of standing up to your equals and treating those who were less fortunate with consideration.

But perhaps one of the things I most miss about Christine is the way she brought intellectual content to the work. She loved the contestation over ideas and connecting best practices of organizing to insightful books such as Richard Sennett's *Fall of Public Man*, Hannah Arendt's *Men in Dark Times*, Mary Midgley's *Wickedness*. She also had a passionate love for Scripture, looking for nuggets of wisdom in the ages of commentary on holy texts of all faiths. She loved to practice what the Jewish rabbis call *havruta*, contestation among a group of people about different interpretations of the meaning of particular scripture passages.

Christine leaves a marvelous and wonderful legacy of leaders and organizers who will cherish the memory of her work and her presence with us.

In Shakespeare's rendition of Mark Anthony's peroration at the funeral of Caesar he proclaims, "This was a Caesar. Whence comes such another?"

I would say, "This was a Christine. Whence comes such another?"

197

■ ■ ■ ■

Editor's Note: Ernie Cortes says, "On a personal note, Christine Stephens was a friend of my family, my wife and three children. She was *madrina* of my daughter Amy at her confirmation; and she, along with our IAF colleague, Sr. Pearl Ceasar, were present at my daughter Alma's and my son Jacob's baptisms. She came to both of my daughters' weddings. She was there for us in moments of joy and sorrow." He also confesses, "One of the things I most hated about Sr. Christine was that when I shared with her an idea or insight or developed a new training session she often liked them so much she would redo and present them in more effective ways than I had thought of. It was hard for me to watch someone learn from me in such a way that she became better than I am at that particular skill!"

Questions for Discussion and Reflection

1. With whom do you collaborate in trying to make the world a better place? Tell a story about what one of those people mean to you. And why.
2. Why is reading challenging books important to leaders and organizers? What book have you read lately? What book is on your bedstand to be read next?
3. Why is being able to laugh at yourself important in organizing?

The Power of Providence

by Elizabeth Valdez

Elizabeth Valdez (born 1954) grew up in a migrant family and became a union organizer with the Amalgamated Clothing and Textile Workers Union (now UNITE HERE). She later became an organizer with the Industrial Areas Foundation (IAF) in Valley Interfaith in the Rio Grande Valley and is now the lead organizer for The Metropolitan Organization in Houston. Valdez has had over thirty-five years of organizing experience with the IAF throughout Texas. In both San Antonio and the Valley, she spearheaded successful living-wage campaigns, and she organized a successful effort to prevent contamination of the Edwards Aquifer in San Antonio. In the Rio Grande Valley, she registered 25,000 voters and then, in partnership with other organizations of the Texas IAF, worked with state officials to pass landmark legislation providing essential water infrastructure to the *colonias* (rural communities outside city limits from El Paso to Brownsville along the entire Texas border). Sister Christine Stephens and Elizabeth Valdez were the co-directors of the Texas IAF Organizations until Christine's death in 2019. Elizabeth continues in that role and is now also a member of the W/SW IAF Executive Team along with Ernesto Cores, Jr., Joe Rubio, and Paul Turner.

grew up in South Texas, in the part of the state that would become known simply as "the Valley." In those days, anything south of San Antonio was barely acknowledged politically and life was hard, especially for the migrant families who called it home. My own family lived there in the winters, but every year (spring/summer/fall) we would follow the crops north to Idaho. Because of that, I would leave school in Texas and enroll part of each year in an Idaho school. My parents didn't speak much English, but I did; and when I was eleven I started negotiating with the farmers for what they would pay us to pick their crops. Our family was one of thousands who took the journey north to work in the fields each year and, as a result, I married young and soon started having children of my own.

We stopped migrating in 1974, and I went to work at the Levi's clothing plant in McAllen, Texas. We were paid piecework: If you worked hard you got decent pay. More importantly, they provided health insurance. Still, I joined the Amalgamated Clothing and Textile Workers Union (ACTWU) to fight the injustices that the company perpetrated on its employees on a regular basis.

■ ■ ■ ■

It was at a training session titled "Power and Pressures on Families" that I met I a young organizer with the Industrial Areas Foundation (IAF) named Ernesto Cortes, Jr. Ernie and I had an individual meeting, and he connected me to the work he had started doing in the Rio Grande Valley, including hundreds of individual meetings and countless trainings. There was another organizer with him—Jim Drake—and the two of them together, working with the Catholic church and the unions, launched the organization Valley Interfaith, which is still going strong today. Jim died in 2001.

It was from Ernie that I learned about my faith and how to build power to bring about change. Though challenging at times, I enjoyed the constant learning and reading he provided me as a young woman. Leaders say IAF is a "mini-university for public life;" it certainly was for me. I would add that for many people of color, the IAF is our *main* university. When the IAF first hired me as a staff organizer in the Valley, my job was to register voters. Valley Interfaith leaders registered 25,000 voters and organized a non-partisan get out the vote that year. This put the valley on the state map…and organizing into my blood.

■ ■ ■ ■

Six months into my organizing with Valley Interfaith, Ernie and Jim left the area and Sister Christine Stephens was hired as the lead organizer. At the same time, the union tried to hire me back, offering to double my IAF salary and promising to make me a lead organizer. It was exciting to be offered so much money, but the IAF had taught me enough to ask, "Who would be my mentor?" The union said, "No one, you'll be the lead." I told Sr. Christine about the offer, and I remember how she looked at me and almost screamed, "What did you tell them?" I told her I understood ongoing mentoring was critical to my development as an organizer and had turned the union down flat.

Christine understood what it meant to my family for me to turn down that job, and from that moment she took seriously being my mentor for the rest of her life.

She was a great organizer and mentor. What made her great was that she was clear about her own anger and was able to teach that anger had to be connected to power. Her anger started with the injustices her father had experienced. (He had been laid off just as Christine was graduating from high school, but he was in the union, so they had to take him back.)

Sr. Christine had been raised on the southeast side of Houston. She saw the flooding that was happening to poor communities, how African Americans and Jews were treated. She saw how Hispanics were treated. And there she was in the Valley, predominantly Hispanic and Spanish-speaking, and she knew not a word of Spanish. But that didn't even slow her down.

Ernie Cortes, Jr., and Jim Drake created Valley Interfaith and organized the founding convention attended by 5000 people. Christine took over and developed it into a power organization.

I learned how to organize from Sr. Christine. In those early days, I was very good at violating the Iron Rule, which is "Never do for others what they can do for themselves." Whenever she would run with me, she would remind me not to violate that rule. I learned how to train from watching her and Ernie train. I would say, "I'm never going to be like you." She would say, "You don't want to be like me, you want to be yourself. Maybe you'll be better than me."

■ ■ ■ ■

Perhaps the most important thing Christine taught me was how to fight and how to build enough power so that you can be at the table. When the *colonias* of Los Milpas were fighting to get water and sewers for their homes, the mayor of Pharr wanted to annex their neighborhood, which would have meant the residents would have paid city taxes for their water, but without a guarantee of the other clear benefits of paved roads, off-street lighting, fire department, stop signs, drainage, police protection.

Carmen Anaya was a leader with Valley Interfaith at the time, and she said not just "no," but "hell, no." Once she had decided something, however, Ms. Anaya could remain stubborn about it. Sr. Christine told me, "You have to teach Carmen that there are no permanent enemies and no permanent allies." In other words, she had to learn to negotiate with the mayor. I repeated what Sr. Christine said, and Ms. Anaya said, "If I'm across the table with the mayor I'm going to punch him." So, I said, "If you're across the table from him, you're going to sit on your hands." We both laughed, but then we role played how to do it.

The bottom line was that Carmen negotiated with that mayor not just for water and wastewater sewers, but also for paved roads and stop signs and other important items. Her *colonia* got annexed, yes, but they got much more than what they were initially going after, much more than what was initially offered. When the city offered to pave Mrs. Anaya's street first, she wouldn't let them. She told them, "When you're paving my street, it's because you've already paved the rest of the *colonia!*" That's how she worked to transform their community.

■ ■ ■ ■

Sr. Christine had a temper. When she needed to scream at you, she would. What I came to learn was that she was upset at the situation, not just by what you were doing wrong. I learned to take those screams as a signal to listen hard: There was a message she was transmitting through that anger. She was relentless, tough, and nothing would break her. If you knew how to take shit, you could give it. This world is not kind. She was the first woman to be a co-director of the national IAF, and she worked with Ernie to build the West/Southwest IAF network into what it is today. It was always she and Ernie. She would say, "Ernie taught me this, and Ernie taught me that," because Ernie was her mentor. Ernie had the imagination of building a network in Texas, and she said he was crazy but would always be there with him. She would push and fight, but she was always there for all of us.

But this was not the only side to Sr. Christine. Most of us witnessed her love and compassion as well. She had a deep love for family. We grieved and mourned with her during the loss of her mom, her father, and her brother-in-law. When I lost my husband and my son had major heart surgery, she was loving and compassionate with me and my family. She said, "Take all the time you need." This empathy was not just during your private pain. When she witnessed the Communities Organized for Public Service leaders on the Westside of San Antonio suffering with major floods, families in the *colonias* along the border without water and wastewater sewers, minority low-income children without access to good public schools, her love and compassion drove her anger to do something about it. Sr. Christine, like Martin Luther King, Jr., understood Paul Tillich's point that "Power without Love leads to brutality, and Love without Power is sentimentality."

In 1987, Sr. Christine told me that if I really wanted to learn how to organize I needed to leave the Valley. She suggested I go to Houston and learn how to organize in a diverse community, how to work in an urban center, how to deal with various religious denominations and faiths. That was another of her strengths—an understanding of how to develop organizers (which she would have told you she learned from Ernie).

In 2013, Sr. Christine was planning to celebrate her Fiftieth Jubilee as a Sister of the Congregation of Divine Providence (CDP). She invited me to join the CDP Associates so I could join her in the celebratory dinner. I said of course; it would be an honor. I did go through the complete process; but because their associate program had changed, I was not able to complete the requirements in time for her jubilee. But it did not matter, because the pure fact that she invited me was an honor.

Christine gave me this card when I became a CDP Associate: "Remember these things: You are talented, you are valued, you are loved. Welcome to the congregation—this is yet another birthright institution we share. Believing in the Power of Providence to bring all things to good, we commit ourselves:

+ to hear the cry of pain and anguish of the poor, immigrants, women, and Earth;
+ to be present as neighbor to all in need;
+ to act with courage and collaborate with others to heal what is broken and celebrate what is good in our world.

■ ■ ■ ■

Editor's Note: On a recent sabbatical, Elizabeth Valdez studied at both Princeton University and the Princeton Theological Seminary. She adds this about Sister Christine Stephens: "The last time I saw Christine while she was well, we were planning my sixty-fifth birthday party. She promised to make a chocolate ganache cake, which is my favorite dessert of all time. She was not just my mentor; she had become my friend. For this I will always be grateful."

Questions for Discussion and Reflection

1. Remember a time you did something for people they could have done for themselves. Or when someone did something for you that prevented you from learning how to do it. Why—and how—do good organizers and leaders refuse to do that?

2 Are Power and Love intertwined? How? Why is that connected to "no permanent enemies and no permanent allies"?

3. What is "providence" in your philosophy or faith? How does it work in building power to get at the root causes of people's problems? Tell a story from your own experience of that of someone you know.

A Good Anger

by Anna Eng

Anna Eng (born 1975) is the lead organizer of Nevadans for the Common Good, an affiliate of the Industrial Areas Foundation (IAF). She has organized for over eighteen years in California, Texas, and Nevada. Here she remembers Sister Christine Stephens, one of the co-executive directors of the IAF, who died in 2019.

A good anger acted upon
is beautiful as lightning
Marge Piercy

I was relaxing in the common area at American Jewish University in Los Angeles after training all day at the IAF National Training in 2015, when suddenly Sister Christine Stephens was standing in front of me. She was not happy. I had done something that angered her and she was coming to confront me in clear, unambiguous terms, no holds barred, forehead-to-forehead. With little regard for who might hear, Christine made her points loudly, persuasively, and directly to my face. I fought back. Whatever the content of the fight, we were on opposing sides taking swings and eventually I made a dramatic closing statement and stormed away.

We had been working that day with a Lincoln scholar, and within the hour a voicemail came through my cell phone. It was Sister Christine. "In the spirit of Abraham Lincoln, I am calling to depolarize," she said. For her, the fight was over.

■ ■ ■ ■

I had met Christine at IAF National Training fourteen years earlier during a time in my life when I felt my anger was a liability to my employability. And I had been told as much by my employer at the time.

At the time, I had very little knowledge about the Industrial Areas Foundation (IAF), but by the end of ten days of training I was intrigued enough to ask for a meeting with Ernesto Cortes, Jr., the supervisor for the Southwest region of the country, including California where I lived. He asked which trainers had impressed me over the course of the week, and without hesitation I said, "Christine Stephens." He chuckled and said, "Yes, yes, she's pretty good." An understatement if ever there was one.

That January I started an organizing try-out in Los Angeles. I was green, clueless, and unimpressive. Years later, Christine told me she wouldn't have given a dime for me when I had first started, yet it was in part meeting her that had made me want to organize in the first place. Christine had a clarity and straightforwardness I admired, and when it was combined with her anger, I recognized that she possessed something I wanted to learn. Here was a woman to be reckoned with, here was a woman whose anger was taken seriously, here was a person of power, fully alive.

I was impressed by Christine's anger because I had no control of my own. My anger was a blurry, hot, impotent mess that led me to do rash and stupid things, cave in on myself, or take myself too seriously.

■ ■ ■ ■

While the first thing that impressed me about Christine was the power and clarity of her anger, the more important thing I would eventually learn from her was the necessity of humor. She understood more than anyone I have ever met the corrosive nature of anger when left to fester into resentment or rage. In order to act on anger, people need power, and if that power is to be relational their anger must come with a sense of humor. Christine's anger was always tempered with humor. Humor is what allowed her to laugh at herself when she was wrong, sometimes uproariously and publicly; her humor is what allowed her to let go of petty differences; her humor is what led her to call me and depolarize immediately after our fight in Los Angeles, even while I was still seething.

In one of the last conversations I had with her, I asked if she ever tired of always being seen as "the bitch." She laughed out loud and said that what I needed to understand is that the price of "being one of the mean ones" is the ability to know when to apologize. She taught me that humor proceeds from having perspective on yourself and the world. Humor is the simultaneous understanding that one day we will all die, and yet that which does not kill us makes us stronger. Humor allows for a generosity of spirit that can embrace humankind in specific and big-hearted ways, which Christine did in thousands of ways for thousands of people.

We need more humor in our politics today, which, in turn, might help us with our generosity.

■ ■ ■ ■

Sister Christine Stephens was a profoundly political person, an extraordinary organizer who, for her part, gave generously to a generation of organizers and leaders who will never be the same because of her example and mentorship.

"Good work." she said to me as she got out of the car at the Harlingen airport on her last day supervising my short stint as the lead organizer with Valley Interfaith in the Rio Grande Valley in Texas. "As you know, that is my highest praise."

Good work is what Christine left behind: a legacy of the deep, solid, long-lasting fruit of anger acted upon in service to the world.

■ ■ ■ ■

Editor's Note: Anna Eng says her niece and nephew, Lena and Alexander, are expert at helping their auntie keep her sense of humor. At the age of five, Lena was asked what Anna does (presumably for a living). After thinking for a moment, Lena wrote down, "loves children." A most noble profession if ever there was one.

Questions for Discussion and Reflection

1. Have you ever experienced the connection between anger and humor? If so, describe what happened. If not, what do you think the author is talking about?

2. How do you deal with your own anger? Be specific, with examples. Does your approach work for you? Why?

3. What does "a good anger acted upon" mean? Tell a story about it from your own experience or that of someone you know. Why is it "beautiful as lightening"?

Oh My God! She's a Nun?

by Lady Coleman Carlson

Lady Coleman Carlson (born 1951) has been an organizer for thirty years in the following communities in Texas—Houston, Fort Worth, Dallas. She has also organized in the following Louisiana Parishes—Rapides, Caddo, Ouachita, East Carroll, Iberville, West Baton Rouge, Pointe Coupee, and St. John the Baptist. She began her organizing career as a leader in Triangle Interfaith in Port Arthur in 1989 and began her professional organizing career in 1991 with The Metropolitan Organization (TMO) in Houston.

I am from the southwestern-most part of Louisiana, which is Port Arthur, Texas! Before you get confused, Port Arthur is geographically and technically in southeast Texas but is culturally southern Louisiana. I am Missionary Baptist, a code to Black folks traveling through the South back in the day that denoted Black-only churches. But when I was growing up, Port Arthur also had a very large Catholic population, both Black and Hispanic, at Our Lady of Guadalupe parish. And my memory of nuns was of women wearing what they called their "habits"—long, usually black, robes that went all the way to the ground and headgear where only their faces peeked out.

■ ■ ■ ■

I began my education in "colored" schools. Oil fueled the local economy, and when I was growing up Port Arthur was prosperous. The schools were segregated, but new schools were built even for us "colored" children; and I remember getting new books, not hand-me-downs. When given the opportunity in the late 1960s to help integrate the white schools, a group of my friends and I attended Woodrow Wilson Junior High and later Thomas Jefferson High School.

Teachers for the most part challenged students to think critically. There were some white teachers, mostly older, who did not like the idea of integrated education, but we Black children had a good educational experience in the schools we integrated.

When I attended school in Port Arthur, we had the best school district in the state. But when my children attended public schools in the 1980s, the district had become the worst school system in the state. Port Arthur also had been a strong union town, but oil prices were declining and the city was no longer prosperous. Jobs were disappearing and so was the power of the union to demand wages and other concessions. And Port Arthur was as segregated in the 1980s as it was in the time I grew up.

■ ■ ■ ■

About the same time my kids were in school, the Industrial Areas Foundation (IAF) had been working on a strategy to equalize funding for public schools in the state of Texas. Then in my forties, I was in New Hope Baptist Church, where I was one of the youngest members of the congregation. I consistently had conversations with the pastor about how the church had to be more than just about God helping us get a better job and a bigger house. So, when IAF organizers approached him, he thought I would be someone they should talk to.

I was so frustrated with elected officials that I had been pursuing running for elected office myself, but the IAF organizer for the area told me that was not the way to build power. The way to really build power, she said, was to build relationships with people who are different from you, organize a plan, and then go to whomever were the elected officials and demand accountability. Before IAF, I thought you voted and you prayed and that was the end of it. But no, the organizer said, you give elected officials your agenda, they agree to work with you on it, then you vote, and if they do not do what they said they'd do, you have a measure to evaluate them by.

Well, durn, that made sense. A justice of the peace told me one time that when a white person got a traffic citation, he or she said, "I am asking you, your Honor, to dismiss this because I voted for you." Blacks on the other hand would tell the same judge what a pillar they were in their church—for example, a deacon and a good family man. What I learned from IAF is that no public official cares about people's status in the church, what they care about was whom did you vote for in the last election.

When the IAF came to Port Arthur, we were dying on the vine. But the women in my church said we couldn't work with Catholics. Duh! People in the church had no conception of power and how we could change the course of the town.

I was determined to be part of this IAF thing, just because it made so much sense to me. The best school district in the state when I was growing up was now the worst school district, and it was more segregated than when I grew up. Something clearly had to be done.

■ ■ ■ ■

It was then I met Sister Christine Stephens. My stereotype of Catholic nuns came from movies and television shows. They showed them working in the shadows to carry out their duties to the Church and sacrificing their lives for all. Or later, like Sally Field as the "Flying Nun," they were renegades who consistently disobeyed orders. I was introduced to the words "women religious" when I met Sister Christine and other Sisters. They didn't wear habits, they had stylish hair styles, and they certainly broke my stereotype of what a nun was.

Before IAF came to Port Arthur, I lived in a very small world. We had clearly defined roles and very little interaction with those that were "different" from us. The older folks in my Baptist congregation decided we couldn't be part of this new group because Catholics were involved in the organizing and Catholics "gambled." I, on the other hand, thought, 'Okay, is that the worse thing we can say about them?'

Here I digress for a moment. The other thing I liked about IAF was the insistence on respecting "older Black and Hispanic people." In the South, a five-year-old white child was equal to all older Black persons, male or female, and hence could address them as "boy" or "girl," or by their first name. One day, my grandmother and I encountered a young white man who spoke to us. He said, "Good morning, Auntie," to my grandmother. Confused I asked her if we were related to him. Otherwise, why did he call her Auntie? "Well, Lady," she said, "whites would never call an older Black person Mr. or Mrs. But out of respect he called me Auntie."

Christine understood that legacy, and hence her insistence on calling older leaders by their formal titles, giving dignity to a group of elders who had not received it before. These were ordinary people—some educated, some not—but in our meetings they were all equal. I cannot describe the powerful emotion evoked in me when in large meetings our leaders were all introduced as "Mr." or "Mrs." Or when I had a one-to-one with a Mrs. Normand or Mr. Jones. It just changed the dynamics of the meeting.

Sister Christine taught us to call all our leaders by their formal titles to give them the respect they deserved. They were Mr., Mrs., Rev., Fr., Sr., or Dr. So-and-So. And Christine always reminded the organizers that we existed only because the leaders existed. They made what we did possible.

■ ■ ■ ■

My favorite personal Sister Christine story is this one. She and I had done a training session in Tyler, Texas, and she suggested we then go to Shreveport, Louisiana, and do a little gambling at one of the casinos there. By then, I guess, I had realized I wouldn't go to Hell if I gambled a little bit, and it might be fun. Besides, I would be with a nun and could explain that to God when the time came!

We got to the casino and Christine showed me how to play a slot machine. We then split up and I played some slots along the wall. Christine disappeared somewhere. Maybe she was at the Roulette wheel or a Blackjack or Craps table. I never found out. Finally, Christine found me and asked if I was ready to go. For the last at least fifteen minutes, however, I had been trying to figure out how to get rid of all those darn credits that kept coming up. Christine told me that meant I had won.

"Wow, you are kidding me, Christine," I said.

"No, you have won a hundred bucks, Lady," she laughed.

Sister Christine Stephens taught this good Missionary Baptist lady named Lady two things that are important: Building power to affect change crosses lines of division, and we need to bust our stereotypes of whom we think we can work with to affect that change. But she also exposed me to a world I did not know existed: I discovered art museums in my forties because of her. She encouraged me to travel both throughout the United States and abroad. And she was my greatest champion, but she also gave me biting critiques because she wanted me to grow.

That was Christine: brutally honest, funny, witty, and always working to teach people like me how to understand the self-interest of others if we were to truly build powerful organizations that would be long-lasting.

I am sure she is now conducting training sessions in Heaven.

■ ■ ■ ■

Editor's Note: Lady Carlson notes, "God admonishes Moses to tell the children of Israel to teach their children the story of the captivity lest they forget and become like Pharaoh. Organizing for me is not only a way to remember the story of riding on the back of the bus, the "colored only" signs, the indignities suffered by my parents and grandparents, but also to constructively work to change racist systems by building the power necessary to change them. Frederick Douglass said 'Power concedes nothing without a demand. It never did and it never will.' That for me summarizes what organizing is about."

Questions for Discussion or Reflection

1. Tell a story of someone very "different" from you in some important way who has influenced your life.

2. Why is it important for organizers to respect leaders…and vice versa? How important is it to use people's formal names and titles in public? Explain your answer.

3. What is the importance of childhood, young adult, and ongoing education in the development of leaders and organizers? Be specific, with examples from your own experience or that of others.

Have You Always Been Ambitious?

by Kristen King

Kristen King (born 1966) is the lead organizer for VOICE and ACTION in Oklahoma. Here she recalls her mentor, Sr. Christine Stephens, CDP, who organized with the Industrial Areas Foundation for forty-five years, including as a co-executive director of IAF from 2008-2012.

H ave you always been ambitious?" she asked me. I felt as if this nun had named a secret part of me. I mean, women aren't supposed to be ambitious—I was very clear about that from growing up in the evangelical church, and her question made me feel exposed, maybe recognized, definitely outed. I stumbled with my answer—"No, um, well...." It was awkward, like a good individual meeting should be when you agitate someone. It gets them to think about themselves in a different way.

That's what I remember about my first individual meeting with Sister Christine Stephens, at national training run by the Industrial Areas Foundation (IAF) in San Antonio, Texas, in 1999.

For years after that, as a beginning organizer, I thought the power of that meeting was in the question. And so I struggled to always ask the right question, assuming that magically things would then start to happen. But the power wasn't in the question, it was in Sr. Christine. The point of institution-based organizing is to give congregations and other civic institutions a set of tools—habits and practices they hone—to form leaders who can act on the traditions of the institutions that formed them. Christine was completely "formed" in both her religious tradition and in the IAF organizing tradition, so completely integrated that she lived out her call with her entire being. Her question to me that afternoon in San Antonio was the result of thousands of individual meetings, of hearing stories from all races and economic levels, of cultivating an imagination for what people could do when connected to real power to take action. Her question came from her own hard work of unlearning all the messages that tell women that we can't pursue our interests, that we have to stay in the background, that we cannot build power.

■ ■ ■ ■

Sr. Christine was excited when I moved to Oklahoma in 2007 to build an IAF-affiliated organization in Oklahoma City. As a young nun, she had been assigned to teach at a Catholic high school in Oklahoma City, and she remembered clearly how much she learned from the Black students she worked with, who were at the time very much engaged in the struggle for civil rights. I can imagine that as a white woman from southern Texas she had a lot to learn, but Christine let those students challenge her and shape her and then carried their stories and their names with her until the end of her life.

Throughout her forty-five years with the IAF, she built projects with African American leaders and worked hard to make our organizations grapple with the racial injustices inherent in our communities. She modeled for a lot of us younger white women how to be an ally before it was a "thing."

What I came to appreciate about Christine Stephens as I advanced in my career is that she was fully present in her public life as an organizer.

- When she conducted a training session, she could make the concepts and the stories come alive. She had clarity and humor. I think she even danced once while teaching the basics of broad-based organizing (a session that in the wrong hands can become a deadly bore).

- In seminars, she could reframe what we were studying in such a way that a room that had all but checked out was suddenly engaged with the text. Once my peer organizing group was reading the biography of economist Albert O. Hirschman and were vaguely summarizing his formative years. She interrupted and said, "Do you all really not care about history? This is the story of Hitler coming to power, and the left could not organize themselves against him because they were too busy fighting each other. That doesn't matter to you?" Her ongoing teaching on the Bible—"the Bible is an organizing story"—helped many of us to see ourselves in the story and the story—the tradition—in all of us.

- In how she conducted business, she had an amazing "turn-around time." That's the time it takes for someone to follow up on a commitment they've made. She usually followed up on commitments within the same day she made them, or the next day at the latest.

⁘ In her individual meetings, she mastered the art of understanding self-interest, which the IAF teaches is the heart of political thinking. Self-interest is a fancy way of saying "the self among or between," or "with whom the self is in relationship." She knew the organizers and their families. She knew key leaders from most of the projects. She knew the history of the organizations and even understood the self-interests of many of the elected officials across the entire southwest region of the United States. And she could agitate them all—stir them up in such a way that they could all imagine doing something better, more decent, more humane than anything politics-as-usual had to offer.

▪ ▪ ▪ ▪

Ernie Cortes, the long-time director of the W/SW IAF, once asked me what I thought of Sr. Christine, and I told him she was "the embodiment of wisdom." It was overwhelming to me to even try to summarize what she meant to me at the time, but I was trying to communicate that Christine knew me and worked hard to make me a better organizer. But if anyone were to ask me again about Christine today, I'd have to add that her energy and her radical sense of urgency—NOW is the time—made her a force to be reckoned with. I am now about as old as she was in our first individual meeting in San Antonio. (How did that happen?) You don't get Christine's level of energy at my age from anything other than being completely grounded in your purpose, and that requires an ongoing willingness to be agitated, to imagine and re-imagine yourself and those around you, to take new risks, and to keep listening to the stories of those who are crying out, begging to be heard.

I think Sr. Christine Stephens, who died in 2019, would be proud of the IAF's ongoing work in the Covid-19 crisis—the global pandemic, the economic downturn, the demand for racial justice—because we kept at the fore her insistence on acting NOW and fighting for the families who are most vulnerable in this moment.

■ ■ ■ ■

Editor's Note: Kristen King continues to organize in Oklahoma, primarily from her home, where she sheltered in place during the entire Covid-19 pandemic and continues to do so whenever possible because, as she says, "At least now there's something always cooking in my kitchen."

Questions for Discussion and Reflection

1. Are you ambitious? To do what? Why?
2. Name some women mentors in your life. Were they different from your male mentors? If so, how?
3. What does "Now is the time" mean to you in today's political environment? Give a couple examples from your own experience or that of others.

Taking My Side

by Josephine Lopez Paul

Josephine Lopez Paul (born 1971) has been a senior organizer with the West/ Southwest Industrial Areas Foundation (IAF) since 2005 and is the Lead Organizer for Dallas Area Interfaith (DAI), a coalition of congregations, schools, and non-profits organizing for local change in Texas. She was born and raised in New Mexico, became a public-school teacher there, and then was elected co-president of the teachers' union in Santa Fe before organizing with the IAF. She has organized with other IAF affiliate organizations in Albuquerque, El Paso, and Fort Worth. Her recent successful organizing campaigns in Dallas include revising the city's housing code to give stronger protections to the 60% of city residents who rent; increasing trust between immigrants and law enforcement through a Catholic parish ID program; designing and implementing an alternative lending program for immigrants, and developing a 30,000-voter bloc drawn from member institutions and surrounding neighborhoods in preparation for the November 2020 election. Here she reflects on how she was mentored as a young organizer by Sister Christine Stephens, CDP.

My first relational meeting with Sister Christine Stephens, in 2005, was memorable to say the least. I arrived in an Austin restaurant to discuss my trying out to become an organizer with the Industrial Areas Foundation (IAF). Over coffee and *huevos a la*

Mexicana, we began our public relationship. I arrived a powerless, burned-out teacher with little hope for organizing institutions. She challenged my powerlessness and held me accountable for my own actions. After I spewed how toxic my school, my union, and the church was, she responded with, "So what do you take responsibility for? Or is it always everyone else's fault?" Her words both stung and invigorated me at the same time. It was the first time someone took me on about my own action or inaction.

I saw her anger. It was attractive, clear, and impressive to me. Her anger was what George Orwell described as "generous anger." Orwell uses this term to describe the appearance of author Charles Dickens: "It is the face of a [person]who is always fighting against something, but who fights in the open and is not frightened, the face of [someone] who is generously angry." This was Sister Christine. While you could be the recipient of her anger, you knew there was truth in what she was saying, even if it was hard to hear. She wanted me to be better and stronger than my foes, and she convinced me I could. I was worthy of her anger. Imagine that!

■ ■ ■ ■

I miss her. Her words come to me often things like "we can make people really boring with boring questions;" "you can only organize what you can imagine;" "good organizing moves toward the center of institutions;" and my favorite, "move it or lose it!" I was terrified of her being my supervisor at first, but I learned as we negotiated our terms of working together that while she would always challenge and critique me she would also be my strongest supporter in times of need. When I was assigned a new supervisor after three years with her, I grieved for six months and frequently would call her. I remember her saying it was time for me to fly the coop and learn from someone new. She said, "I like hearing from you, Josephine, but only if you call your supervisor first."

One of my favorite memories of Christine was after an accountability session attended by more than 2,000 residents and three chiefs of police from the Dallas Metro area in which Dallas Area Interfaith (DAI) won acceptance of a parish-issued ID for undocumented immigrants to present during any encounter with local police. DAI leaders secured a front-page story in the *Dallas Morning News*, and Christine sent a text that was emblematic of who she was to me. "Congratulations, you're making history. Now get ready for your enemies to come after you." She recognized the victory, but she didn't let me gloat either. Our enemies never did mount much opposition, but even so Sister Christine took a moment to recognize the victory, while reminding me to stay alert.

■ ■ ■ ■

She taught me to never become sentimental about my situation. An IAF universal principle is that our organizations' diversity should be reflective of the communities in which they operate, working across lines of race, class, age, and geography. When I began working in one IAF organization, I found a mostly white, upper-middle-class group of leaders who operated as a board of directors instead of a power organization. Christine told me this needed to be disrupted. Well, I took "disrupt" literally and created extreme conflict. When I told her what I had done, she said, "Josephine, I told you to disrupt it, not to blow it up." Even though she was angry with me, she never left my side during that fight or any other fight. But she also never *only* took my side.

I will never forget our last relational meeting at a three-day training in Dallas. Most conversations with her were memorable, and this one was no different. She helped me see how far I have come as an organizer. "Look at what you have become," she said." Thank you, Sister Christine, for your public friendship and never letting me take the easy way out.

■ ▨ ▨ ▨

Editor's Note: Josephine Lopez Paul says, "One of the tough lessons Sister Christine Stephens taught me was that you are responsible for your inaction or the consequences of your actions. She never let me off the hook for what I did or didn't do. Once I tried to blame a failed organizing effort on other people and made excuses for myself. She wouldn't let me blame others. She said that I was the one responsible for the failure, and she was right. She was incredibly forgiving about the situation but wouldn't let me take a pass and blame someone else."

Questions for Discussion and Reflection

1. What is the difference between supervision and mentoring? Explain with examples.
2. Name two or three people who have "had your back." How did that feel? Have you ever had someone else's back? Name them.
3. How can anger be a good thing in organizing? Have you ever given or received "generous anger"? Tell the story.

Sister Christine Stephens

by Pearl Ceasar

Sister Pearl Ceasar (born 1943) is the Superior General of the Sisters of the Divine Providence and a long-time friend and colleague of Sister Christine Stephens. This essay is adapted from Sister Pearl's eulogy for Sister Christine Stephens, CDP, who died at age seventy-eight in 2019. Sister Christine did not leave many writings, so several people have contributed essays in this book about the woman who was a key "founder" of the modern Industrial Areas Foundation.

Sister Mary Christine Stephens: Woman Religious, Organizer, Mentor, Leader, Agitator, Historian, Daughter, Sister, Aunt, Cousin, Friend.

■ ■ ■ ■

On Thursday, July 11, 2019, at 10:30 am, Christine went to her regular physical therapy appointment. At 11:40, she told the therapist she was leaving because she had a splitting headache. She drove herself to St. David's Hospital in south Austin, went to valet parking, gave her car keys to the attendant, went inside, pointed to the left side of her head, and collapsed. In the days that followed, her condition worsened. A large hematoma had caused severe swelling in her brain.

230

For seven days, several times a day, the doctors and medical personnel would come in, say Christine's name loudly, poke her, and ask her to open her eyelids, squeeze their finger, or wiggle her toes. I told one of the doctors I knew she was unconscious because she would have knocked him silly if she had been awake.

During those days, I, her long-time IAF colleagues Elizabeth Valdez and Ernesto Cortes, her family, many leaders from COPS/Metro in San Antonio, the sisters of our community, and many, many others went to the hospital and talked to Christine. We knew she could hear us. Periodically, tears would flow down her cheeks. We each told her what she had meant to us and to other leaders throughout the years. There were more tears.

Finally, the neurosurgeon recommended that based on her continued unresponsiveness we consider disconnecting Christine's ventilator on Thursday, July 18. That was a very difficult decision. However, Christine had a living will that directed that no extraordinary means of life support be used. She had been very clear, and her next level of life-support would have been a permanent feeding tube and a tracheotomy for breathing. We all knew what her wishes were.

■ ■ ■ ■

Then a miraculous thing happened. On that Thursday, July 18, at 6:30 AM, the Intensive Care Unit doctor went in to her room for his usual daily exam. He said, "Christine, open your eyelids." She did. He then said, "Christine, squeeze my finger." She did. "Christine, wiggle your toes." She did. He announced that Christine was breathing on her own! She did not need the ventilator. None of us knew what this meant.

Looking back, the miracle of that final day was that Christine had once again drawn us out of our grief and sorrow. For eight days we had been consumed by the thought of losing her. All week we had sat with a body that we knew was not Christine. We were like Mary Magdalen, who went to the empty tomb after the Resurrection. Magdalen was so consumed by her own grief, sorrow, and tears that she did not recognize Jesus in the person she met at the tomb until Jesus called her name. She had thought Jesus was a gardener.

Christine came back to us in a very real way on her final day and called our names one last time, if you will. She told us by breathing on her own and mustering whatever strength she had that she was not afraid to die. She conveyed to us that she was meeting her God, whom she had been seeking all her life. She showed us by her calmness and peace that she was a Woman of the Resurrection, a Woman ready to be transformed into a new state of being, more fully alive than when she walked the earth. We knew Christine had taught us how to live; on her last day, she showed us how to die.

We got to tell her how much we loved her and how much she meant to us in our lives. We prayed with her and sang. We sang the "Salve Regina." We were singing her father's favorite hymn, "Amazing Grace," when she died at 5:20 pm on that Thursday, July 18, 2019.

■ ■ ■ ■

Sister Mary Christine Stephens: Woman of Faith, Vision, Conviction, Anger, Humor, Simplicity, Integrity, Compassion, Kind-heartedness, Empathy, Conscience, Fidelity, Justice. A true Woman of the Resurrection.

We miss you, dear friend. You will forever live in our hearts and lives. Your legacy will continue in all of us. Amen.

■ ■ ■ ■

Editor's Note: Christine Stephens, CDP, was a pioneer in organizing for many reasons, not the least of which was her mentoring of so many others. Many of the current organizers in the Industrial Areas Foundation (IAF) point to her as the person who taught them about power...and about themselves, and several of them tell stories about her in their essays in this book. She is the first of the current generation of leaders in IAF that includes Ernesto Cortes, Jr., Michael Gecan, Arnie Graf, and several others to pass away. Stephens organized with the Industrial Areas Foundation for forty-five years, including a serving as a co-executive director of IAF from 2008-2012. Stephens often said, "What you pay attention to will happen," which on one level is like, "Duh!" But Paul Turner says that what Stephens meant is critically important and often overlooked: Organizers and leaders have limited time and energy. We can fall prey to magical thinking. Bottom line is, whatever we *want* to happen *won't* happen unless we *make* it happen. Or—as Sister Christine pointed out in shorthand thousands of times to those she taught, supervised, and mentored—"What you pay attention to will happen."

Questions for Discussion and Reflection

1. Name personal mentors or heroes in your life, living or dead. What made them so important to you? What is one lesson you learned from them that you use almost every day?

2. Are there special challenges for women in being a leader or an organizer in a power organization? What are they? What can help them overcome those challenges?

3. Should religious leaders, especially those called, vowed, or ordained to formal church ministry, be involved in organizing? Defend your answer.

Crossing Race in Mississippi

by Ronnie Crudup

Bishop Ronnie Crudup (born 1953) is the Mid-South Diocesan Bishop of the Fellowship of International Churches and the Senior Pastor of New Horizon Church International in Jackson, Mississippi. New Horizon has over 3,000 members. Bishop Crudup has been a leader with Industrial Areas Foundation (IAF) projects in Mississippi since 1994.

In late 1993, my best friend in ministry, Rev. Phil Reed, who was at the time the pastor of Voice of Calvary Fellowship, the first deliberate attempt in Mississippi at developing a multi-racial church, called me and asked me to meet with a friend of his, Perry Perkins, a native Mississippian who was an organizer with the Industrial Areas Foundation (IAF).

Phil is Caucasian. I am Black. We had been drawn together in mutual ministry for almost twenty years at the time of my meeting Perry. We had been drawn together by a mutual concern for racial reconciliation and the effort to do ministry that crossed racial lines. I didn't know it at the time, but we were searching for ways to develop a "ministry of public life" together.

In that first meeting with Perry, Phil and I were introduced to a systemic and institutional approach to crossing the civic, religious, and political segregation that had emerged in the aftermath of the Civil Rights era in Mississippi. IAF, while recognizing the importance of movements, and the Civil Rights Movement in particular, offered us a broad based and institutional response to public life.

■ ■ ■ ■

As a Black pastor, I had always been politically active in my ministry. However, there had always been two things missing in my approach to public life. The first missing ingredient was my response was an isolated response coming out of a Black church, with little interaction with the dominant white community. This fact is what drew Phil Reed and I together.

Phil, as pastor of Voice of Calvary, which he described as "a deliberate attempt to attack the most segregated hour in American life," and me, as pastor of rapidly growing Black church, had committed to develop joint ministry together. But we weren't sure how to go about it. IAF introduced us to a potential path of bridging the continued systematic civic and religious segregation of our city and state. Perry talked to us about bringing institutions together to create a space of political equality that did not exist at the time in Jackson or any other place in Mississippi. A space where institutions—white, Black, and eventually Hispanic; rich and poor; Christian, Jewish, Muslim; and the secular—could come together. This coming together could get beyond the paternalistic patterns of past cross-racial efforts and create a space where institutional interest was placed at the forefront of our public work.

The building of relationships based on the historic and contemporary interests and traditions of our diverse institutions was at the center of the partnership with IAF that began in that three-person afternoon meeting. From this tiny initial relationship, we worked together to develop a measure of public trust with religious and civic leaders we had never worked with before. We moved from the traditional clergy-based public responses, which we were familiar with, to a congregational and institutional leadership-development methodology, where our lay leaders were developed for public action. The measure of trust they developed across racial and religious lines allowed them to share leadership in public action together.

Through this partnership with IAF, we have built an organization which has become the most diverse public organization in Mississippi, Working Together Jackson (WTJ). WTJ created a process where people who previously would not have dared to cross color, religion, political, and economic chasms not only ventured across them but were welcomed into spaces they never dreamed they would be welcome and allowed to speak and enjoy fellowship. These new relationships changed what hadn't been possible in Mississippi to that point and opened the door to all kinds of interactions and ventures. We learned that we not only had shared interest but that that interest could be harvested for mutual benefit.

The second missing ingredient of my previous attempts at cross-racial public life was the reactive nature of most of our public work. We would experience a racial incident and come together for the moment to react to it. But most of our work was not strategic or sustainable. IAF introduced us to more thoughtful and strategic response to political action altogether.

The following are three brief examples of the work that has come out of our organizational work over the last twenty-five years.

■ ■ ■ ■

Black-controlled banking institutions and access to credit has been a major problem facing Mississippi and other southern states. Over twenty years ago, we partnered with the Enterprise Corporation of the Delta, a secular member institution of the IAF work in Mississippi, to form Hope Federal Credit Union. Hope is now one of the largest Black controlled financial institutions in the Mid-South, with branches in Mississippi, Arkansas, Tennessee, Louisiana, and Alabama.

■ ■ ■ ■

In 2014, the late Mayor Chokwe Lumumba of Jackson proposed passage of a one-cent sales tax to be used exclusively for infrastructure improvements in Jackson. This proposal was aimed at dealing with decades of neglect in dealing with basic street, road, drainage, and water and sewer projects in Jackson. WTJ discovered that even though the mayor had called for a referendum in early January there was no organized campaign or messaging in favor of it. We were concerned that the proposal would not pass and this would continue the deterioration of Jackson.

We attempted to get a meeting with Mayor Lumumba to discuss our concerns and develop a plan of action. We were not successful in arranging the meeting. We then took two steps: first, we commissioned our own poll to gage public opinion on the proposal; and second, we called a breakfast meeting at my church of key white and Black business leaders and several city council and state legislators. We told the mayor's staff of the meeting but had no reason to believe he would show up.

Five minutes before the meeting was to start, however, I received a call that the mayor was on the way. The mayor, because of his Black Nationalist, past was not fully trusted by business leaders, white or Black. As he came in, the mayor immediately approached Leland Speed, the most significant white business leader in Jackson. I knew that politicians like to take over meetings, so I called the meeting to order immediately and the mayor sat down.

After preliminary introductions, I said, "Mr. Mayor, it is late November and you are calling for a tax election in mid-January. We do not see an organized campaign ready to pass this new tax. Because of that we have commissioned a poll that Working Together Jackson is paying for, with no money from the business leaders here. The poll will run this weekend and we will have the results by Tuesday. We ask you and the city council members here today to delay the vote if this poll indicates we are not ready for the election. We also offer our organization as the lead group to develop an organized campaign to pass this critical infrastructure tax."

You could cut the tension with a knife. The mayor smiled and said, "I thought I was talking to the right people about this election, but it's obvious I wasn't." He looked at the city council members in the meeting and said to them, "Will you work with me to delay the election if the poll shows that is necessary?" They all nodded their agreement. We committed to sharing the results on Tuesday, and Mayor Lumumba agreed we would work with his staff to develop the campaign, with WTJ leading the effort.

Under state law in Mississippi, a tax referendum requires 60% of the vote for approval. Our poll showed that 55% of the voters and 60% of Black voters would support the new tax. However, when informed of items that were exempted from the tax, such as groceries and prescription drugs. the support rate went to 90%. We informed the Mayor of these results and began the work to develop a successful campaign. In the two weeks between New Years and the Mid-January election, our leaders took their church membership rolls and began to call congregational members seeking a commitment for affirmative votes. We secured over 4,000 yes votes from our members, and the referendum passed with a 90% margin. Black and white precincts had overwhelmingly supported a tax increase for infrastructure improvements. At the celebration of the referendum's victory, the first words out of the Mayor's mouth was "I want to thank Working Together Jackson for their leadership in this critical election."

■ ■ ■ ■

In 2020, during the national protests led by Black Lives Matter, we got a call late on a Wednesday afternoon and were informed that the governor and leaders of the Mississippi State Legislature were going to have a critical meeting the next day to discuss removing the Confederate Battle Flag from a corner of the official Mississippi State Flag. Governor Tate Reeves was attempting to send the question of changing the flag to the voters in what was sure to be a very contentious referendum. We were told, "Working Together Jackson and Working Together Mississippi [our new statewide organization] are the only groups in the state that can convene religious leaders across racial lines on such short notice and stop the disastrous possibility of a divisive statewide flag referendum."

The next morning, on the steps of St. Peter's Catholic Cathedral in Jackson, the Catholic Bishop of Jackson, the Episcopal Bishop of Mississippi, the Methodist Bishop's representatives, the Church of Christ Holiness Bishop, representatives of National Baptist President Dr. Jerry Young, and female and male lay leaders and clergy from our individual religious institutions around the state including Muslim, Jewish, Cooperative Baptist, Independent congregations, and AME leaders—all properly socially distanced and wearing masks—called for the immediate removal of the Confederate Battle Flag by a vote of the legislature rather than by a referendum. We said:

> As people of faith, we believe that repentance is a necessary part of our personal and corporate faith journey. Enslaved African's were brought to this continent 401 years ago. A theology of white supremacy was constructed to justify this brutal kidnapping and enslavement. The most destructive war in our nation's history was fought to protect the economic system that slavery produced. It was fought under the battle flag that is contained in our State Flag. Many religious leaders of the Confederate States defended slavery with a theology of white supremacy. We stand today as a diverse group of religious leaders saying that as a state we need to repent and make amends for these corporate sins.

The brutal public death of George Floyd by a police officer shocked the country. George Floyd's death occurred on Memorial Day, a day that began in Columbus, Mississippi, with the decoration of graves of Confederate Soldiers with the Battle Flag of the Confederacy. We as Mississippi religious leaders know that much work is to be done to assure equal treatment under the law. We also know that police and law enforcement reform will only work if it is rooted in corporate racial reconciliation.

The immediate removal of the Confederate Battle Flag from the Mississippi State Flag will be an important public symbol of our willingness as a state to seek repentance and racial reconciliation. We call on our elected leaders to act now.

In the following days we worked with Southern Baptist Leaders, gaining their support for the immediate replacement of our state flag and paving the way for the historic vote of the legislature on June 28th to overwhelming pass a law removing this racist symbol from our state flag and setting the groundwork for a reluctant Governor Reeves to sign this bill on June 30, 2020.

■ ■ ■ ■

Editor's Note: Bishop Ronnie Crudup says: "A flag is a symbol; however, I believe that the critical and historic move to remove this racist symbol from our public space in Mississippi could not have happened unless we had built the public infrastructure of equality, trust, and strategic power over a twenty-five-year period. Relational organizing is more than a symbol. It is a new way of being together."

Questions for Discussion and Reflection

1. Give examples from your own experience or that of others about how racial divides have or have not yet been crossed in your community. What are you doing about it either way?

2. Why are symbols so important when it comes to race? Name three good symbols on race and three that absolutely have to go.

3. Why is building a "public infrastructure of equality, trust, and strategic power" over a long period of time important? How is it done?

Reveille for a New Generation

by Martin Paul Trimble

Martin Paul Trimble (born 1956) has been an Industrial Areas Foundation (IAF) co-director since May 2019. He started as a leader in Philadelphia Interfaith Action (PIA) in 1989 and joined IAF as an organizer in 1995. Trimble has been a lead organizer and supervisor with IAF projects in Delaware, Maryland, Virginia, North Carolina, and Washington, DC. Prior to organizing with IAF, he was the founding director of Opportunity Finance Network (OFN)—the national organization that establishes and enforces performance standards and raises hundreds of millions of dollars of below-market-rate capital to support community development financial institutions' efforts to provide affordable housing and economic development lending nationwide.

W hat's the matter? Don't you like my cooking?" Mary Lee Higgs, head of the Church of the Advocate's Willing Workers, barked at me. Ms. Higgs, Bertha Cohen, and a posse of other retired women labored all morning to make lunch for members of Church of the Advocate—a predominately African American Episcopal Church at 18th and Diamond Streets in North Philadelphia—seven blocks west of Temple University. I had wandered into the Advocate that Sunday seeking to revive my dormant religious faith. Little did I know that it would change my whole life.

Mary Lee Higgs was always direct when she spoke. That first day I had offended her and her Willing Worker compatriots by returning my lunch plate with uneaten collard greens and yams.

Mary Lee Higgs grew up in North Carolina and was part of the Great Migration north that brought her to Philadelphia. She worked as a housekeeper at downtown hotels for forty years. Mary organized with her fellow housekeepers to unionize Philadelphia hotel workers and create UNITE HERE Local 274, from which she had to retire due to a stroke. In the union, Mary found a place where her fighting spirit was valued and respected. The union made it possible for Mary to buy a house four blocks west from the Advocate—where she joined so her children could sing in the choir.

In retirement, the Advocate became Mary's life. Her stroke made the left side of her face droop, affected her gait, and slurred her words. Mary did not look like a leader. But Mary led the Willing Workers—an ad-hoc group of the most important leaders at the Advocate—who made things happen like baptismal and wedding celebrations, church fundraisers, bereavement visits. All major decisions at the Advocate required the support and informal ratification of Mary and her crew.

That first day, I had done a bad power analysis from which I thought that I would never recover....

■ ■ ■ ■

Six years after that initial introduction to Ms. Higgs, I was sitting alone in the Church of the Advocate—a Gothic stone monument built

245

by a previous generation of white Episcopalian brownstone owners and rowhouse mill workers who had fled the neighborhood for the suburbs after World War II that was now a predominately Black Episcopal Church surrounded by 40,000 abandoned homes that radiated for miles, stacked like junk cars end to end waiting to be crushed.

Above me were four murals painted by Walter Edmonds depicting the African American religious experience in all its anger and hope, suffering, and redemption. Walter Edmonds was a neighborhood artist whom the Advocate's long-time pastor Father Paul Washington had invited during the height of the civil rights movement to paint the murals. These murals and the history of the Advocate as the center of Philadelphia's Black Power movement during the civil rights era had drawn me in that first Sunday. The Advocate was always open, a place to learn to organize from the street corner to the nation, a place to launch and shout demands and campaigns for justice—all under the protection and blessing of the Angel Gabriel who sat atop the Advocate's spire. Angel Gabriel towered over 18th and Diamond proclaiming God's command, as Advocate Rector Father Isaac Miller put it, "To Love God's People of North Philadelphia."

When I had first seen these murals, I had the same sense of awe that I felt in visiting San Salvador's Roman Catholic Cathedral, the one where Archbishop Oscar Romero had stopped construction and where he had been murdered by military death squads while saying Mass. Six years previously, I had sat, inspired by the silence and the courage of the San Salvador *comunidades eclesiales de base* that had stood up to the Salvadoran junta and fled to the cathedral for sanctuary, where Romero welcomed them, protected them, and died for them. The military junta murdered Romero to murder the people, they thought. But their resistance endured, and they came to pray daily.

I wandered into the Advocate, son of an Episcopal priest, cynical about the church and angry and grieving the slow death of the city that I loved. In the mid-1980s, Philadelphia was hemorrhaging thousands of jobs and residents monthly and was besieged by the crack cocaine epidemic. I lived on the demilitarized zone of this devastation at 23rd and Poplar in lower North Philly: a mainly white, working-class neighborhood integrated with Philadelphia Housing Authority scattered-site properties. Here, white and Black working class managed to co-exist through a shared fear of and determination to resist the devastation on the horizon for their children and the way of life they had scratched out for themselves mostly as city workers—at the gas company, school district, water or sanitation departments.

This area had two other saviors besides my hardworking neighbors: first, a city residency requirement for all city employees—like most of my neighbors—and second, Girard College, a city-run boarding school, just one block away, that protected our modest island of integration ironically, since Girard College had been segregated until 1968.

As a young boy, I remember when Rev. Dr. Leon Sullivan, an African American pastor in Philadelphia close to Rev. Dr. Martin Luther King, teamed up with Episcopal Bishop Robert Dewitt, my hero growing up, to launch a campaign with 200 multi-racial and multi-faith clergy to integrate Girard College successfully. I grew up with reports of the unfolding drama of this campaign, and Rev. Dr. Sullivan's and Bishop DeWitt's public leadership as frequent conversation topics at our family dinners. We lived in the large house reserved for the chaplain of the Episcopal Academy, where my father worked for eighteen years. My brother, Philip, and I attended and graduated from Episcopal Academy as proud and rebellious faculty-brat scholarship kids who always knew we were the sons of hired help who were ministering and teaching the sons of wealthy Philadelphia families.

■ ■ ■ ■

Mary appeared from nowhere and sat next to me that day, knowing that I was struggling as I stared intently up at the Advocate murals to understand my mother's death from a sudden heart attack at age 62. Putting her hand on my knee, she said with her touch: "Do it." Mary knew from conversations she and I had had over the last two years that I was considering leaving the national non-profit community development financial institution I had started and grown successfully to become an on-the-ground organizer with Saul Alinsky's Industrial Areas Foundation (IAF).

Mary and I had forged a bond of understanding in battle—as leaders through the Advocate in Philadelphia Interfaith Action (PIA), IAF's new local affiliate—fighting city hall to clean and seal the abandoned properties around the church, to force Philly cops to get out of their cars to walk a beat in Mary's neighborhood so that she could walk to Bible study on Wednesday evenings without being mugged, and to build new affordable homes in the shadows of the Market Street subway line in West Philadelphia to revitalize the blighted land and provide homeownership and wealth creation opportunities to first-time, mostly Black and Latino, homebuyers.

Mary Higgs took no prisoners. Just ask Philadelphia's former Mayor Ed Rendell. Father Isaac Miller, the Advocate's rector at the time, united Mary and me in an organizing team to teach Mayor Rendell some respect. Fifty leaders from Philadelphia Interfaith Action (PIA) and the Advocate waited anxiously on the sidewalk outside Ms. Higgs' one-story, flat-roofed home on Gratz Street on a sweltering June evening in 1992 for the first meeting of PIA with Philadelphia's newly elected mayor. Father Miller and other leaders were crammed into Mary's small living room. Mayor Rendell's seat—Mary's deceased husband's rocking chair—was empty. It was 8:15 PM. Mayor Rendell had promised to arrive at 8:00 PM sharp. At 8:20, Mary rose from her chair and walked to the door, planning to tell those of us assembled outside to go home since the Mayor was not coming.

As she got to the portal, however, a squad of police cars leading a black town car came down the 1800 block of Gratz Street towards Mary's house and stopped out front. Mary hobbled down her front path to the street. As Mayor Rendell emerged from his car, smiling and ready to work the crowd, Mary declared, "You're late! You said that you would be at my house at 8:00 to talk with me and my neighbors about these abandoned houses," pointing to an entirely vacant block across the street.

Stunned, Rendell tried to offer a half-hearted apology, but Mary and her neighbors walked back inside, and this time they offered the mayor a seat on a sagging couch between three angry and besieged homeowners. Ed Rendell was now in Gratz Street City Hall, before Mayor Mary Lee Higgs and the Gratz Street City Council, for an abandoned property hearing! In thirty minutes, Mary and other PIA/Church of the Advocate/Gratz Street leaders negotiated a pledge from Rendell to clean and seal 100 abandoned buildings and remove the garbage and burned-out cars from another fifty abandoned lots the team had meticulously catalogued on a series of neighborhood inspections on previous Saturdays.

Ed Rendell had just become Philadelphia's mayor—heralded by the business class as the rescuer of downtown Philadelphia for promises of a Market Street shopping mall, hotels, a new convention center, and river walk esplanades like Baltimore's Inner Harbor. But Rendell, former tough-talking District Attorney for Philadelphia, was viewed suspiciously on Gratz Street. During his entire campaign, Rendell—who once had been spotted as a part of a group of inebriated fans at Veterans Stadium throwing ice balls down on the Dallas Cowboys at a December Eagles game—uttered not one word, made not one commitment, offered not one pledge to reclaim the devastation in North Philadelphia, of which 18th and Diamond was the epicenter.

That night, though, Ed Rendell got schooled about a new kind of power emerging in Philadelphia—citizens' power rooted in a broad-based, city-wide organization called Philadelphia Interfaith Action. It was made up of diverse institutions committed to make the city work for everyday residents like Mary Lee Higgs and her neighbors, who had a vision for something better for themselves and their families, and who now had the power to demand and fight for it.

Ed Rendell left Mayor Mary's house, the unofficial Gratz Street City

Hall, that night with a roster of abandoned buildings he promised to clean and seal and a pledge to return in thirty days for a citizens' inspection where a former housekeeper, a retired school cafeteria worker, and others from Gratz Street would grade the mayor's performance. After he left, Ms. Higgs and her fellow PIA leaders plotted about how to share their assessment of the mayor's work at the next city-wide Union League meeting—where Rendell's business and financial patrons gathered monthly—if our group decided his performance was unsatisfactory.

In fact, not much work got done on those abandoned houses and lots in the first three weeks after the PIA's Gratz Street action. But on the last Monday of the month, a battalion of city trash trucks, bulldozers, and dump trucks loaded with two-by-fours and door-and-window-size sheet metal panels barreled down Diamond Street and pulled up on the Church of the Advocate's broad sidewalk. An army of city sanitation workers jumped out and descended on the neighborhood. Under the watchful eye of Mary Higgs, her compatriots, and the Angel Gabriel, every house and lot got fixed in time for Mayor Rendell's return the next week to receive his "A-minus" grade. At the end, however, Mary and the other PIA leaders raised the mayor's grade to an "A" because he arrived ten minutes early that Saturday for the inspection.

In that moment, and still now thirty years later, I am motivated to organize by the profound lesson I learned from Mary Lee Higgs about the purpose of organizing: helping ordinary people create and lead an organization through which they can build, wield, and maintain power—to get to the table and fight for their families and make meaningful change.

And my reward, my joy, my drive in organizing then and today is rooted in this blessing: to experience, to bear witness, and to cherish having watched Mary Lee Higgs and the thousands of leaders I have trained and worked with over my thirty years with IAF exercise their agency and achieve through organizing what the late historian Lawrence Goodwin, author of *The Populist Moment*, called "political self-respect."

■ ■ ■ ■

So this is my Reveille for a New Generation: Be on the ground, stay on the ground, invest in the extraordinary leaders—people like Mary Lee Higgs—of your generation or the next by organizing side by side with them to build a broad-based citizens' organization within the IAF network, a labor union, or some other kind of institution that poor and working poor people own and lead so they can exercise power to change their city, their state, and our country.

Go to 18th and Diamond and listen: the Angel Gabriel is trumpeting: Where is the next Ella Baker, Diane Nash, Fannie Lou Hammer, John Lewis, Bob Moses, Caesar Chavez, Fred Ross, Dolores Huerta, Edward Chambers, Ernesto Cortes, Sister Christine Stephens, Arnie Graf, Michael Gecan, Sister Mary Beth Larkin, Jim Drake, Frank Pierson, Sister Pearl Ceasar, Jonathan Lange, and so many others?

This is generational work. We need you.

■ ■ ■ ■

Editor's Note: Martin Trimble says: "This reflection was written on the 80th anniversary of the Industrial Areas Foundation and in honor of Mary Lee Higgs, Rev. Isaac Miller, Rev. Mary Laney, Rev. Kermit Newkirk, and other leaders in Philadelphia Interfaith Action to whom I owe so much for the first relationships, fights, and victories in organizing that molded me into the organizer that I am. They taught me about organizing, being an organizer on the ground, and living up to my birthright as a Philadelphian and as a citizen. I will also write additional reflections about these and other extraordinary leaders who have taught me so much in hopes of imparting to a new generation of organizers the rich, meaningful, and abundant life that organizing with the Industrial Areas Foundation has bequeathed to me and I hope by extension in some small measure to my wife, Colette, and our children Elias, Delia, and Shane."

Questions for Discussion and Reflection

1. What does it mean to you to be a leader or an organizer "on the ground"? Explain your answer from your own experience or that of others.

2. When did the "light" go on for you about the power of collective action? Tell the story in as much detail as possible.

3. Do you want to be part of the "generational work" of organizing? Why? How and when will you get started and make it happen? Be specific.

PART THREE

Future of Organizing

Future of Organizing

Unlike many eighty-year-old social justice organizations, the Industrial Areas Foundation (IAF) is not resting on its laurels. Instead it has doubled down on it rich tradition while experimenting with new ideas and methods and is looking to increase its outreach to people (especially women, people of color, members of the LGBTQ community, and young adults in their late twenties and thirties) who want to learn how to organize the IAF way.

That is one of the reasons this book is being published. The IAF has developed a collection of first-person books and booklets on organizing, and it continues its local and national leadership training. There is now a cadre of established organizers and leaders in the IAF who are under fifty years old and will become the next generation of local and national supervisors.

Part Three includes sixteen articles by current IAF leaders and organizers: Cheri Andes, Stephen Applegate, Larry Gordon and Burns Stanfield, Chevon Chatman, Bob Connolly, Dean Deida, Keisha Krumm, Alicia Glassman, Matthew Marienthal, Cynthia Marshall, Adrienne McCauley, Malik Mujahid, Perry Perkins, Amy Totsch, Richard Townsell, and Paul Turner. Perhaps some readers of this book will want to join them some day.

■ ■ ■ ■

Birth of the Affordable Care Act

by Cheri Andes

Cheri Andes (born 1965) organized with the Industrial Areas Foundation (IAF) from 1994 to 2013. She was part of the founding team of United Power for Action in Justice in Chicago, Illinois, working under the leadership of then IAF Executive Director Ed Chambers. In 1999, she returned to the Boston area as part of the Greater Boston Interfaith Organization team. She became the lead organizer there in 2004, where she worked on one of the largest health-care issues ever tackled and won by an affiliate of the IAF. Here is that story.

I n 2000, under the leadership of Industrial Foundation (IAF) organizer Jim Drake (now deceased), the Greater Boston Interfaith Organization (GBIO) came roaring into existence at the start of this millennium with a campaign that won the first increase in affordable housing spending in years in the state of Massachusetts—a $100 million Trust Fund to subsidize the construction of new affordable housing across the state. This victory was intended to be localized by building hundreds of affordable units in Boston that members of GBIO congregations could enter a lottery for. In a stinging defeat, those homes were never built.

The GBIO co-president at the time, the Rev. Hurmon Hamilton, recognized that GBIO needed local victories to strengthen its base, which it proceeded to go out and get over the next few years. Here is just one exam-

259

ple. Using the leverage of its member institutional deposits, GBIO negoti-ated with Citizens Bank for what would become a $1 million investment over a ten-year period to fund a debt reduction program for low-income and moderate-income members of GBIO congregations. Members re-ceived twelve hours of financial literacy training, three one-to-one sessions with a financial counselor, membership in an ongoing peer support group, and a $500 check they could use to either pay off debt or start a savings plan. 1000 GBIO members ultimately went through this program—orga-nizational patronage at its best!

■ ■ ■ ■

It was 2005. I was the lead organizer for GBIO, and I was sitting in my office contemplating this win and other specific local victories, trying to imagine how to parley them into a bigger campaign that would unite the entire organization around one meaningful fight. At that moment, the phone rang. John McDonough was on the line, and he wanted to meet.

McDonough was a former Massachusetts state legislator with a pas-sion for health care justice. He had left the legislature in 1997, frustrated because he did not have enough power to move his progressive agenda. In 2003, he took the job of executive director for Health Care for All (HCFA), a top-flight think tank and health care advocacy organization. His mission was to spearhead a state-wide health care reform campaign. He believed that the moment had arrived in Massachusetts when it would be possible to win real change—not yet for single-payer coverage but for a hybrid model of universal health care coverage.

Through both financial literacy workshops and other campaigns with Haitian nursing home workers, GBIO had become aware that there was a massive problem of health insurance coverage in the state: One out of every ten people were uninsured. And through house meetings in the suburbs, we knew this was a middle-class issue too. I pressed McDonough—would his plan help those working in the nursing home industry who could not afford employer-sponsored coverage? Would it help suburbanites who had been downsized and were now working as "consultants" instead of as "employees" and were therefore now uninsured? I sat up straight when McDonough's answer was yes to all these questions. Perhaps, I thought, this health care campaign could unite GBIO's city and suburban bases into a regional campaign that would benefit both.

McDonough laid out to me the details of the policy he was proposing: ending the waiting lists for Medicaid; a major expansion of Medicaid eligibility, including for legal immigrants; subsidized coverage for low-moderate income individuals and families who could not qualify for Medicaid, including pharmacy and dental coverage; keeping children on their parent's plan up to age 26; no pre-existing conditions, etc. This expansion and new coverage would be paid for by matching federal dollars and by a "business mandate" (the latter was a controversial idea that all businesses over a certain size would be mandated to either offer employees a health care insurance benefit or alternatively pay a fee to fund the *public option* for those employees.)

But still, I needed to hear about the politics. Why was the 2006 legislative session the right political moment? McDonough argued thus:

1. Bill Clinton had been replaced by George Bush II and, therefore, there would be no health care reform coming from the federal government, especially considering the earlier Hillary Clinton health-care debacle.

2. At the state level there was both a new Democratic Speaker of the House (Salvatore DiMasi) and a new Democratic President of the Senate (Robert Travaglini), each of whom could conceivably be open to a new initiative for state-wide universal health care.

3. The new Republican Governor, Mitt Romney, was rumored to be interested in a run for president and was looking for a signature issue to run on.

4. The state was due to renegotiate its Medicaid waiver agreement with the federal government, which required it to come up with a new plan for covering the uninsured or the state stood to lose some $350 million in federal funds.

5. If it could be done in any state, Massachusetts was well-positioned because it had one of the lowest numbers, per capita, of uninsured in the country

6. The economy was slowly recovering, and state coffers were beginning to replenish, yet awareness of the pain of the uninsured was growing and becoming a widely felt public problem.

7. The key stakeholders—the hospital systems, the health care insurance companies, businesses, government, and the whole

spectrum of the state's health care "consumers"—would all have to agree to participate in sharing the burden of this transformation from the status quo to a new system of providing affordable and quality to everyone. Most of these stakeholders seemed ready to do so, as the mantra of shared responsibility started to catch on.

8. And finally, while the strategy would begin with the creation of a new coalition to push the reform, it was *essential* that GBIO be a partner to ensure that the coalition in fact would have the power to do the on-the-ground organizing necessary to build the political will in the legislature to enact it.

McDonough's analysis got my attention. I find that many groups come knocking on an IAF organization's door saying, "Hey, do you want to join a coalition?" They often have a particular policy—sometimes even a good policy—that they are pushing, but rarely do they have a power analysis and a strategy needed to win the way John McDonough and HCFA did.

■ ■ ■ ■

I brought the question of our joining a state-wide health care coalition, to be led by HCFA and GBIO, to pursue such massive legislation to our strategy team. We had a strenuous debate that included engaging great questions like: How can we trust the large hospital systems and insurance companies? How can we not address the question of increasing medical costs? Are we not better off going after a single-payer system? The strategy team voted to bring the issue to our entire GBIO membership.

At our February 2005 delegates' assembly, the GBIO membership debated and then voted to bring the campaign to a much larger number of members through a house-meeting campaign. A consensus was growing. That campaign concluded with a GBIO "internal action" of over 1,000 people in June 2005. The delegates from our member institutions voted to announce the campaign, and GBIO joined the coalition that was to lead on the issue. The building of such deep consent provided the energy enabling GBIO to ultimately deliver 55,000 signatures towards the total 130,000 statewide signatures needed to put an initiative on the ballot to force the needed legislation in the event the legislature would not do so on its own accord.

■ ■ ■ ■

The campaign was fast and furious and lasted from June of 2005 to the Spring of 2006, with what seemed to be a major event at least once a week. Here are three key actions I observed and helped organize:

+ An action on ourselves. In September 2005, GBIO's ballot-initiative-signature collections were flagging. Our public reputation and the coalition's goal of insuring nearly half a million people were on the line. We gathered 200 top leaders together, and campaign co-chair Rabbi Jonah Pesner led us in a collective "gut-check." He called us out, charged us up, led us in re-committing to quotas, blew the shofar, and sent us out to "walk the talk" in building power. 55,000 more signatures later, the action was a success.

• An action on Massachusetts Speaker of the House Sal DiMasi. From June–December 2005, DiMasi became the "champion of health care reform" and the tough guy standing up to the business community, which had become our main opposition. A high point of one action was DiMasi raising his fists in the air in front of 400 GBIO leaders at Pastor Ray Hammond's Bethel AME Church and shouting: "Yes, Hallelujah! I will stand up to the business community!"

• An action on the coalition itself. In early spring 2006, support for our initiative was collapsing. Speaker DiMasi was getting pummeled by the business community and in the press. GBIO got a call from his press secretary asking us to publicly call out Senate President Robert Travaglini by announcing that his intransigence was putting at risk the lives of hundreds of thousands of people of the Commonwealth. GBIO was inclined to run this action, but we needed the blessing of our coalition partners to do so. The coalition was not in favor of such polarization. It turned out that some of them had other interests at stake with the Senate President in addition to this health reform bill. I called the Speaker's press secretary back and told her that it was imperative for the coalition to meet with the Speaker the following day in order to give DiMasi an answer in person to his request. The appointment was set. I then told McDonough and the coalition that we had an appointment

with the Speaker the next morning and it was critical we give our
lead ally an answer face-to-face. So we all gathered in DiMasi's
office—John McDonough, the Rev. Hurmon Hamilton, Celia
Wcislo from SEUI 1199, Tim Genz (now deceased) from the Mass
Hospital Association, Judy Meredith, the HCFA's lobbyist, and a
representative from Neighbor to Neighbor. DiMasi came in late,
strode to the head of the table, slammed his hands down on the
table and barked, "Let me ask you all something. How much of
my bill is in *your* bill? 5%? 10%?" "Oh no, Mr. Speaker," someone
in the group piped up. "85-90%!" "Then why," he raised his voice,
"won't you all *say* that? Let me ask you another question. How
much of the *Senate President's* bill is in your bill? 85-90%?" "Oh no,
Mr. Speaker, only 5-10%!" "THEN WHY WONT YOU SAY
THAT?" thundered DiMasi. "Look," he said, pointing his finger at
Rev. Hamilton. "I came out to your church and promised to stand
up to the business community, and I have. And now I'm asking
you to stand up for *me*! And if you *do* this (he dramatically pointed
his finger all around the table at each person), we will win! And if
you do *not* do this, we will lose!" Then he turned on his heal and
walked out of the room. DiMasi had run one of the best actions I
had ever seen on the coalition. In the evaluation after the meeting,
the coalition leaders agreed—to a person—that GBIO (though
not the coalition itself) could and should hold that polarizing press
conference calling out the Senate President, which we did the next
day. It proved to be an important turning point in the campaign.

(Note: Some years after this campaign, and in an unrelated matter, Speaker DiMasi was convicted of a bribery charge and spent several years in federal prison.)

■ ■ ■ ■

On April 12, 2006, Governor Mitt Romney signed into law Chapter 58—Massachusetts' state-wide Universal Health Reform Law. With the stroke of a pen, nearly half a million uninsured residents in the state became eligible for insurance, insurance that GBIO and its allies would have a hand in crafting. The bill also became the model for the nation, forming the blueprint for the Affordable Care Act (aka Obamacare) a few years later.

Big change is possible. In 2006, we got affordable quality health care in Massachusetts. But, of course, the story did not end there. Who would have thought that a provision of this reform would show up as a contentious point of debate between Democratic Party Presidential candidates Barack Obama and Hilary Clinton in 2007-2008? (They split during the presidential race over whether the national government should *mandate* that everyone had to get health insurance, a solution that Massachusetts pragmatically settled on in order to insure everyone.) Then again, after the 2008-2009 banking debacle, and after—at least the pundits claimed— Obama and his advisors felt they had to come up with some alternative compelling national issue to focus on, who would have predicted they would choose the health care model that had been fought and won by the organized institutions of the State of Massachusetts. Indeed, this same controversy would spill over again in the 2012, 2016, and especially the 2020 presidential campaigns (with Democrats at loggerheads over single-payer "Medicare For All" vs. an insurance-based hybrid and a Republican President making every effort to destroy health care reform altogether). GBIO's state-wide actions, in coalition with other allies, had leveraged a national debate and national action on healthcare that continues to reverberate throughout the country today.

■ ■ ■ ■

Editor's Note: Cheri Andes is now working in the field of mental health care. In reflecting on this story, she said: "While progress has been made, the 2020 world-wide pandemic laid bare the ongoing gaping wounds in America's health care system. So much more is asked of us as human beings caring about our fellow human beings. The only thing leaders and organizers have to fear are the limits we place on our own imaginations. Big change is possible when organizers and leaders understand that the solutions we seek to enact must be creative, but also that the process of our exercise of power must be creative as well."

Questions for Discussion and Reflection

1. What are the limits on imagination about what is possible if people and their institutions organize for power? How do you do a power analysis to see what might be possible?
2. What are the positives and negatives of allying with other civic organizations and/or politicians? Give examples from your own experience or that of others.
3. Are housing, jobs, health care, and education a right or a privilege? Explain your answer and its implications for your organizing.

A Sermon on Anger

by Stephen H. Applegate

Stephen H. Applegate (born 1952) was the interim pastor of All Saints Episcopal Church in Chicago when he delivered this sermon on July 5, 2020, in the midst of the Covid-19 pandemic and protests over racism and systemic injustice. Prior to this stage in his career, where he had been taking various interim assignments for three years, he had been pastor for fourteen years at a parish in Granville, Ohio, which he considers to be his home. In response to a request from Richard Townsell of the Lawndale Christians Development Corporation (who wrote an essay later in this book), All Saints raised over $200,000 in "The Greenlining Campaign" to help build the first model home in the Lawndale community for an effort organized by United Power for Action and Justice to build thousands of affordable homes controlled by the residents on the south and west side of Chicago, controlled by the community and built to scale according to an organizing model on the Nehemiah Homes built by East Brooklyn Churches in New York City.

We had just finished Morning Prayer about a week and a half ago when one of the participants asked a question. She noticed that a good-sized chunk of one of the readings had been left out. An entire eighteen verses from the Old Testament Book of Numbers had been omitted. And she wanted to know why that had happened.

There are different reasons this kind of deletion of verses occur in a service. They depend on the readings themselves. Sometimes verses get left out because the lesson is long enough and the omitted verses don't add anything or move the story along. Sometimes the passage includes hard-to-pronounce Biblical names that are better avoided. And sometimes the omitted passage is just plain offensive. There are whole sections of the psalms, for example, where the psalmist asks God to do unspeakable things to his enemies. That sort of ugliness is hard enough to listen to when it's shared in political rallies or it gets re-Tweeted by the Tweeter-in-Chief. We hardly need to read Scripture in church that add more cruelty and viciousness to our current already unpleasant world.

The reason I'm talking about leaving out verses from readings is because when I started to prepare for this sermon I noticed that the Gospel passage for this morning had a big gap in it. Six verses had been left out. When I discovered what they were, I added them back in. I've indicated which verses they are by putting them in italics in the service leaflet in your hands: "*Then Jesus began to reproach the cities in which most of his deeds of power had been done, because they did not repent*"(Matthew 11).

In these restored verses, Jesus calls down calamity on the cities where "most of his deeds of power had been done." Jesus does this, Matthew says, "because they did not repent." In demanding disaster, Jesus singles out three villages—Chorazin, Bethsaida, and Capernaum—and predicts that these three villages will come to a worse fate than some other places that were far more notorious or nefarious.

I can't tell you exactly why the people who put together the lectionary

271

readings for us left out the "woes" that Jesus proclaimed over the villages, but I have a theory. I suspect the people who compiled the readings wanted to protect us from such an angry Jesus. And he certainly was angry!

Jesus let fly on these cities where he had worked the hardest. "Doom to you, Chorazin!" he said. "Doom to you, Bethsaida! If Tyre and Sidon had seen half the powerful miracles you have seen, they would have been on their knees in a minute. But not you! And Capernaum! You think you're pretty darn special, but you're going to end up in the abyss. If others had had the same chances you've had, they would have changed their ways!"

■ ■ ■ ■

Ouch! What happened to the Jesus of the Way of Love? Where is *that* Jesus? This story about Capernaum, Chorazin, and Bethsaida is probably news to most of us and, to be honest, we don't like it very much. It doesn't jive with our image of Jesus, and it's going to take some serious work to integrate it into our understanding of the Jesus we know and love.

But here's the thing—when Jesus gets really angry, doesn't it get your attention? Isn't it interesting?

We all know that Jesus is fully a human being, but sometimes that fact gets lost in all the lofty words used to describe him: "God from God," "Light from Light," "True God from true God," "seated at the right hand of the Father"—those kinds of words.

I am more drawn to the human Jesus: the one who weeps when his friend Lazarus dies, the one who shouts at Peter when he doesn't "get it" for the umpteenth time, or the one who laughs with his friends as they share a joke around the table. Because Jesus did laugh. A lot. In contrast to the exalted language often used to describe him, the Gospels portray Jesus as a flesh and blood human being—a passionate person who cared deeply about others, who was moved with pity because of the situations people brought to him, someone who, in today's reading, could be wounded by criticism and injured by apathy.

When I read today's story, I want to know more about this Jesus, what got under his skin, and what he did about it. Because I'm convinced that when Jesus got angry it was never about trivial or petty things. His anger was aroused by things that really mattered to the reign of God he was trying so hard to inaugurate.

Don't you wonder what these towns and villages did that made Jesus so angry? I do. Capernaum, Chorazin, and Bethsaida were all nondescript little fishing villages in Galilee. There was nothing "notorious" or "nefarious" about them. They were the same small villages that most of his disciples came from. Nothing in the Gospels points toward these villages as being full of terrible sinners. Jesus' main complaint, apparently, was that the people in them were apathetic. They literally "didn't care." Jesus had preached and healed in each of them, performed what Matthew called "acts of power," and they remained unmoved. They weren't transformed; they just went on about their business of catching fish.

Jesus compares them to children in the marketplace: "'We played the flute for you, and you did not dance; we wailed, and you did not mourn.' For John came neither eating nor drinking, and they say, 'He has a demon';

the Son of Man came eating and drinking, and they say, 'Look, a glutton and a drunkard, a friend of tax collectors and sinners!"

The people of those three towns don't seem to want the tough asceticism of John the Baptist. Nor did they seem to want the lighter touch of Jesus, who welcomed everyone and hung out with sinners. My sense is that they probably wanted someone to bless them the way they were, rather than challenging them to rise to his challenge of building a Kingdom of God "on Earth, as it already is in Heaven." It was their apathy, indifference, and comfort level with the way things always were and therefore had to be that really bothered Jesus. And he was angry to the point of telling them to go to hell. After all, that is what he was saying when he told the village of Capernaum that they would "be brought down to Hades."

■ ■ ■ ■

Anger is not something we talk a lot about in churches (or, I'll bet, in most mosques, synagogues, or temples). Congregations typically avoid conflict if at all possible. Fighting seems un-God-like, and at least a few of us have been part of religious institutions when things blew up and war broke out and people we cared deeply about were badly hurt in the process. Those situations are blessedly rare, but if we've ever been in the middle of one of them, we don't ever want to repeat the experience. Those of us who serve as clergy learn pretty quickly how to navigate conflict and negotiate disagreements and soothe hurt...or else we don't last very long in ministry.

But there's a different kind of anger that can be healthy and motivating, and that is the kind of anger that Jesus displays in today's Gospel. It's the anger that flares when it sees injustice, that refuses to accept "the world as it is" and is impatient for "the world as it should be."

I came to Chicago nine years ago for community organizing training with the Industrial Areas Foundation (IAF). Before I arrived, I had to read two books—Michael Gecan's *Going Public* and Gregory Pierce's *The World as It Should Be*. The books are still on the bookshelves in my office at All Saints'. Tom Lenz, our main trainer, was the lead organizer for United Power for Action and Justice at the time—the same IAF affiliate All Saints' now belongs to.

I still remember a lot about that week: about relational meetings, which are part of All Saints' DNA, about relational power, and about self-interest. But what I remember the most about that week is what happened when I went back to the congregation I was serving. What happened was that I worked with the parish leadership to disorganize and reorganize our Outreach Committee! The chair of the committee had recently stepped away, and this gave the rest us an opportunity to do something different: The Outreach Committee of the parish needed to go in a whole new direction if it was going to be transformative, not only for others but for ourselves too.

We conducted forty one-to-one meetings. In those meetings we were trying to identify people's anger. What I'd learned in the training was that it's anger that ultimately motivates people to act for justice. It turns out that people who are angry make good leaders. That may seem surprising. I know it was to me at the time. After all, anger is often presented as the antithesis of what should motivate the hearts of good people. But it is not.

Organizers point out that the word *anger* derives from an old Norse word meaning "memory" or "grief." The late Rev. Jeff Krehbiel, who was the pastor of the Church of the Pilgrims in Washington, DC, for sixteen years (and also has an essay included in this book), wrote that "healthy anger is deeply related to loss." He said, "If you cannot remember what you really value, if you do not grieve over the ways things are that do not respect those values, you cannot sustain the struggle to organize for change."

If you're looking for a scriptural basis for healthy anger, it's in today's Gospel. Jesus shows us what healthy anger looks like. He looked at the very people he had known all his life, the people from whom he and his disciples had come, and he couldn't believe that they could look at the world as it was and remain apathetic, immobile, not caring. He knew that change, repentance, transformation—whatever religious words you want to use—are impossible unless something affects our indifference and lack of concern. So, he let them have it.

■ ■ ■ ■

The anger and frustration that have erupted in so many different cities and communities since Memorial Day weekend of 2020 are giving people of all religious and philosophical backgrounds the energy and resolve to look at the world very differently and begin to change things. We see now how monuments to those who fought to preserve slavery honor the wrong values, how schools named after racists at Ivy League colleges shouldn't be named after them (whether those names belonged to the former president of the United States or not). how wrong it is that Black and brown men go to prison in numbers all out of proportion to their representation in society, how the redlining of neighborhoods has made home ownership impossible for generations of people while, at the same time, massive amounts of money have been invested in our own neighborhoods.

Here we are already on Independence Day weekend, and so much has changed just since Memorial Day because of righteous anger. What makes you angry about the world as it is? What injustice makes you so darn mad you want to do something about it?

All Saints' has picked out just one wrong and is working to right it through the "Greenlining Campaign" we are conducting to help our allies in the Lawndale neighborhood of Chicago. But transforming redlining through greenling doesn't have to be what *you* care about. It could be something entirely different. Whatever you do, though, don't be complacent. Don't be apathetic. Don't live in Capernaum, Chorazin, or Bethsaida for the rest of your lives.

Our not caring, evidently, made Jesus really angry. Energized by his own righteous anger, he ushered in a different kind of kingdom. We are invited to join him.

■ ■ ■ ■

Editor's note: The Rev. Dr. Stephen Applegate was raised in upstate New York and went to Hamilton College and seminary in New York City after a short career in business. He plans to return to Granville, Ohio, when he is done with his interim assignment at All Saints' Episcopal Church in Chicago. Applegate is sixty-eight years old and is now wondering what productive work he could do in southern Ohio. He is open to suggestions.

Questions for Discussion and Reflection

1. What does "righteous anger" mean? Have you ever experienced it in yourself or in others? Tell the story.

2. What does your religious or philosophical tradition teach about anger? How is that teaching modeled? How was anger handled in your family of origin or extended family? Give examples.

3. Discuss how anger is handled in politics, business, not-for-profits, schools, law enforcement, ethnic organizations, civil rights organizations. Name three public figures who expressed their anger in helpful ways.

A Reckoning of Sorts

by Chevon Chatman

Chevon Chatman (born 1986) published this essay in the *Mississippi Free Press* on July 2, 2020, right after the decision by the Mississippi State Legislature to remove the image of the Confederate battle emblem from the state flag of Mississippi (the last state from the Confederacy to do so). Chatman has been an organizer for Working Together Jackson (WTJ), an affiliate of the Industrial Areas Foundation (IAF) in Mississippi, since 2016.

My introduction to Mississippi took place during the summer of 2007. I was a student at Grinnell College and had travelled to Mississippi for an internship at the federal court in downtown Jackson. At the time, the federal courthouse was located on Capitol Street and was named after infamous segregationist Sen. James O. Eastland. His name was displayed prominently on the marble sign in front of the building.

My first assignment was to sit in for the trial of former Klansman James Ford Seale who in 1964 had helped abduct, torture, and drown two Black teenagers, Charles Moore and Henry Dee. My roommate, who was also an intern from Grinnell, and I sat right next to the bench, in view of everyone in the courtroom, including the aged killer himself.

We listened to accounts of how Seale and his co-Klansmen picked up

Dee and Moore as they were hitchhiking in Meadville, took them into the woods and beat them, and then tied their bodies to Jeep engine parts and dumped them into the Mississippi River—all because they suspected the young men of participating in planning uprisings against whites. No detail of the brutality was spared.

On June 14, 2007, a federal jury convicted Seale on one count of conspiracy to kidnap and two counts of kidnapping. He was sentenced to three life terms for his part in the murders, but he died in prison four years later. No one else involved served any time for these crimes.

It had taken forty years for any semblance of justice to be served.

I was deeply angered.

Any person of good conscience would find this story disturbing. But I was particularly affected for deep personal reasons. It had hit me hard why my ancestors left this place a half century before.

■ ■ ■ ■

You see, I'm a Black woman who's originally from Chicago, born and raised on the south side. And like many Black folks who experienced racial terrorism and second-class citizenship in the South, my family had fled to Chicago for better jobs and overall quality of life.

Growing up, I had heard about Mississippi. I knew what happened to Emmitt Till. I had read about the Confederacy and Jim Crow. I had seen "Mississippi Burning." I saw the Confederate battle emblem displayed above and inside the government buildings when I arrived here.

But I did not truly understand until the end of that trial.

In Chicago, my family never talked about living in the south. My paternal great-grandmother, Juliet Horton, who was born in Vicksburg, Mississippi in 1899, lived with us in her later years until she died at age ninety-four, but she had declined mentally so I never got to speak with her about it. There was no contact with anyone in Mississippi, no visits to relatives "down south" during the summer, no phone calls, nothing.

■ ■ ■ ■

Fast forward to my 2014 return to Mississippi as a mom and lawyer. I was hired to serve as a law clerk in the federal court, a job that entailed performing legal research and drafting opinions in cases. It was then that I began to witness how the hatred had seeped into the younger generations.

I worked on a case involving a group of white teens, boys and girls from Rankin County who had made a hobby of travelling to Jackson (or "Jafrica" as they derogatorily called it) solely to attack random Black people. In June 2011, on one of these trips to "f*ck with some n*ggers" as they put it, they found an unsuspecting James Craig Anderson in the parking lot of a south Jackson hotel. They beat Anderson while yelling racial slurs, and then one of them ran over him in a Ford F-250 truck. They all fled the scene and left him to die.

About a year later, there was a moment when I had to fight back tears of rage as I listened to my son sobbing about an experience he had while playing with a white boy at a nearby park. The boy's dad had seen the two together and called his son over to tell him he couldn't play with Black kids. When my son tried to re-engage the boy, he told him what his father said. My son was seven.

I was angrier than ever.

By this time, I had begun dealing with my anger through my broad-based organizing with Working Together Jackson, the local affiliate of the Industrial Areas Foundation (IAF), which engages in the building of power through institutions. Having returned to the South, I had started to understand my work as an organizer as a reckoning of sorts.

Indeed, I was here working to deal with the same evils that drove my family away from here long ago, "evils" that now present in the form of disinvestment in poor Black communities, failing to adequately fund public schools, failing to expand Medicaid ("because...Obama"), and other issues that keep Mississippi in last place among the fifty states.

■ ■ ■ ■

For 126 years, that evil was embodied in the state flag. And while many try to claim otherwise, indisputably the Confederate battle flag had racist origins. It was a constant reminder of the collective pain, trauma, and systematic subjugation of all Black people.

So for me, bringing down the flag marks a new season for Mississippi. And it gives me a renewed sense of hope for Mississippi because, if we can do this now, so much more is within our grasp. When the votes came in last Sunday, I exhaled both literally and spiritually. A weight was lifted from my consciousness that I had not realized was so heavy.

I also felt a tremendous amount of pride. As the senior organizer with Working Together Mississippi, our statewide organizing vehicle, I worked with clergy from various faith traditions across the state in the fight to remove the flag. We worked with Jews, Muslims, and Christians from many different religious denominations and organizations, including Catholics, Methodists, Episcopalians, Presbyterians, Mennonites, COGIC, the Cooperative Baptist Fellowship, and Southern and Missionary Baptists. It was the honor of a lifetime, an ode to the ancestors and others who championed this cause long before me.

Admittedly, I have mixed emotions about what this moment means because I understand that changed hearts are not what gets us to the finish line. Hell did not freeze over when the state flag was changed. The Confederate ethos is still very much alive in Mississippi. Instead, it was the political dynamic that changed. State leaders' interests in the status quo were superseded by unprecedented pressure. It meant economic prospects were dimming in the state, and real consequences were imminent.

Good will alone is not enough. It's always about power—the ability to act and compel a reaction.

Ultimately, I could not prevent my son's heartbreak at the park. But at least I could help stop that flag from waving to him as he walks into his school building. And I also can keep working with courageous, thoughtful Mississippians to create a better future for everyone.

In closing, I'm reminded of a recent comment from Working Together Mississippi leader Bishop Ronnie Crudup, Sr. "We can't change evil hearts," he said, "it's up to the good Lord to do that." But we can change the landscape that evil hearts create.

That's the real reckoning. And like my hero Ella Baker said, that's the slow, patient work of organizing.

■ ■ ■ ■

Editor's Note: Chevon Chatman earned a law degree from the University of Iowa College of Law, where she was active in the Black Law Students Association and wrote for *The Journal of Gender, Race, and Justice*. Chatman clerked for two years for the United States District Court for the Southern District of Mississippi before becoming an organizer.

Questions for Discussion and Reflection

1. Why are symbols so important? Make a list of symbols you feel have power in some people's lives—for good or for evil. What can you do to make symbols reflect the common good? Be specific.
2. What places do you have embedded in your heart, even if you do not live there? Why? What is the power of place in organizing?
3. Why do you think the Industrial Areas Foundation (IAF) organizes only what it calls "people's institutions" (institutions that are controlled by the people in them) rather than individuals?

Building Common Ground

by Robert Connolly

Robert Connolly (born 1949) is the founder and a leader in Common Ground, the Metro Industrial Areas Foundation affiliate in Milwaukee, Wisconsin. He is also a founder and former CEO of The James Company, a fundraising consultant organization that has raised more than on billion dollars on behalf of religious congregations and other not-for profit institutions throughout the United States.

S aul Alinsky was one of my heroes when I was attending Marquette University in Milwaukee in the 1960s. I read everything he ever wrote and laughed out loud at his irreverence. My instinct at the time, in the midst of so many activist movements back then, was that he had the most practical strategy for bringing about real social change for real people.

After graduate school, I went on to work for Alinsky's Industrial Areas Foundation (IAF). He and Ed Chambers had set up an institute to train organizers in the early 1970s. I organized with IAF over a 10-year period in my thirties in Pittsburgh and Harrisburg, Pennsylvania; Buffalo, New York; and Madison, Wisconsin. Even though I did some of the organizing really well, I was not flourishing in the IAF culture of the time. I did not have the self-esteem to be able to handle the confrontational style within the IAF training model nor the confidence to be able to stand up for my own organizing instincts, which I discovered years later are pretty good.

I left IAF feeling like a failure, and it took me two years to organize myself a new career. I did over 100 "research meetings" with a range of people trying to figure out what I might be able to do with my life that would both make a contribution and provide a living for my then-burgeoning family. I ended up meeting a Lutheran layman named Jim Harrison, and together we built a company we called The James Company. It was a fundraising consulting firm that helped churches and non-profits raise money for their ministries; but it was also about helping congregations of various denominations build their organizations.

Jim and I ran the James Company over the next 25 years, We went from two people doing about $300,000 per year in sales to 19 people doing almost $3 million per year. It was a very successful venture—we helped a lot of congregations raise a lot of money—over one billion dollars in total.

I still knew how to organize. I organized a new career, a new company, and hundreds of church fundraising appeals.

■ ■ ■ ■

In my mid-fifties, however, I began to get restless. I had been out of community organizing for almost 25 years. All I did was work and take care of my family. But I remember vividly watching the evening news quite often and yelling at the TV. The social anger I felt in my twenties had never left me. I had just ignored it or tamped it down. For some reasons, I'm not sure exactly what they were, I decided it was time for me to see what kind of organizing was going on in Milwaukee, where my wife Lynn and I have lived since 1986.

There was an organization in Milwaukee called MICAH, part of the national Gamaliel network. Our Catholic parish was a dues-paying member of MICAH, so I got involved in our parish core team and started to check out the organization. I spent almost three years digging into what MICAH was doing, building relationships with their local organizers, and becoming their treasurer (I knew how to raise money).

The more I was involved, however, the more I saw how much better MICAH could be. I thought that the Gamaliel staff was not offering the MICAH staff and leaders the time, training, and advice we deserved. So I started raising questions about MICAH's relationship with Gamaliel and in so doing discovered I had violated a sacred taboo. I got into a lot of trouble with those who were really running MICAH and ended up leaving— or getting "thrown out"—depending on how you interpreted the story. In either case, I was out. That is a special kind of powerlessness.

■ ■ ■ ■

I did not like being powerless in an organization in which I was supposed to be a leader. Soon after I "left," I decided to call Ed Chambers, then executive director of the IAF and Saul Alinsky's successor. To enjoy this story, you have to understand that to me Chambers was the most intimidating person I had ever met in my life. In my early IAF organizing days,

I had never quite figured out how to deal with him, so I had more or less avoided him.

When I had left IAF, though, Chambers had said to me, "You can always come back." Well, after twenty-eight years I was going to try to "come back"—but as a volunteer and a leader, not as a paid organizer.

That meeting with Chambers was the first time in my life we could do a real "relational meeting" where I felt like an equal. I was a successful small-business owner who had built one of the best church fundraising consulting companies in the country. I also had the courage and curiosity to try to get to know Chambers as a human being, not just my old "boss." The meeting was a redemption for me.

After three meetings, Chambers and I shook hands on a deal: I would raise $750,000 in seed money for three years of organizing by the IAF in Milwaukee, and he would send me an experienced organizer who knew what he/she was doing. "Not a rookie," I specified and he agreed.

It took me twelve months and 150 one-to-one meetings to build the Greater Milwaukee Sponsors Board of forty people, who began to raise the seed money to start the organizing process. Eighteen months into our work together, Chambers called me to say that he had an organizer ready to go. We only had about $250,000 committed, but we said "Okay, let's go."

We hired Mark Fraley and began organizing and raising the rest of the money at the same time. This is not the way its written in the mythical "IAF manual," but we live in the real world of grabbing an opportunity. It took us another eighteen months and hundreds of one-to-one and small group house meetings before we were ready for our founding convention.

On April 13, 2008, we turned out 2,300 people at the downtown Convention Center and we launched what we still call Common Ground.

■ ■ ■ ■

As I have mentored younger organizers and new leaders over the past ten years, there are two questions you have to answer for yourself: Can you get people to follow you? Can you lead them to issue-campaign victories?

We had proven that we could get people to follow us into Common Ground, now we had to see if we could turn this potential power into real power. With the help of IAF senior organizers Arnie Graf and Jonathan Lange, we learned that most new organizations need a signature victory to establish their reputation and their real power. Ours came in seizing the opportunity that the mortgage-foreclosure crisis of 2009 presented to us.

As a young organizer back in the day, I would never have recommended that we take on five of the largest banks in the world as our first campaign, but we did it anyway. I and many others were angry about what the banks were doing to our neighborhoods and hungry to use the potential power we had spent the last five years building. It was also time for me to learn to be a real leader.

We began the campaign in 2009 as more and more vacant, boarded up homes began to appear all over Milwaukee, particularly in the Sherman Park neighborhood where Common Ground had eight member institutions. We went door to door, talking to residents about what they wanted to improve in the area. Over and over we heard stories about the crime and deterioration that the foreclosed homes presented. There were 300 vacant foreclosed homes in a 25 square block area of Sherman Park, all immediately around St. Joseph Hospital—an anchor institution in the neighborhood and one of the largest employers on the north side of Milwaukee. We asked people if they wanted to go after the people who were responsible for this mess. It was not hard putting a team of 50-60 leaders together to begin the fight.

The research revealed that the largest owner of foreclosed properties in Milwaukee was Deutsche Bank. We were astounded. We had no idea who or what Deutsche Bank was, since they had absolutely no retail establishments—not only in Wisconsin but in the entire United States of America. We also did not know why they owned so many residential properties in Sherman Park or why they were foreclosing on people's mortgages. (No one we found had gotten their mortgages originally from Deutsche Bank.) If you have seen the movie or read the book *The Big Short* by Michael Lewis, you understand why. The answer is that banks were purchasing "subprime" mortgages from other banks and then packaging them and selling the packages to unwary investors. But it took us another six months of research actions with bankers (including a lot of good ones), lawyers, realtors, mortgage companies, investors, and many others to understand the whole story in Milwaukee.

After doing this research we were able to explain the whole story to a broader group of our leaders in Common Ground so they would be prepared for the subsequent campaign. We held a hearing with 300 of our leaders and invited in the best experts we had found to do the power analysis of the foreclosure crisis. We invited the five banks we had identified as the primary "pushers" (that's what we called them) of the subprime mortgages that had led to the crisis in Sherman Park and the rest of Milwaukee: Bank of America, Chase, Deutsche Bank, Wells Fargo, and US Bank. None of them showed up. Wells Fargo responded to our letter with a form letter saying they "would look into our mortgage." We voted that night to release a report on our findings and go public with our demands that these banks clean up the mess they had created.

On January 16, 2010, one hundred of us gathered for a press conference in the heart of downtown Milwaukee in front of Wells Fargo to release our "Faces of Foreclosure" report. The banks started to react. Wells Fargo tried to get us to stop the press conference by calling various state legislators. I was one of the leaders of the action, because my company was also a Wells Fargo customer. When I walked into the bank with copies of the report to give to them, they tried to stop me, but I showed them a deposit I was making into my business account!

We were now into the campaign full force—lots of small and large actions, coming at all five banks from many angles. Our biggest event was in October of 2010, where we got representatives from all five banks to stand in front of exactly 1,124 Common Ground members and promise to meet with us to solve the problem of their vacant, abandoned, crime-infested foreclosed properties. It was a classic organizing action: show the pictures, tell the horror stories, and then demand accountability.

■ ▨ ▩ ▦

We got the banks to recognize us, but getting a deal was the harder fight. We met with each of the five banks, and they all sent people who appeared to have attended the same public relations school. They came in being nice, telling us what great things they were already doing, and offering us very little.

But we were prepared. The toughest meeting was the one where we told five representatives from Wells Fargo "to please leave now" after we forced them to say "no" to the three demands we had sent them in advance of the meeting. (We still role-play that action today at what we call Common Ground University training.)

Despite the tenacity of our leaders and our creative tactics, there were moments during the two years of this foreclosure campaign when we doubted we could win it. Things finally broke our way, however, after a small group of us went to the Deutsche Bank shareholders meeting in Frankfurt, Germany. That tactic is still spoken of with awe in Milwaukee when people talk about Common Ground.

We actually went to Frankfurt two years in a row. Thanks to the help of our sister IAF affiliates in Germany the second time, we got the attention of the German media. We were on the "60 Minutes" of Germany. We also had a German TV station come to Sherman Park to see the devastation. It worked. At the shareholder meeting, we were able to confront Dr. Josef Ackerman, the CEO of Deutsche Bank. Our theme was that Germans had built Milwaukee and now the Germans were destroying Milwaukee. We had a simple demand: STOP IT!

We also went to the Wells Fargo shareholder meeting that year and had an 80-year-old grandmother, who lived in Sherman Park and whose family had owned stock in the bank for decades, stand up and tell John K Stumpf, the CEO of Wells Fargo, that her grandfather would be rolling over in his grave to know what Wells Fargo was doing to her neighborhood and her property values.

All five banks reached an agreement with Common Ground during 2012 for what amounted to $33 million in grants, mortgages, and properties so that foreclosed properties in Sherman Park could be acquired, rehabilitated, and resold to owner occupants. As I write this piece in 2020, we are about to close on the 91st property we have restored in Sherman Park. Millions of dollars in home equity has been recreated. Thousands of new property tax dollars are going to the City of Milwaukee. There are no longer any vacant, abandoned properties in Sherman Park.

Organizing works. Common Good does have power in Milwaukee, and I am proud to have helped to build a tri-racial, broad-based organization that fights every single day to strengthen the common good. As journalist Eugene Robinson of the *Washington Post* has said, self-interest and the common good are the same thing.

■ ■ ■ ■

Editor's Note: Bob Connelly is retired from The James Company but continues to be active with the Industrial Areas Foundation (IAF), conducting seminars and workshops around the country on "How to Raise Money for Anything." Connelly has published two related books: *How to Raise Money for Your Community Organizing* and *Raising Money for Your Congregation*. He and his wife, Lynn, still live in Milwaukee and have two adult children and six grandchildren.

Questions for Discussion and Reflection

1. Why is "organized money" important to people's institution power? Where should an organization's money come from? Where should it go?

2. Some people go back and forth between being a paid organizer and being a volunteer leader; or between being involved in an organization and taking time off. Tell the story of how this has happened to you or to someone you know. What was the result?

3. What does it mean to think "outside the box" in organizing? Give examples from your own or others' experience.

Fighting Poverty

by Dean Deida

Dean Deida, pronounced "Day-da" (born 1976) is the son of Puerto Rican and Cuban Immigrants. His last name is Portuguese, a remnant of the Portuguese slave trade. His parents moved to America to escape the economic destabilization of their countries. He says, "They would not have moved if they had another choice for survival." Deida was born into poverty in the American slums of the South Bronx. There he struggled as a youth between "the urge to honor my parents' dedication to lawful obedience in a society that ruthlessly exploited them" and his own rejection of helplessness. He says, "Something in my DNA, perhaps my melanin or the spirits of the Afro-Caribbean diaspora, provoked me to seek out power. Having no access to reliable male role models, I filled the void with the examples of gangsters on the street corners." Dean Daida is now an organizer with South Bronx Churches and Manhattan Together, two affiliates of the Metro Industrial Areas Foundaiton (IAF) in New York City.

Grieving with a Tec-9 in hand, I walked the streets back then like a soldier alongside my mentor—One-leg John, a fifty-something Puerto Rican gangster. I was fifteen; my father was already dead from cancer. John needed a scapegoat and I needed a father. In that way we found safety in each other. Schools, hospitals, and social services didn't fail us; they were designed to exploit us. Poverty pimps and

Medicaid-mills functioned to thrive off our misery.

Luckily, I found myself a new mentor, a man named Paul Auerbach. He was a New York State Department of Education librarian, and I was the head of the largest Latino gang in New York at the time. We met inside the most violent place in America—the adolescent building in Rikers Island. I was stuck in the system, feeding into the expectations of the Prison Industrial Complex, a fact my friend Paul was eager for me to question. Fresh perceptions I gleaned from him urged me to use my status at Rikers in new ways.

■ ■ ■ ■

Let me tell you about my first organizing experience.

On a hot summer morning on the way to the school floor in Riker's. I found myself in the middle of a riot, surrounded by about 300 teens animated by rage. I had been tasked with the responsibility to respond to an unprovoked act of violence against one of my newer comrades. They cut him from ear to lip, so that his tongue was hanging out of the side of his mouth. A terribly gruesome sight for anyone to see, but I had grown up watching heads get blown off since I was fourteen years old, to say nothing of the violence some of the young endure at home. Violence seemed normal to me.

Ironically, my sixteen-year-old heart was filled with a deep respect for the leader of my sworn enemies. Respect that I didn't understand. It caused me to hesitate as my heart filled with truths I'd need many more years to understand. Up until that moment, I had spent the previous six months meeting the leaders of my gang's enemies in an attempt to diffuse the violence and figure out how to compromise. We didn't trust each other. "Mike-mike," the head of the Bloods, could just as easily kill or cut me as he could talk to me. But I wagered my life that he was just as tired as I was of the constant violence. Eventually, over time he came to trust my intention to keep the peace. That was how I earned the nickname "Preacher."

Mike-mike and I began a daily diet of playing chess and cards as we discussed the minor squabbles within and between our warring factions. It was peaceful, and we were able to act like kids for a time. But nothing lasts very long in the ghetto. Mike-mike and I had spent so much of our time meeting with each other that we had both forgotten to relate to the new members of our factions. Eventually many of those who respected our efforts to keep the peace had been released and moved on, a testament to the new culture Mike-mike and I had cultivated in Rikers Island. However, this also made the tide of rising tensions between the new members of our two gangs at the jail impossible to hold back.

■ ■ ■ ■

There I was, face-to-face with my enemy, Mike-mike, who also happened to be someone I had deep respect for. He walked right up to me, looked me in the face, and asked, "What now, Preacher?"

Tension thickened the spaces between everyone in the room so that we all froze. All went silent as my lips began to move. I simply looked at Mike-mike and said, "No! I can't fight you." Mike-mike looked at me confused. I respected him. In fact, I considered what we had a kind of public friendship, so I refused to hurt him. But I turned to look at the stranger next to him. A member of his faction, whom I was told had started this whole mess. I knocked that boy out with one punch, and the riot began. I plowed through the angry crowd like a garden rake through loose dirt.

Eventually, Mike-mike was face-to-face with me again. The crowd around us stopped. The same process repeated itself.

"What now, Preacher?"

"No! I won't fight you, Mike-mike!"

This time the guy standing next to Mike-mike backs up a bit. I have to lunge forward to reach him. They catch me off balance and I fall to the ground. By this time most of the members of my faction had run for their lives. I was surrounded by enemies and getting stomped pretty good. I was about to lose consciousness when I saw Mike-mike. He picked me up from the ground and helped me stand. Other older leaders among the adolescent gangs I had related with circled around me to protect my rear, left-and-right flank. Mike-mike, the most influential of them all, cries out "Alright, anyone who still has beef with the Preacher can line up and face him one at a time."

I wipe the blood and sweat out of my eyes. This was all very shocking to me. My enemies were protecting me? I prepared to fight, but no one would face me. There I stood, alone. But somehow I couldn't be any safer. The riot was over.

■ ■ ■ ■

Once I was free from jail, Paul Auerbach encouraged me to enroll at Bronx Community College. There my curiosity caused me to become elected the vice-president of the student government. I began associating with electoral politicians. Eventually, this led me to become the chief-of-staff of the Bronx Democratic county machine. For over a decade, I was in charge of exploiting the naive and ambitious to turn out the vote. The others—party cronies all—understood their jobs depended on the machine. Occasionally it was my job to remind them of that. But the culture of electoral-gangsters left me burned out, and I eventually quit.

A friend I had stayed connected with from my days with the machine encouraged me to apply for a position as organizer in the Industrial Areas Foundation (IAF), the oldest and biggest network of community organizations in the world. He told me he had thought of me when he saw that one of the IAF's criteria for hiring an organizer was anger. My childhood, along with party politics, had left me with plenty of anger to go around, and I am now on a tryout with IAF.

Today I digest political theories and debate with organizers from different backgrounds, affording me a new scaffolding with which to examine the trajectory of my life. The IAF teaches that our collective choices and relationships shape our experience of community.

■ ■ ■ ■

I have learned that I am a proud American! This country has not always been kind to me or people like me, but I still believe in democracy and authentic people having power to fight for the common good. I wouldn't be alive today without them. The racial and gender lines of control over productivity in America tell an old story of who is still missing and neglected. Race and gender are tools to restrict access. The ability for anyone to be someone in America, "if they work for it," is still not true for everyone in the same way. America was developed in defiance to British oppression over the colonies, yet those same brave settlers utilized slavery to help them develop this country. We must organize across all dividing lines to overcome our shared history.

Democracy is a fragile thing that requires constant attention—like a child does—the kind of attention I couldn't freely get or give because I was born into poverty. Attention is recognition, and recognition requires power. When a child is born and raised a commodity, power is not their inheritance. Unless they organize.

■ ■ ■ ■

Editor's Note: Dean Deida has become one of the most dynamic voices on the New York City poetry scene, performing with great passion—often about the duality of love and hate—at such venues as The Inspired Word, The Bowery Poetry Club, and The Nuyorican Poets Café. He attained his Graduate Equivalent Degree (GED), learned about Dharmic meditation, and started writing poetry while a teen inmate on Riker's Island in the 1990s, where he became a student of the Manhattan Theater Club's "Writers On The Edge" program that assisted him in writing his play *Choices*.

Upon being released from Riker's, Deida matriculated at Bronx Community College as a Fine Arts major and shortly thereafter was elected the student government's vice-president for two years. Deida was also chief-of-staff for the Bronx Democratic Party for three years and worked as a computer instructor at Neighborhood Networks for eight years. He has continued to maintain a relationship with Manhattan Theater Club (MTC) as a spokesperson during its fundraisers and makes frequent visits to Riker's to speak with incarcerated adolescents. He says he is "still working on honing his craft and finding the depth of his voice."

Questions for Discussion and Reflection

1. Name three things that can overcome violence. Give examples from your own experience or that of others.

2. Do you think people who were formerly incarcerated can make good leaders or organizers? Explain your answer with specific reasons for your opinion.

3. Are poetry, meditation, theater helpful to leaders and organizers? How? What other kinds of things help you understand power?

Don't Win Too Quickly

by Alisa Glassman

Alisa Glassman (born 1967) is the lead organizer of Virginians Organized for Interfaith Engagement (VOICE) in Northern Virginia. Over her twenty-four years of organizing with the Industrial Areas Foundation (IAF), she has led organizing campaigns from the very local to those that have had national impact. These efforts have addressed some systemic issues of racism and economic equity, such as the passage in Maryland of the DREAM Act in Virginia, returning the driving rights to 627,000 Virginians whose driver licenses were suspended solely for unpaid court debt; and working to ensure hundreds of thousands of mostly African American and Latinx families are not evicted from their homes during Covid-19. Some of the names of people mentioned or quoted in this article were changed for their comfort or protection.

Whatever you do, do not win this campaign too quickly." Three months into my new job as a community organizer in 1996, this was not what I was expecting to hear from my boss. We were sitting outside the president's office at Johns Hopkins Hospital, discussing our negotiation with Mr. Sunshine, a man whose unlikely name belied his indifferent reception to our demands.

As was our organizing practice, we brought both new and veteran leaders to the meeting, people directly impacted by the issue at hand and those with a measure of power. There was Chris Jenkins, a Broadway Service janitorial contract worker who grew up and now lived in a row home a walk away from where we were standing, Jonathan Lange, a veteran organizer with the Industrial Areas Foundation (IAF), a pastor from East Baltimore whose 100-year-old Baptist church was in the shadow of the hospital, and me, the rookie. My job was to organize with Broadway Service's janitorial and security guard workers. Just fifteen minutes earlier, while still in Mr. Sunshine's office, Mr. Jenkins had looked the hospital president in the eye from across the boardroom table and implored, "I do the same work as the Johns Hopkins janitorial staff that you hire, often buffing the same hallway floors. We want you to pay us the same wages."

At this point, my organization, Baltimoreans United in Leadership Development (BUILD), had already won the first Living Wage campaign in the United States. It created a new standard for thousands of public contract workers such as Baltimore public school food servers, school bus drivers, janitorial workers, and security guards. After this victory in the public sector, BUILD was now strategically going after the largest private employer in Baltimore, Johns Hopkins Hospital and University. The demand was simple. Do what BUILD made Baltimore City do— pay all of your contract workers a living wage.

I was troubled because I wanted to win. I like winning, a lot. When Jonathan Lange said those words to me that day, "don't win this campaign too quickly," I wasn't sure if he was right in the mind. Do not win too quickly? Isn't winning the point? I had been in Mr. Jenkin's home and the homes of hundreds of other Broadway Service contract workers. I had seen again and again what $4.25 an hour meant for a family in Baltimore City: It was, simply, not enough.

As I got into my car after our meeting with Mr. Sunshine, I heard Jonathan's words reverberate in my head: "Don't win this campaign too quickly." I felt betrayed by them. I had become an organizer to win, and to win as quickly as I could. This is what the world needs, I believed. I felt the deep righteous anger of my profession as I drove through East Baltimore to my apartment. I passed kids playing outside a home that was boarded up, next to a house that reminded me of pictures I'd seen of bombed-out buildings in Iraq. I thought, *This can't be; I want to be about change.* What I didn't know then was that organizing is about so much more than victories.

⬛ ⬛ ⬛ ⬛

Seven years later, I learned this same jarring organizing lesson all over again. This time, my teacher was Ms. Bette Johnson, the six-foot-tall matriarch of a historic African American community who had just saved her neighborhood from being turned into horse stables. Ms. Johnson grew up in the Scotland Community, in Montgomery County, Maryland, which was now surrounded by the town of Potomac, called by some "the Beverly Hills of the East." Ms. Johnson led the successful organizing effort to "Save our Scotland" that won affordable housing and a community center. But now the prized center was showing its age after years of neglected upkeep by the county government.

As we walked from Ms. Johnson's home to the community center one block away, we stopped often to greet and be greeted by neighbors, or for Ms. Johnson to share with me a story about what once was. When we finally arrived at the center, there were about a dozen teenagers leaning against the community center wall listening to music and talking with one another. Ms. Johnson turned to me, "The kids are waiting their turn to go inside." She explained, "The community center is only big enough for one activity at a time, and from 3:00-4:30 PM it is the seniors' hour." I looked at my watch, it was 4:17. As we walked down the stairs into the building, Ms. Johnson made sure I saw the sandbags alongside the outside of the brick wall: "Those sandbags are for when it rains." The tour was quick as there wasn't much to see—a computer room with four computers, a couple of other rooms, and the space that was called the basketball gym but in actuality was an old trailer.

Back outside on the sidewalk, I found myself relearning the lesson I was first taught as a green organizer in Baltimore. Ms. Johnson asked me what I thought of their community center. She listened intently to my response and then said, "I'm seventy. I don't want to organize a campaign to rebuild our center like I did years back." She paused and I had the sense she was revisiting those days. When she returned her attention to me, she said quietly, "I don't want you or your group to win it for us either. I showed you that center because we need to use it for something." I was starting to wonder where this conversation was going. and I had to get on to my next meeting. Ms. Johnson then went on to explain, as my former boss did seven years ago, "Whatever we do, we can't win this campaign too quickly. I'm old, and the generation who saved Scotland is gray like me. What Scotland really needs a new generation of leaders, more than it does any new center."

The important lessons about power we learn anew, again and again. This lesson, while hard to recall in the heat of campaign, is that the focus of organizing is not victory. The focus is power. If we say we care about the people we organize, then we need to ask ourselves how the people and the structures that impact them are different at the end of every issue campaign. How are leaders connected to their own power in new ways by winning something they care about? We need to ask ourselves if we have instilled in people the habits they need to build relational power. Are the underlying systems that created the conditions we are organizing against being addressed? All of this takes time. That's why we can't win too quickly.

■ ■ ■ ■

I still recall clearly a woman named Nellie Cunningham showing me around her home and then offering me a chair in her narrow row-house living room. About twenty minutes into our conversation, I asked her, "Do you want to help lead a campaign to win a Living Wage for workers at your school?"

"What?" she replied, looking at me like I was from another world, which indeed at that moment for her I was. Ms. Cunningham continued, "I have three children and I am a housewife. Politics is for others, not me." Then in a quieter voice, "I've never even left East Baltimore."

But it turned out that Cunningham did lead the campaign at her school, and this quiet housewife who had never left East Baltimore helped launch a national campaign. After we won the Living Wage for Baltimore City contract workers, we could have stopped. But then, to our fortune, the next leg of the Living Wage Campaign was handed to us by President Bill Clinton when, in 1997, he suddenly announced he planned to undo welfare reform.

Clinton had decided it was better to subsidize companies like Aramark, the national food services company, than mothers. He pushed thousands of former welfare recipients into the labor market and did so by telling companies that if they hired welfare recipients the government would give them the equivalent of their employee's former checks to subsidize their wages. Thus he created a whole new group of subsidized workers. Not surprisingly, smart companies like Aramark started letting go of their former workers in order to hire a new class of less-costly subsidized-by-the-government workers. Nellie Cunningham was one of the Aramark workers who were in danger of being replaced.

Here was step two of BUILD's Living Wage campaign. It wasn't intuitive at first. Why should workers who were being pitted against one another—former welfare recipients and the low-wage worker they were replacing—come together? And why would middle-class church leaders, who through hard work and grit had moved themselves out of poverty, align with welfare moms who many saw as taking the easy way out?

This tension was voiced one night, three days before Christmas, at a BUILD action filled with hundreds of church folk, Living Wage janitorial workers, and three pews filled with former welfare moms. I can still hear the pastor of that Baltimore church lift up BUILD church leaders in one sentence and then slam lazy welfare recipients in the next, not recognizing that some of those so-called "lazy moms" were sitting in his church at that moment listening to him preach, as we were all now working together to change Baltimore.

That pastor, however, preached a very different message nine months later after a successful voter participation campaign where BUILD church leaders were matched with Living Wage and former welfare workers who went door to door to get out the vote in some of the hardest-hit Baltimore neighborhoods. The pastor spoke at the celebration, highlighting the recognition Baltimore's newspaper, *The Sun*, had given our campaign. He then went on to poke fun of himself. "As I went door-to-door in the Patterson Park area with Patricia Edwards, I was humbled. Not only were her twenty-year-old knees a lot stronger than my old rickety ones, but it was apparent that she has been there for her neighbors emotionally and monetarily in ways I was not when I was her age. Or perhaps even today. Nine months ago, I would have been Patricia who? Latonya who? But now, I know that these former welfare moms are 'we.'"

In East Baltimore, some twenty-two years ago, the real victory was that the Living Wage Campaign spun a web that connected communities of working-poor and the very-poor with middle-class church folk where very few deep or meaningful connections existed before. And then, with that new relational power, not only was the first Living Wage won but "higher education" now counted as a valid welfare work activity. BUILD became known anew in Baltimore City because with its new relationships the leaders were instrumental in the 1998 election. And all that led to

BUILD being a central player in many future economic decisions, including an important redevelopment plan for the national company Under Armor. And *that's* why it was good that we didn't win too quickly.

Authentic, meaningful relationships take time. Building relational power takes time. If we want long-lasting power, we must give the building of new relationships the time it takes for people to learn to trust one another. We must give these budding relations the time to gel and become real. This happens through many actions, big and small, as people see others actually show up and be true to their word. This is how trust and new relationships are formed. This is the work of organizing. In this way, we develop leaders, build relational power, and then direct that new power to address the systemic racism and inequality that exists in the economic structures that had kept Ms. Cunningham, Ms. Edwards, and that BUILD pastor from being their best selves.

■ ■ ■ ■

Now in my twenty-fourth year of organizing, in Virginia, the dual pandemics of Covid-19 and systemic racism are threatening to cause 550,000 mostly Black and Latinx families to be evicted from their homes, making me revisit yet again this central lesson in my organizing. At night when I close my eyes, the fears that I brush away during the day come out. I see the faces of Winnie Dickerson, Yolanda De Leon, and others who do not know how they will pay next month's rent. With so much on the line, is it ethical to focus on anything else but winning the issues looming in front of us as quickly as possible?

We are in the midst of our organization's campaign to stop evictions as I write this piece. The reality is that each day a certain number of families will be evicted. We must work quickly. Yet, just as importantly, it is too costly to win at the expense of building power.

What I learned from Mr. Jenkins in Baltimore and Ms. Johnson in Scotland applies today in Virginia: All good organizing is about building new power. The work is always about building new relationships among and between communities that did not exist before and focusing that power to address inequities. Virginia needs big power to undo the racist housing systems that led to Ms. Dickerson, Ms. De Leon, and other families facing evictions today.

Our job is not to let the win be our sole objective...or even the top objective. The irony is that unless we prioritize other areas besides winning, we will always lose. Without this clear focus, we sabotage the very communities we say we care about.

■ ■ ■ ■

Editor's Note: Alisa Glassman was a Peace Corps volunteer in Ecuador, South America. Her husband, Mike Mangiaracina, gave substantial help in developing the ideas and writing this essay. He is an elementary school teacher in the District of Columbia Public Schools who incorporates organizing principles into his teaching, including running listening sessions for parents and students in the school community. Regarding her current work on the housing crisis in Virginia, Glassman adapts a comment by Kerry Cavanaugh, an editorial writer for the *Los Angeles Times*, for organizers and leaders everywhere: "There's simply too much at stake for us to be passive observers of any eviction tidal wave. We have a moral obligation to save our communities from another housing crisis."

Questions for Discussion and Reflection

1. What else in life is best if not done quickly? Explain each example.
2. How can organizers and leaders balance the need for results with the need to build an organization? Tell a story from your own experience or that of someone you know.
3. What does the phrase "relational organizing" mean to you? What is its opposite?

How Basketball Changed My Life

by Keisha Krumm

Keisha Morris Krumm (born 1973) is currently the lead organizer with Greater Cleveland Congregations (GCC). She has been an organizer since 2001 with the Industrial Areas Foundation (IAF) in Milwaukee, Wisconsin; Los Angeles, California; and Tacoma, Washington.

I t's a beautiful fall morning in 1995; I am twenty years old and wake up in my bed at Tabor College in Hillsboro, Kansas, to prepare for battle. My every thought and move equips me for the basketball game of my life. Tonight, I go back to Friends University in Wichita, Kansas, to defeat all the people who have sought to bring me harm my entire life.

■ ■ ■ ■

As I prepare for this confrontation, the story my grandmother told me about my great-great-grandfather, Jeff Pendergrass, comes to my mind. It's early 1900s in a small town in Texas, and Jeff, a black man in his early twenties, heads to town to buy flour, sugar, and other essential supplies for his mother. He rides his horse into town. It is a beautiful, sunny day, full of possibility and hope. Plus Jeff knows he will bring back the goods to his mom and she will make him his favorite meal.

312

As he enters town, Jeff nods to the folks he knows and keeps his eyes forward to avoid the people who are not interested in observing a black man with money in his pocket. He gets off his horse, loops the reins around the wooden pole, and steps up on the boardwalk. He ambles slowly, looking in the windows of each store. Ahead of him, he sees a group of three white men. He takes a deep breath and cautiously continues forward. As he gets closer to the men, he squares his shoulders and raises his chin. One of the white men says to him, "Move, boy." Jeff keeps walking. The second white man yells, "Boy, if you don' move it, we'll MAKE you move it." Jeff keeps walking.

Finally, the third white man reaches out to push him off the boardwalk. Jeff sidesteps to miss the man's hands. Then the other white men began reaching for their guns. With lightning speed, Jeff draws his own gun from its holster, cocks it, and shoots one of the white men stone dead with a single shot. Before that man's body hits the ground, Jeff takes off running, jumps on his trusty steed, and hightails it home. He knows he is now a wanted man.

Jeff is proud of standing up for himself, but he also knows that for a Black man in Texas this kind of pride will get you lynched. So when he gets home he tells his mother. "Mama, I shot and kilt a white man; I gotta git outta town." He hides her in a flour barrel and gallops north.

After many other adventures—and now with a new name, Jeff Hunt—my great-great-granddaddy finally lands in Pawhuska, Oklahoma, where he meets and marries Bessie Berry and they have thirteen children together, one of whom is my great-grandmother, Helen Maxine Hunt.

■ ■ ■ ■

Fast forward to 1995. My team, the Tabor College Bluejays and I arrive in the parking lot of Friends University in Wichita. I calm myself as I take a look at the outside of the gym. It looks the same; not much has changed since the previous year when I had played as a freshman for the Friends University women's basketball team. I take a deep breath and get out of the van with my new team and walk into the gym. The lights are dim and the bleachers empty. The referees are just arriving. The scorekeepers are setting up.

Friends University is where my college career started. I walk toward the guest locker room but stop when I turn the corner to look up the stairs that leads to the Lady Falcons' locker room, remembering the time when two men from the Friends men's basketball team stood at the top of the stairs and spat on me as they called me nigger. This memory put a crack in the armor I had donned before coming here today.

As I undress and put on my Tabor uniform, my time at Friends University started to flood my mind. The spiteful practical jokes my teammates played on me, the lies they told about me, the hostility we felt for one another, start to crawl up my skin and absorb into me like lotion. I suddenly realize, "I'm here for payback."

■ ■ ■ ■

When I had been a student here, the Lady Falcons and I had an unspoken agreement: We tolerated each other off the court so we could win basketball games on the court. This worked with basketball, where we were quite successful, but it was torture for me at practice, in the locker room, and during our travels to and from away games. I had refused to deal with this reality one year earlier and had left Friends University to attend Tabor College, where I am now a sophomore.

As I sit in the locker room before my "return" to Friends University, I try to shake off my feeling of revenge, I get dressed and put on my basketball shoes. I sit and bow my head to pray, *"Dear God, thank you for this opportunity to be back in this place. I am honored to be in Wichita, my hometown, and playing before my mom, grandma, cousin Travis, and friends. Please help me make them proud and represent them well. Give me strength to play with courage and grace. Let my actions glorify you and be a witness of your love in my life. Help me play my best game ever, and give Tabor the ability to win. In Jesus' name, I pray."*

I go out early to warm up and say hi to my mom, grandma, cousin, and friends, who are all there to cheer me on. My grandma, Mildred Shorty, says, "Go get 'em, Stink." I smile and give her a hug and kiss. My mom, Johnnie Freeman, gives me that quiet look she has that communicates, "You got this, Keisha!"

■ ■ ■ ■

Back in Tabor's locker room, my team huddles and vows to win. I lead our team onto the court. We run our warm-up routine. I'm feeling good. My shot is on and I am ready! I pause for a minute and look over at my old coach; then I see my main nemesis when I was at Friends—let's just call her "#6"—and we glare at each other. I see another girl—the Lady Falcons' new addition and my replacement—and she looks mean and tough. I grin inside because I know I'm meaner and tougher than she is.

Warm-ups end and we go to the bench and wait for the announcer to name the visiting starters. I am the last to be called. The announcer says, "And finally, playing center for the Tabor College Bluejays—from Wichita, Kansas, at 5 feet, 10 inches—number 25, sophomore.... My fan club starts chanting, "Keisha, Keisha"...and the announcer, continuing with a grin, yells to the rafters, "And the Kansas Collegiate Athletic Conference 1994 Rookie of the Year: Missss...Keee...shaaaaa...Morrrr...isss!"

■ ■ ■ ■

#6 and I meet at the half court for the jump ball. We stand toe-to-toe, eye-to-eye. She says, "Keisha! With a tone of disrespect." I reply. "Number #6! With venom dripping from every syllable." We look each other in the eye, wordlessly shake hands, and square up to jump for the first possession of the game.

The referee tosses the ball in the air. I jump faster and higher than #6 and Tabor gets the ball. I post up; Carman passes me the ball; I take a shot and miss. The Falcons rebound the ball. The Bluejays hustle down the court and set up our defense.

#6 posts up in front of me. I elbow her and push her. She gets the ball and goes up for a shot; I try to block it but foul her instead. Hard. "Foul, number 25," shouts the referee.

"Dang! First foul in the first three minutes of the game," I kick myself. We all run a few more times up and down the court. The game seems to come down to #25 vs #6. We both sneak in a shove here, an elbow there, which causes the referee to pull us aside and say, "Take it down a notch, ladies, or I'm going to call a flagrant foul." His warning goes in one of my ears and out the other. #6 gets the ball and squares up for a shot; I jump and come down on her. Hard, "Flagrant foul, number 25," shouts the ref. "Falcons number 6 gets 2 shots." Both teams stand at the half court line to watch #6 shoot. As she shoots, shouts from my personal fan club yell, "Miss! Miss! Boo 6!" She makes the first shot but misses the second one. Our fan club cheers her miss. We resume the game. I now have two fouls within the first ten minutes.

Our coach calls a time out and says to me, "Keisha, you have to calm down and relax or you're gonna foul out the game." At this point, I'm in my own world. My personal vendetta against #6 and the Lady Falcons is all I can think about, but I say to my coach, "Ok, got it, Coach. Just put me back in the game. I'm good."

I back off for a few plays, but then the moment presents itself. #6 posts up, I elbow her before she gets the ball, and then step back ready to bring down the hammer when she shoots. The ball releases from her hand,

I tip it as it goes toward the backboard, but then I hit her. I hit her so hard she slams to the ground as her shot swishes the hoop. Referee yells, "Flagrant foul, 25. Yer outta here!"

I proudly stand over #6 and say, "That's what you get for messing with me!" I turn and walk off the court.

As I walk to the end of the bench, my coach gestures for me to come to him, but I ignore him and sit at the end of the bench, away from my team, by myself for the remaining minutes of the first half.

I mentally check out during the half-time locker room talk. Our team is losing the game big time. The second half starts. My team plugs away, but Friends has the home court advantage…and Tabor doesn't have our starting center.

The Falcons plan to make me irrelevant worked. I sat at the end of the bench for the whole second half. Here I am, twenty years old, thrown out the game in my hometown, in front of my family and friends. I start to obsess on all the wrong that had been dealt to me by the Lady Falcons, and then on all my negative life experiences—in Wichita, in my neighborhood, in my country. I'm on a roll of hopelessness and feel my life-force fill with rage. The more I remember all the wrongs I have had to put up with—all the racism, all the struggles, all the injustices—the more it consumes me. I fall into a pool of powerlessness. I am drowning.

Suddenly, I remembered the story of my great-great-grandfather, Jeff Hunt. I decide I will be like him: I will stand up for myself; I will not let #6 take me down; #6 is going to pay for it ALL.

■ ■ ■ ■

The final buzzer goes off; Friends easily wins the game and I am the first to head to the locker room. As I walk down the hallway, I stop and wait at the stairs for #6. She comes around the corner, our eyes lock, my wrath touches her like an electric current. She halts; I stand still. Then she slowly ambles toward the steps and I charge toward her. Just as I get ready to throw my first punch, though, I feel four hands grab me from behind. I try to get away from them, but the hands pull me back. Hard. Then they push me into the Tabor locker room. I fight to get away, but they block my escape.

I suddenly realize the four hands grasping me are my mom's and my grandmother's. They surround me with their arms; they anchor me, they pull me to themselves. I cry for the longest time. I had lost the battle; we had lost the game; I had lost myself.

■ ■ ■ ■

The great thing about basketball is that you usually get a second shot. Later that season, Friends University's Lady Falcons had to make the reverse trip of 53 miles to Tabor College. This time I would be prepared and centered. The Monday after the Friends vs Tabor brawl, I had asked my teammates to meet with me so I could explain why I had been in the space I was in; what my mother and grandmother had done; and about Jeff Hunt. I apologized to my sisters and committed to not repeat what I had done in Wichita—to them and to myself. They cried with me, we hugged, and we all left our locker room with our minds set on redemption. I made a promise, then and there, to become the woman of God I know I am and want to be. And I did.

The day of the rematch, the Lady Falcons try to get me to lose my cool again, but this time I am not alone; I am with a real team, the Tabor Bluejays, and we are calm, focused, and ready to win. It is a tough game still, of course; and I force myself to keep my head in the game and cheer for my teammates whenever I am on the bench. I dig deep and play with control and focus. I help foil the Falcons' final attempt to get to the hoop by stealing the ball as they in-bound it. Then the final buzzer goes off.

We won the game by two points, yes, but I also began the process of remaking myself. It was basketball—and my mother and grandmother, and the story of my great-great-grandfather—that put me on the path to become the woman, the wife, the mother, and the organizer I am today.

■ ■ ■ ■

KRUMM • HOW BASKETBALL CHANGED MY LIFE

Editor's Note: Keisha Krumm is married to Stuart and is the proud mother of Olivia. She is beginning her writing career with this article.

Questions for Discussion and Reflection

1. What are you angry about? How do you express your anger? Do you try to control it? Why? How?

2. Have you ever been the instigator or the target of bullying or discrimination or prejudice? Describe what happened and what you did about it.

3. Have you ever been a member of a team—athletic or otherwise? What kind of relationships did you have with your teammates? Give examples of how teamwork (or lack of it) helped you succeed (or fail) in building power.

People Need More Power

by Matthew Marienthal

Matthew Marienthal (born 1988) is the lead organizer for Queens Power, a new Industrial Areas Foundation (IAF) affiliate in New York City.

like people more than power. That's why I became an organizer in the first place. I have spent the past eight years meeting and working with thousands of local leaders from across Brooklyn and Queens. In many of these meetings, I hear stories about the injustices facing New Yorkers. For example, public housing tenants often wait months, or years, for urgent repairs like getting their gas or heat turned on in their apartments. These stories make me angry as they would anyone with half a heart.

Yet I leave the majority of my meetings hopeful. That's because I encounter people like Vincent Hall, Jr. Mr. Hall is a retired postal worker and veteran. In the 1970s, thousands of residents were fleeing Mr. Hall's neighborhood, Bushwick, in part due to increased crime. Property values dropped so steeply that landlords set fire to their own buildings to collect insurance payments, often with little notice or concern for tenants inside. Through all this mayhem, Mr. Hall stayed put. He purchased a home, taught religious education at his church for decades, and invested his time in building a citizens organization, East Brooklyn Congregations, an affiliate of the Industrial Areas Foundation (IAF). Through their organization,

Mr. Hall and hundreds of other leaders helped drive crime to historic lows, opened two quality public schools, and built thousands of affordable Nehemiah homes.

Mr. Hall's persistence changed Brooklyn. His never-give-up attitude is one of the many qualities I admire in the leaders I work with.

■ ■ ■ ■

When I started organizing in Bushwick, a team of leaders identified six parks that were in horrendous conditions—no toilet seats in the bathrooms, broken lights on pathways, sprinklers that didn't sprinkle. Residents had petitioned for improvements for decades, yet nothing had happened. At the same time, privately-funded conservancies had revitalized huge public spaces such as Central Park and Prospect Park, and real estate developers had built gleaming new parks like Domino Park in Williamsburg or Brooklyn Bridge Park in Dumbo. The neglect of the parks in Bushwick wasn't an oversight or a policy puzzle, it was a question of power.

So we went through the painstaking process of building power—I did over 300 individual relational meetings, and volunteer leaders then hosted dozens of house meetings with their neighbors and fellow congregants. We organized multiple tours of each park, so we knew them better than anyone else; and then we organized our first action with the Brooklyn Parks Commissioner.

There were sixty-five of us sitting patiently in a public-school gymnasium when the commissioner walked in with his entourage of about eight deputies and assistants. The commissioner's staff began setting up a projector and a screen. At this point, Father Joseph Hoffman politely stood up and ask the commissioner what he was doing. He responded, "I'm preparing for my presentation." Fr. Hoffman said, "There must be a mistake, we are running this meeting. Please take your seat."

The commissioner was shocked. He bashfully took his seat and listened as one leader after the next demanded that he make specific improvements to their parks. After reviewing the issues for each park, we asked the commissioner to answer each demand with a simple "yes" or "no" on whether he would resolve it. Surprisingly to us, he agreed to twenty-four out of thirty-two demands. After the meeting was over, the commissioner proceeded to try to greet every person who attended the meeting. After a while, however, Fr. Hoffman approached him again. The priest thanked the commissioner for coming and asked him to leave, indicating that it was time for us to evaluate with our team.

That is when the tension of the meeting boiled over. The commissioner exploded: "I don't know who you all think you are to make demands on me and then kick me out, but this isn't how you get things done." He and his crew stormed out.

By this point, Fr. Hoffman had been pastoring churches in both Brooklyn and Queens for decades. Respectfully standing up to people with power was nothing new for him. On the other hand, being held accountable by everyday citizens was something new for the commissioner.

I was a young and inexperienced organizer at the time, and frankly I thought we'd blown the action. I figured that we'd pissed off the Parks Commissioner of Brooklyn so much that he would never meet our demands as he had promised. As I walked back to my car, with my easel and notepad in tow, I honestly thought my nascent organizing career was over. That evening I called my family and told them I'd probably need to look for a new job soon.

A couple days later I got a call from Jesus Navarette, a leader from St. Joseph Patron Roman Catholic Church. He told me that the Parks Department was mowing the grass at Green Central Noll. Jesus and others from his church ran a youth soccer league and they were always looking for parks where they could play. The league hadn't been able to use Green Central Noll for years because the grass was up to the children's knees. Now it was in good condition. I got calls like this every day for over a week. Ultimately, the commissioner resolved all twenty-four issues he had committed to address.

That first action taught me that—although not everyone is willing to admit it—you get things done by building and wielding power, and power comes from organized people and organized money. As our team grew to several hundred, we were able to win more than $5 million in park renovations.

After all the repairs were made in the Bushwick, we invited the commissioner for a tour of Green Central Noll. He did not try to set up a slide show. He didn't bring his entourage. We had earned his respect and, by delivering results, he had earned ours. Mr. Navarette thanked the commissioner for his work, showed him how much more the park was utilized now that it was kept up, and then pointed out a scoreboard where the paint needed to be touched-up!

The tour went well, but at the end Mr. Navarette turned to the commissioner and said, "You know, Commissioner, we shouldn't have had to fight with you to get this done. You should have done it on your own. It's your job."

Jesus Navarette is right that in ideal world we shouldn't have to hound city officials to do their jobs. But the world we live in is far from ideal—whether you're in Brooklyn, New York, or Puebla, Mexico, from where Jesus emigrated decades earlier, that will always be the case.

Liking people, and caring about their circumstances, came naturally to me, as it does to many leaders and organizers in our network. I learned through experience that, contrary to the commissioner's counsel, building power and confronting others with power is exactly how you get things done. I still like people more than power; but organizing has taught me that this affection is futile unless I work with leaders to earn respect and win results. In a world with mounting injustices, people need more than a shoulder to lean on. They need an organization with power.

■ ■ ■ ■

Editor's Note: Matthew Marienthal was born and raised in Chicago and has spent the past eight years organizing in Brooklyn and Queens, the two largest boroughs of New York City. Having grown up in a big and bustling city, Marienthal believes that New York, Chicago, and other American cities are unique places where people from all backgrounds can live decent and productive lives. He says he is committed to helping make this a reality through building broad-based citizens organizations that push forcefully for improvements.

Questions for Discussion and Reflection

1. Why don't things get done just because they are the right thing to do? Give examples from your own experiences or that of others. If you can, tell a story like this one.
2. Is it always necessary to polarize or cause tension over an issue? Why? Is it also wise to depolarize once the issue is resolved? Explain.
3. Give three reasons why people and their leaders who are most affected by a situation or problem have to lead the fight to get something solved or resolved.

Unbelievable and Dazzling

by Cynthia Marshall

Cynthia Marshall (born 1975) has been an organizer since 2005. She is now the lead organizer of the Maryland Industrial Areas Foundation (IAF). This essay is adapted from a sermon that Marshall gave on July 26, 2020, at the Unitarian Universalist Congregation of Columbia in Columbia, Maryland, which was inspired by something she wrote elsewhere: "Beyond rescuing our democracy, building power to act in the public sphere is necessary on a deeply personal level. Most of us have felt powerless in the face of trying to make things right in the world. It demoralizes us, and at its worst makes us cynical. Paradoxically, our drive to make the world right is only possible in a significant way by acting as a collective, where we change others and others change us. The IAF focuses on building relationships across our differences and discovering that we are not alone in the values we espouse. By acting as a collective of people's institutions to right the wrongs in our community, we can act on the power God gives each and every one of us from the start. It changes us profoundly, both in our public and personal lives.

Still, what I want in my life
is to be willing
to be dazzled—

Mary Oliver, "House of Light"

When were you last dazzled by the world? Standing on a mountain watching the sun rise? Having a child put a treasure she found into your hand? Finding a helpless white grub in the dirt you dug for your garden?

How does it feel when you are dazzled? Do you get a sense of the expanse of time and space, how small we each are? Yet understanding that our actions and existence matter, at least to our tiny part of the universe? Does the hair on your scalp prickle, your chest feel like it's opening up, like mine does? Do you feel pain in your heart when witnessing beauty, like I do? This is central to how I experience what I now call the holy, but it did not start out this way.

I grew up on Jesus jokes, my primary entree into learning about his life, death, and resurrection. It wasn't what you would call a formal religious education! My first wanderings into what Henry James referred to in *The Varieties of Religious Experience* was time spent in nature. Watching animals and plants, digging in dirt, and learning about the astounding natural world. The more I learned, the more my wonder grew. To me, biology was the most beautiful explanation of the world we live in. The more I delved into genetics, ecology, and especially evolution, the more I was in awe.

329

■ ■ ■ ■

Take anteaters. Who would have thought that an animal that sleeps most of the time; has an incredibly long, sticky tongue, and no teeth; and subsists exclusively on ants could fill a special niche in the world and survive for thousands of years? Not only that, but that creatures with these characteristics would evolve completely separately at least four different times? Unbelievable. Dazzling.

A key element of evolution is that creatures strive, in whatever ways they can, to live and pass life on to the next generation. In their attempts to carry life forward, there are many more that fail than succeed. It is impossible to know ahead of time what attributes will lead an individual animal, or species, to survive or thrive, and for how long. Often species that succeed for millennia, like the enormous reptiles we call "dinosaurs," ultimately fail. For someone who was taught to follow the rules, the chaos and unpredictability in evolution could be unsettling; but to me it is dazzling.

Yet when I am feeling most cynical, the evolutionary drive to live and to pass on life gives me hope. Even if we humans completely destroy the world as we know it, seeds that survive thousands of years will spring up out of the rubble. A random tiny creature, like a cockroach, will live to fight another day. These meager beings will expand to new generations and species, and eventually the world will again be teeming with life under new parameters. This has happened multiple times already on this planet. Unbelievable. Dazzling.

■ ■ ■ ■

At the risk of anthropomorphizing, I feel these lessons from nature do translate to humans. Aren't we all stumbling around, half-blind, constantly striving in our own flawed ways? We want to do something, be something, have an impact on the world. Isn't that part of what it means to be alive? To want to carry on with living, except in extreme circumstances, while making all sorts of missteps along the way, often even working at counter-purposes to our own goals? Attempting to be able to point to something and say, "I was here."

I believe this desire to make a mark is innate in each of us. My children made me feel this before they were even born. They would hold dance parties in utero, often at the times when I most wanted to sleep. Already signaling to me, "I am my own person." Tiny, pre-birth beings. Unbelievable. Dazzling.

I have a practice of carrying around particular poems and songs that I recite when I struggle to feel hope, when my own mistakes and misdeeds seem too large, or when I cannot see what mark I am making on the world. They help me return to these feelings of hope and wonder.

I found my way to a Christian church about fifteen years ago. I fell in love with many older traditional Protestant hymns with grand, poetic language that stirred something deep in me. A few of my very favorites invoked stunning nature imagery and became my touchstone recitations. "This is My Father's World," for example, includes the lines:

And to my listening ears/ All nature sings and round me rings/
The music of the spheres.

I rest me in the thought/ Of rocks and trees/ Of skies and seas/
His hands the wonders wrought.

In the rustling grass I hear him pass/ He speaks to me everywhere.

Many hymns use nature imagery to show the wonder of the world. The Christian hymnology recognizes, and offers tribute to, this type of holy experience. They ultimately arrive at the same destination as the mystery of science, with similar sentiments of "Unbelievable! Dazzling!" I could end this reflection here, with that parallel alone.

■ ■ ■ ■

Instead, I am going to dive into a harder part to say, at least for me. More difficult because I am much less certain about this. I feel concerned that I'm unable to articulate what I mean well enough to be understood. This section is also harder because I know the Christian church has, at times, willfully hurt people and abused their power against people of other faiths and those of no faith and perpetuated systematic oppression against those who are not in power.

For me, there is another deeply felt aspect to these Christian hymns, something that explores the ways in which our world is unbelievable and dazzling, ways that evolution and connection to nature touch upon but do not delve into as deeply. In "How Great Thou Art," there are moving verses about nature, "When through the woods, and forest glades I wander, and hear the birds sing sweetly in the trees. When I look down, from lofty mountain grandeur, and hear the brook and feel the gentle breeze. Then sings my soul!" After two nature verses, the hymn transitions to the life of Jesus as the primary example of God's deep love for the world.

How did I, an avowed evolutionary biologist raised a non-believer, end up embracing Jesus? I started going to church soon after I became a community organizer. I went because I met so many people in religious congregations, believers deeply dedicated to social justice, who had a beautiful combination of deep humility and love. They carried a specific type of assurance that led to a lack of unnecessary criticism of themselves and others. It was clear that their faith was nourishing them, and that they were experiencing something I was not. Going to church made me deeply uncomfortable at first. I wasn't taught to have faith, and deep down felt that Christian faith is gullible, and that it is naïve to believe. I nearly bolted many times, except that the welcome I received always included the line, *"No matter what you believe or doubt, you are welcome in this place."*

After some time, the story of Jesus became profound to me personally. The story is about an all-powerful being willing to be so vulnerable as to become a helpless infant. Someone who put love into as the world, faced cruelty and systematic oppression for doing so, and did not intervene with violence even when faced with death. The church I was part of, inspired by Jesus' life, practiced in word and deed an unconditional love that was a balm against self-inflicted criticism and doubt. This love opened me up to being more vulnerable to the world and gave me the space to more fully reflect on the many times I choose what is expedient, easy, or self-serving over what is most loving—both to the individuals I encounter and through the systematic oppression I organize against. If you can strip away all the ways the Christian story has been misused, at its heart it is truly unbelievable and dazzling.

Central to the story is anguish and suffering. Isn't that the flip side of unbelievable and dazzling? That the world can be unbelievably painful and cruel? All of us flawed humans contribute to that pain, even those who are deeply loving and compassionate. Doesn't that make the times when the power of love happens that much more incredible? At the end of the day, the Christian story of love and pain gets me to a profound feeling that the rationalism and reason of science does not. My religious faith may not provide the Truth of science with a Capital T, yet it is an equally deep Truth for me. It lets me access a profound tenet of what it means for me to be alive with all of my own and the world's contradictions and messiness. And I find that dazzling.

Being vulnerable to and accessing these contradictions and messiness of the world both motivates me to organize and helps me be a better organizer. At the end of the day, what drives me to do this work is bringing people together to stand up against cruelty and building the power to enact more love in the world.

I will conclude with a quote from Yann Martel's novel, *The Life of Pi*. Pi Patel, the main character says, "If you stumble at mere believability, what are you living for? Love is hard to believe, ask any lover. Life is hard to believe, ask any scientist. God is hard to believe, ask any believer. Reason is excellent for getting food, clothing, and shelter. Nothing beats reason for keeping tigers away. But be excessively reasonable, and you end up throwing out the universe with the bathwater."

For me, choosing to believe in and pursuing encounters with that which is unbelievable and dazzling challenges me in ways that rationalism and reason do not. It challenges me to become more fully human, in all the frailty that encompasses.

■ ■ ■ ■

Editor's Note: Cynthia Marshall says, "One of the biggest challenges of our current political moment is the allure of hopelessness. Many people in our religious congregations of all faiths and denominations feel unable to shape their lives and the world in a meaningful way. Daily, in large and small ways, we experience the world as not fair nor right nor just. Often our attempts to address obvious wrongs fail; or at best they succeed on a much smaller scale than we had hoped. These internalized lessons grind at us and make us angry. This is not the way we have been taught by our religious traditions, not how we want to imagine our own lives or how the world should and could be. Our inability to act in effective ways is undergirded by the crumbling of the people's institutions of public life: congregations, unions, social networks, political parties, even our nuclear and extended families. These people's institutions have traditionally pooled together our passion and our values and our resources and helped us wrestle with how to collectively act out our values on a larger scale in the public arena. These various kinds of organizations join people's lives and action to something larger than themselves, whether tangible—creating a building or program—or intangible—being connected to God, 'moving Earth closer to Heaven' as we say in the Christian tradition." Marshall is married to Jason Roberts, and the couple have two children, Dylan, ten, and Ingrid, seven.

Questions for Discussion and Reflection

1. List three things you find unbelievable and dazzling at the same time. Why?

2. What does organizing for power have to do with religious faith? Give examples from your own experience or that of others.

3. How do religious institutions of all faiths and denominations overcome their own sins and failings? How could belonging to a community organization help do so? Be specific.

My Father's a Union Member

by Adrienne McCauley

Adrienne McCauley (born 1983) has been an organizer for over fifteen years in both W/SW IAF and Metro IAF affiliates in Arizona, Texas, and Illinois. She was until recently the lead organizer for DuPage United and the Fox River Valley Initiative in the western suburbs and exurbs of Chicago for nine years, where she has worked on issues of housing, the incarceration of the mentally ill, health care, gun safety, accessible and affordable housing, and incidents of ethnic and racial hatred.

My daughter and her friend work for Grub Hub and live off tips," said Donna, "and they live with me because there is no way they can afford to live on their own." Donna's story bit me hard and here is why. My dad made a choice at eighteen that if he was going to make a decent living he could never do so off our family's struggling cattle ranch in Arizona. So he hired out on the railroad, and with that he joined a union.

The first fifteen years of Dad's career were rocky. He was often laid off, sometimes for six months at a time (priority in scheduling went to railroaders with more seniority). Then Mom would get a job, Dad would create a side hustle—working for his father's plumbing business, hauling freight in a semi-truck, working the family ranch, selling pipe for corrals—

and my parents would nervously piece together their $250 weekly meager income to cover our their bills for a family of five.

As the years went on, Dad rose in the ranks. With more seniority, he gained more "trips," and in time our family financial picture changed enough for us to gain our place in the middle class. Just this year, Dad retired with a generous employee-sponsored pension and a halfway decent 401K.

Life would not have even existed for me if it were not for my father belonging to a union that was powerful enough to fight for our family. Union benefits that insured a hospital stay and a respirator for a month while my premature-baby lungs developed both saved my life and did not bankrupt us.

Even as my extended family was counting down the months leading up to my father's retirement, the picture for most American workers became much bleaker. The bubble of decent union jobs in my railroad hometown are now an anomaly. Just ten percent of American salaried and hourly workers are in a union today, and even they are under attack from everyone from the White House to the state houses to the Supreme Court.

■ ■ ■ ■

When I was a freshman in high school, a family driving a Ford Fiesta on a rural road crossed the railroad tracks just a couple miles in front of the train my dad was driving. The mile-long train was going seventy miles per hour and while Dad pulled the brakes there was no way to stop the 4,000 tons of cargo from sliding across the rails. Their tiny car was stuck. As the train brakes shrieked, Dad wailed. He saw the fate of the trapped family in clear view. After impact and as the train slowed down, Dad jumped out of the cab. The three adults in the car were dead, but from behind the smashed passenger seat he heard a little voice crying, "Help me!" He delicately pulled the child from the car and held him until help arrived. Dad came home that night a different person. About a week later, the little boy died in the ICU. My father was never really the same after that, nor am I as I retell his story.

Soon after the tragedy, the railroad began an investigation. There was a sense of unease in our house. We knew that the train wreck was an accident, but what if Dad lost his job? With representation by the United Transportation Union, he attended numerous hearings to testify in his case. He also attended counseling for PTSD. Over the course of several weeks, my father, Kelley McCauley, was cleared of any wrongdoing and returned to work without being penalized.

But this kind of employee protection in the USA is dying. We are now tied with Malaysia in being the easiest places in the world to terminate employees. Furthermore, we are pushing out stable jobs with the expansion of "alternative work arrangements," like that of Donna's daughter and her friend. According to federal employment numbers, the USA economy grew 94 percent from 2005-2015—not in union jobs but in freelance and subcontractor jobs, with temp agencies, and in what is hilariously yet tragically called "the gig economy." There is a straight line from the decline of unions to the rise in crappy jobs. Union members do not have "gig" jobs.

Back in October 2019, pre-Covid-19, I traveled home for Dad's retirement party in Arizona. As we gathered in the American Legion Hall, half of those in attendance had been, like my dad, newly minted into the challenging club simply called "retirees." And while my father and his colleagues have the protection of their union in retirement, the employees that follow them may not.

⬛ ⬛ ⬛ ⬛

In January of 2019, *The New Republic* magazine reported that Elwood, Illinois, (population 2000) near where I live and work as a community organizer with an affiliate of the Metro Industrial Areas Foundation had been completely taken over by entrepreneurs whose "business plan" was to staff warehouses surrounding Warren Buffet's Center Point Intermodal Freight Terminal for retailers such as Walmart, Ikea, Home Depot, and Amazon. Elwood was promised a bill of goods: good jobs being the main one. Instead, the temp agencies have consistently hired people (in situations similar to Donna's daughter and her friend) on ninety-day trials, most of which never lead to full time employment. These non-unionized workers are often "let go" and then hired for another ninety days by one of the temp agencies in Will County (which are sometimes owned by the same "entrepreneurs"). They never land that full-time job with benefits they need and crave that is part of the American dream that my dad and mom achieved.

Here is what makes me so angry: The same railroad that my father just retired from is the same railroad that stops at Warren Buffet's Intermodal Freight Terminal in Elwood, loading and unloading large heavy freight cars, running back and forth across warehouses the size of five football fields, and then driving it to our house—in two-days or less for our personal convenience. And many of us think that is great! It's not great. It is wrong. Period.

Marilyn Robinson in her book *The Death of Adam* writes that worker protections, the two-day weekend, and the living wage with benefits were "largely willed and reformed into existence" following the carnage of slavery and the industrial revolution. Is another revolution needed to help us see that our instant consumer gratification has a human cost? Is another revolution needed to stir the imagination of American workers to see the inherent value of organizing and collective bargaining? I personally believe so. I think you do too. Let's do something about it.

■ ■ ■ ■

Editor's Note: Adrienne McCauley is currently the co-trainer with Greg Pierce of the Metro IAF workshop, "Writing for Leaders and Organizers." She is married to Chris MacInness, and the couple have young children.

Questions for Discussion and Reflection

1. Should workers have the right to join a union and bargain collectively with their employee? Why or why not?
2. If workers have a right to join a union, should they be protected by state and federal law from being harassed or even fired for encouraging their colleagues to also do so?
3. What does your religious or philosophical tradition say about the right to organize a union? What could you do personally to support that right? Will you do so? When?

Building Relationships Before You Need Them

by Abdul Malik Mujahid

Abdul Malik Mujahid (born 1951) is a leader in United Power for Action and Justice, the Industrial Areas Foundation (IAF) affiliate in Chicago and Cook County, Illinois. He is an Imam in the Muslim community, president of Sound Vision, and a leader of Justice For All. He is also former chair of the Council of Islamic Organizations of Greater Chicago, as well as Chair Emeritus of the Parliament of the World's Religions.

was raised by parents who cared deeply for justice. My very first memory of my father is seeing him behind bars. At that time, I did not know why he was arrested. However, I do remember one of his students taking me to see my father in prison. I have never forgotten that.

My father was never convicted or tried for any crimes. But it became a routine. He would be arrested any time he took a stand for justice, democracy, or for his faith, Islam. He was a victim of leftover British colonial laws, a remnant of pre-independence India. These laws allowed the government to "preventively" detain people without any evidence or commission of a crime. He was almost always released through a writ of *habeas corpus*. I heard that term so much that, as a child, I thought *habeas corpus* was the name of a friend of my father who helped him get out of jail!

My mother not only never complained about running the home in the absence of my father, but she herself was busy doing justice work of her own. Her primary concern was the poor people around the neighborhood, as my father fought the oppressive systems and policies he was protesting. Together, they made a complete social justice couple.

Mother would cook for the poor and I was her delivery boy. The poor were also always at our home. Years later, in my twenties, I once returned late at night from work and found a family of four strangers sleeping in my living room. I was surprised and a bit upset, but I knew it had to be my mother's doing. She had invited those poor strangers to spend their nights in our small house during that blustery winter. Our home would remain open to any in need of help or shelter.

Among the poor were many "undocumented people," to borrow a term from our time. "Sakina" was one such economic migrant. She had been living in a shanty town that had popped up on nearby grounds the city had designated for a public park. While the municipality wanted to throw the squatters out, Mother would always welcome them into her home to the distinct distaste of some of our neighbors.

Sakina was one of the many women whom we used to call "Auntie" in consideration of our mother's friendship with her. She was an older lady who was married to a much younger man. She and her husband were a part of an untouchable Indian tribe who had wandered into our town in Pakistan. We did not understand their language, but Sakina would sit with my mother telling her all sorts of things, and somehow my mother would understand. She would listen to Sakina's painful stories and cry with her. She would shelter her, feed her, and sympathize with her. Mother became her mentor, therapist, and banker.

I don't remember how, but we later found out that Sakina's husband used to beat her. That was our first encounter with domestic violence. It prompted my siblings and I to engage in a swift boycott of her husband's vending business. That was our first boycott of any sort, as we were learning ourselves to stand up for justice.

My father was a successful businessman. He never failed in business, but whenever he was arrested, the other employees would be unable to sustain the business and soon my mother would be left with no money. But somehow she would manage to keep things going until my father came back and started yet another business, which would once again be successful—at least until his next arrest.

To sum up: My parents' entire life was defined by their struggle for justice and the sacrifices resulting from it.

■ ■ ■ ■

Justice is a religious duty in Islam. God has told us in the Quran that all Prophets were sent by God to help people establish justice, fairness, and equity in society (Quran 57:25). In Prophet Muhammad's last sermon, delivered 1,431 years ago, he assigned that Prophetic responsibility to Muslims as he was leaving this world.

When Muslims circle the building dedicated to God called the "Kaba" in Mecca, Saudi Arabia, a rite which is part of the mandatory Hajj pilgrimage, we reaffirm our commitment to carry out this prophetic mission by uttering the word *Labbaik* or "at Your service, my Lord." God's peace and blessing be upon the Prophet.

Justice, democracy, and Islam were synonymous for my father. I remember he took me to hear an Islamic scholar campaigning on behalf of Fatimah Jinnah, a woman leader who was contesting the presidential election challenging the military dictator Ayyub Khan in 1965. I was barely fourteen years old when Father took me to rallies in support of her presidency. He firmly believed that democracy was a sure way to justice and a corruption-free way of life.

Growing up with my parents was a journey and a lifelong lesson in justice. It became a part of who I am. While in fourth grade, I marched with others in school to get a high schooler released from police custody; in fifth grade, I delivered my first speech; in sixth grade, I marched on the streets of our little town against a military dictator.

My commitment to fight against injustice and demand democracy became stronger as I entered college. At that time, Communists and semi-Communists were all over my campus, with their red flags supported by a democratically elected leader of the country who turned into a tyrant, killing his opponents and tossing opposition leaders into prison. The dreams of democracy under this populist, the late Zulfiqar Ali Bhutto, had started fading. This is when I took it upon myself to read different constitutions from around the world. If I remember correctly, I read around ten of them from across the world, including that of the United States of America.

I liked the preamble of the Pakistani constitution, but I really fell in love with the American constitution. I am just happy that I read it together with all of its amendments, rather than reading the version in which women didn't have a right to vote and Black people were not even counted as human beings.

Struggling against democratically elected but unjust and tyrannical leaders led me to see a whole lot of injustice in society. While we succeeded in mobilizing the country against this elected leader, the army once again took over, unleashing another nightmare just as the opposition and the government were about to reach a compromise for a fair election.

I felt powerless. Would I spend the rest of my life like my father—struggling for justice, Islam, and democracy, making all of the sacrifices without achieving power for the powerless? Or could I chart out another course for myself? I kept struggling with these questions for a while. A political party nominated me to stand in elections against a former Air Marshal, but I did not campaign even for a day. It felt like it was a game to participate in another fake election. Those elections never happened.

It was during that period that I received an invitation from an American Muslim student organization to address their convention in 1977 in the United States. I was in the U.S. for just five days or so, but every day I was in two different cities giving lectures. This is when I noticed American sidewalks. At every corner, they tapered to the street level. It was explained to me that this was to accommodate people with wheelchairs. That had been a gift to disabled Americans on the country's centennial. That realization was the moment America touched my heart. Americans cared enough to actually accommodate a small minority. My lecture tour was a short trip, but I decided I would return.

■ ■ ■ ■

Back in Pakistan, a college graduate by now, I led the work of building a think-tank and Gallup Pakistan, a polling organization. This is when people started telling me, "Malik, you are doing things which are only done in the United States. Why don't you go there to study?" Eventually I did just that and returned to America in 1981.

I had an option of going to three different cities, since universities in each one had accepted me as a graduate student. I really wanted to join a university that had sent me the photos of their hilly green campus, but I ended up choosing the University of Chicago after I learned that President Abraham Lincoln was from Illinois. As a child, I had read about President Lincoln ending slavery. Illinois seemed to be a good state to be in.

During my very first days in Chicago, as I took the Green Line in downtown Chicago from the Jackson subway station to Hyde Park where I was living, I noticed something disturbing. All the Black people were standing on one side of the platform, while everyone else was on the other side. There seemed to be tension in the air. Everyone was dead silent. I was concerned. Had some fight broken out? Why were they standing apart like that? My train came and I jumped on. When I mentioned that incident to my friends later, they pretended to be worried about what I had seen until someone broke into laughter and explained: The people were all silent because it was the end of the workday and they were tired, and the people were waiting in different areas for their trains because the housing in Chicago was segregated and they were going in different directions. That was Chicago 101 for me.

Within a few months a Black acquaintance of mine was arrested at the Joseph Regenstein Library on 57th and Ellis Street. This is where I spent most of my time while at the University of Chicago. He was a PhD student and a former Greek Orthodox priest who was so against technology that he did not even have a phone or a television set. A white woman pointed him out as having stolen her TV while he was studying at the library, and that was enough for this obviously innocent graduate student to be arrested. That was Racism 101 for me.

I ended up marching in protest on behalf of this student with ten to twelve other students. There were not many Black students at the University at that time, despite the predominance of Black residents in the surrounding neighborhoods. This incident took me to a nearby church where we used to meet to plan the next steps. That was how I discovered the part of Christianity which cared for justice as much I did. I ended up visiting the Cook County jail and an American courtroom for the first time. Our lawyers were good, and we were able to get all charges dropped against the student. That was American Justice 101 for me.

■ ■ ■ ■

It seemed to me that the U.S. Constitution I had read and loved so many years before didn't quite match the reality of race in America. Since those years as a graduate student, I have become a part of the peace and justice movement in the United States. I realized that the struggle for justice is not limited to one country, and that democracy does not necessarily guarantee justice. I have known Muhammad Ali and Malcolm X, but until I arrived in America, I did not fully understand the struggles of the justice movement in America.

Prophet Muhammad told us that faith does not stay at one level. It either goes up or goes down. So we must continue to strengthen our faith through building our connection to humanity through service to others and our connection with God Almighty through worship. I came to feel that the struggle for justice and democracy is an ongoing process as well, rather than a destination.

In doing so, it seems I finally understood the depth of my parents' struggle.

■ ■ ■ ■

Years passed, and one day I was rushed into a room in my office in Chicago where a television set was on. I saw live the second plane hitting the World Trade Center towers. *Oh God*, I thought. *I hope it isn't Muslims.* We started hearing back pretty soon that they were Muslims. This had happened once before, when the Oklahoma City bombing was initially blamed on Muslims and the killers turned out to be white supremacists.

So we were hoping that the story would change. But it did not. Those terrorists *were* Muslims. But not Muslim as my parents were Muslim. Not Muslim as my wife and I and our children are Muslim.

I had just moved a few weeks before to my new office in Bridgeview, a southwestern suburb of Chicago. Within hours of the 9/11 attacks, there were people demonstrating in front of my office. (Before we moved in, the location had been a Middle Eastern restaurant, and naturally had a sign with some Arabic on it, which is what they were demonstrating against.) I was worried about my children in school a few blocks away. Police officers came in and offered to escort us to our homes. I let my staff go, but I decided to stick around. This was around 5:00 or 6:00 PM on 9/11. Finally, at around 11:00 PM, the usually busy Harlem Ave suddenly fell silent. It turned out that the police had blocked the entire street for several blocks, and when the traffic disappeared the protestors took it as their cue to head home.

Throughout the country the next day, Muslims were being attacked and harassed. Several years later, Michael Rolince, FBI Special Agent in Charge of Counterterrorism in the Washington office, told me that about 700,000 American Muslims were interviewed by the FBI in search of clues for 9/11. He stated, "I'm not aware of any single person in your (Muslim) community who, had they stepped forward, could have provided a clue to help us get out in front of this."

Just imagine the level of terror our community felt, in a situation where the doors of almost every Muslim home in America were knocked on by the FBI. Many Muslim charities were raided by the federal government, at the very time when Muslims and others needed real help from them. And it was not just the FBI. Profiling of Muslims, use of secret evidence against them, and Islamophobia all constituted a major attack on Muslim Americans, although none of these foreign terrorists were ever a part of any mosque or community in America.

■ ■ ■ ■

Muslims had been busy pursuing their American dream instead of developing relationships, coalitions, and alliances in society. The impact of 9/11 was a wake-up call for them. Not many non-Muslim organizations in America did anything to fight against these injustices which Muslims were facing. But one did: United Power for Action and Justice (UPAJ) in Illinois, which several mosques and Muslim organizations had joined as full dues-paying members during its founding convention in 1997.

The Council of Islamic Organizations of Greater Chicago (CIO-GC) chair, Mr. Kareem Irfan, and Mr. Ed Chambers, then the executive director of the national Industrial Areas Foundation, held several meetings with the leadership of their respective organizations. These conversations resulted in CIOGC leaders, including myself, being invited to a meeting of UPAJ leaders. We first met in the basement of the Old St. Patrick's Catholic Church in the Chicago Loop. There were about 100 people in attendance.

Mr. Chambers proposed the idea of CIOGC and UPAJ organizing a large gathering of solidarity with the Muslim community. There was debate about it, but the decision was to stand by the Muslim community by organizing "Chicago and Islam," the largest welcome of any religious or ethnic group in history on November 18, 2001—two months after 9/11.

That Sunday afternoon, about 2,000 Muslims and 2,000 of our neighbors of other faiths and spiritual philosophies gathered at Navy Pier. This was still the post 9/11 time when we Muslims, out of fear, would normally not have ventured out on our own to Navy Pier or any other public arena to avoid hatemongers and "those eyes."

There were speeches. Some better than others. But the highlight of the afternoon was the introduction of one-to-one relational meetings to the entire assembly. I had never seen 4,000 people turning towards one another in conversation at the same time. It was a unique experience. The buzz of 2,000 individual meetings between Muslims and non-Muslims filled the Grand Ballroom at Navy Pier. My son Bilal conversed with a Catholic lady who told him that her husband did not attend the program despite her effort because he hates Muslims.

Power is in relationships, we were taught from the podium, and one-to-ones were the tool we use to begin relationships. We also learned that relationships must be built *before* you need them, not *when* you need them. It is too late then.

I am proud that the Council of Islamic Organizations of Greater Chicago was a founding member of the United Power for Action and Justice and proud that that relationship resulted in this timely action for justice. Muslims have now joined other IAF organizations around the country. Going forward, I hope we Muslims and our neighbors continue to learn how relational organizing can help us fight for justice, democracy, and Islam—just as my parents taught me.

■ ■ ■ ■

Editor's Note: Imam Abdul Malik Mujahid offers this excerpt from the Quran for those not familiar with its demand for justice: "O ye who believe! Stand out firmly for justice, as witnesses to God, even as against yourselves, or your parents, or your kin, and whether it be against rich or poor: for God can best protect both. Follow not the lusts of your hearts, lest ye swerve, and if ye distort justice or decline to do justice, verily God is well-acquainted with all that ye do" (Quran 4:135).

Questions for Discussion and Reflection

1. List at least two or three followers of another faith or philosophy whom you know personally. What are some of the things you have in common with them? How could you act together with them for justice or democracy?

2. What did you learn from your parents about justice and democracy? If you have children, what and how are you teaching them? Be specific.

3. What does it mean that "relationships must be built before you need them"? Tell a story about this from your own experience or that of someone you know personally.

Lessons from the Dark Room

by Perry Perkins

Perry Clifton Perkins, Jr. (born 1951) is the supervisory organizer for the Industrial Areas Foundation (IAF) affiliates in the South. He is currently working on projects in Mississippi and Georgia. He has been an organizer in Houston, Fort Worth, Beaumont—all in Texas—and in New Orleans, Monroe, Alexandria, Shreveport, Baton Rouge in Louisiana.

remember the Dark Room. I do not know what was in it, but I do remember it was my parents' bedroom. This room was in what we children referred to as the "Old House": the parsonage of First Baptist Church West Point, where my father was pastor. West Point was a small town in northeast Mississippi of about 10,000 residents—approximately fifty percent Black. My family was white. In the early fifties, when these stories occurred, the town was deeply segregated and divided.

The Dark Room stands out in my earliest memories. The memories are not vivid in terms of detail, but the emotions and feelings associated with them are fresh and palpable. The Dark Room was the place where the secret wisdom of the adults was imparted to me. It was a wisdom that would teach me how to interact and navigate the world beyond the Old House. The conversations were serious and somber.

■ ■ ■ ■

I don't remember having babysitters often, but this night there was an important meeting at the church. Both of my parents had to be there. My sister, Beth, four years older than me, was not yet old enough to watch me at night, so Mrs. Annie Harris came over to stay with us.

Mrs. Harris was a short, stocky, very dark-skinned woman. She was pleasant and extremely courteous, but—at least as I remember—not overly deferential (as most African Americans of that era were expected to act toward white people). We always called her "Mrs. Harris," not by her first name as most white children did. I do not remember being told how to address Mrs. Harris. I just remember it was a rule in our house and that my white friends thought it strange.

The night began quite uneventfully. My mom gave me a kiss on the cheek and told me to be good and obey Mrs. Harris. These were the days before we had a TV in the house, so Beth and I played a board game.

At one point, Mrs. Harris told me it was time to take a bath and get ready for bed. I do not know what provoked me, but the words just came out of my mouth—words I had often heard from the adults in the world beyond the Old House, though never from either of my parents.

"You cannot make me take a bath. I do not have to listen to you. You are just an old nigger."

The look on Mrs. Harris's face was one of extreme hurt. She remained calm, but the pain I had caused her never left her face. Sixty-five years later, that look still haunts me. I still see the shock and disbelief on her face. Her hurt cuts through my spirit today, but it did not stop me that night.

■ ■ ■ ■

I do not remember the details of what happened after I uttered what is now called the "n-word" because it is so dehumanizing, especially when uttered by a white person and even more especially when said by a little white boy who has no idea the pain it causes. But I can still hear the voice of my sister: "Perky, you know we don' talk like that and I'm gonna tell Momma and when she gets home you are going to get a whipping."

The thought of a whipping stopped me in my tracks, but I didn't apologize to Mrs. Harris. I just went to my room and cried and waited for my mother to return.

Mrs. Harris came into the room to check on me, but she didn't utter a word. Her silence made the anticipation of the return of my mother more intense. Then I heard the car pulling up and suddenly realized it was not my mother I needed to worry about. It was my father.

I heard the back door open, and Beth the Tattletale went running. During our growing up, she reveled in telling on me for my various transgressions. I heard her loud, excited, high-pitched voice. I heard my father's voice and my bedroom door opening in the same instant: "Perk, you better come out here right now and apologize. You know that we do not call anyone by that name in this house. You tell Mrs. Harris that you are sorry."

My tears were coming hard, and I could hardly speak. I was ashamed at what I had said, but I was more afraid of the wrath of my father than anything else.

"Mrs. Harris, I am sorry for what I said."

Then almost uncontrollable crying came upon me. I guess she accepted the apology, but I don't really remember. What I remember is that I was left with my dad and his wrath. He did not administer corporal punishment often, but that night he did.

■ ■ ■ ■

After my punishment, my parents and I were in the Dark Room together. I sat on the bed, my dad sat in a chair, and my mom sat down on the bed next to me. She lightly touched my head. I saw the concern on her face. It was palpable. But I also felt her love, maybe more strongly than I had ever done before in my young life. My fear was no longer as intense, but then I looked at my father's face. His permanently wrinkled brow was even more wrinkled, and the broad public smile he was known for was nowhere to be found.

Dad's gravelly baritone voice was stern, as it always was when he scolded me, but this time the parental voice was even more serious. I knew from the top of my head to the bottom of my feet and deep into my soul that this was going to be a serious talk.

I had finally stopped crying by this point and looked at him fearfully and expectantly. He said, "I am ashamed of you. Your mother and I have taught you and your sister better than that."

I knew this was not just another, Your-mother-and-I-have-taught-you-better-than-that talk. Dad's voice was stern and still angry, but the seriousness of his love for me was penetrated the usual stern demeanor and anger I always feared from him.

Then he said, "Perky, the Bible teaches us...."

I remember saying to myself: Oh no, not the-Bible-teaches-us talk.

But this was no ordinary the-Bible-teaches-us talk. It was the best the-Bible-teaches-us talk I ever heard, and I remember it to this day. Dad's words came clearly, but his stern tone gave way to a kind of moral clarity that was his hallmark. His teaching that night in the Dark Room was a moral and political teaching that has guided my life in the sixty-something years since that night. His teaching is at the center of my work and my spirit. But it is also at the center of the anger that has led me to a lifetime of organizing.

That night, my father taught that we are all created in the likeness and image of God. He said this means—in no uncertain terms—that all human beings are completely, unequivocally, and radically equal. Black and white (and by extension yellow and brown and any other color); male or female or other-gendered; rich or poor or middle-class; young or old; Christian, Muslim, Jew, Hindu, or not one-iota religious—no one, not one person, is better than another in the sight of God. Period.

Dad's teaching did not stop there. He told me, without using the terms, that Scripture has political implications. that the story of our creation meant that segregation of any kind was wrong. His clarity on this point penetrated my young mind.

Then a strange thing happened. My fear of punishment receded. I was listening in awe and quiet wonder to my father's words, and they were being imprinted on my soul.

He went on: "Segregation is wrong, and it is going away. There will be a time in this town, this state, and this country where white people and Negroes (as Dad always called them respectfully) will live side by side, go to school together, and treat each other as God intends."

I had not noticed the Devil, the Master of Deceit, coming into the room, however. My dad's moral clarity and theological teaching had seemed to keep him at bay. But in Satan came, entering the room and using Dad's voice as he kept talking, now offering me a different lesson. "Segregation is wrong," Dad/Satan explained. "It is evil. It is going away; but, Perky, there is not much we can do to hasten its demise. All we can do is treat Negroes as we would want to be treated and let God do the rest. These things are in God's hands."

These words came out of Dad's mouth, and even as a child I saw his own fear move into the center of the room. The Devil was standing there, but he never pulled up a chair. He spoke not a word. He didn't have to. My dad's moral certainty and theological strength had given way to his fear. I didn't understand this at the time. I thought my father had spoken all these words in one voice and with one spirit. But looking back, I know now that Dad was speaking with two voices. One was with the clarity of the biblical Prophets; the other with the voice of the Evil One. Some call him the Devil, others Satan, but I call him Fear.

■ ■ ■ ■

Fear spoke, but not in an audible voice. He did not have to. My dad

360

spoke for him. "Do you understand what I am saying, son?"

I nodded my assent.

He continued, "We have to be careful who we tell this to. Not everyone thinks as we do. So, you must be careful."

Fear smiled and left the room, but his spirit remained.

Over the years I have wrestled with these conflicting teachings from my father. My increased determination not to live in a world where fear is promoted to maintain the social order has drawn me toward organizing. However, it has been the melding of disciplines of planning, acting, and reflecting on action with the spiritual disciplines of daily journaling, interior dialogue, prayer, and now writing that has begun to give me very concrete victories over the demons of inherited fear that I met for the first time in that Dark Room in segregated West Point, Mississippi.

My father spoke two opposite and completely incompatible voices that night because he felt powerless. He knew deep down that the social system that was based on white supremacy was in direct conflict with the biblical teachings he and his congregation claimed to follow. He knew all too clearly that the biblical teaching that all are created in the likeness and image of God wages an attack on white supremacy. Yet the fear within him left him speaking with two voices. I inherited this fear.

■ ■ ■ ■

Through the process of organizing I came to understand that much of what brought me to organizing was the experiences that I learned in the Dark Room. I grew up not wanting to live in a society based on fear and intimidation. My anger drew me into organizing. Even as that young boy, I knew that segregation was wrong, and as did my parents, but I wanted to be a part of bringing about the change that was required, not leave it to God alone.

Organizing has deepened inside of me a confidence in my own abilities. It also deepened my commitment to collective action with other organizers and leaders who are willing to combat their own personal fears and publicly act in response to the many griefs in their lives.

The day before my mother died, I was blessed to have a last conversation with her. I told Mom about my response to a particular political problem I was working on at the time that had deep implications for a new project I was developing. She said, "You're not anxious about this situation, are you, Perk? You're not afraid of anything."

The hold of the One I met in the Dark Room many years ago, was being broken.

■ ■ ■ ■

Editor's Note: Perry Perkins has been organizing with the IAF for over thirty-five years. He says, "I believe that thinking and reflection require the deeper discipline of writing. A writer I know says that we must write to think. I am instinctual and intuitive in my organizing style, but a daily writing regime deepens the most important part of my understanding of my own self-interest. As I grow older, the desire to have a deeper spiritual life has become more integrated with my organizing. Engagement with others through writing is a way for me to communicate in a different way."

Questions for Discussion and Reflection

1. How do you feel about the author's use of religious language and imagery in telling his story? Be specific in your feelings.

2. How has racism affected you or someone you love personally? Tell a story about that in as much detail as possible, including your emotional reaction to it. How might organizing help you deal with the racism you were taught?

3. What other words beside the "n-word" are used to divide people and make them afraid of others? List them and share the list with others. Vow to one another to stop using these words yourself or ignoring it when others do so.

Power of Public Prayer

by Burns Stanfield and Larry Gordon

Rev. Burns Stanfield (born 1959) was president of the Greater Boston Interfaith Organization (GBIO), the Industrial Areas Foundation (IAF) affiliate in Massachusetts at the time of these events, and a co-founder of GBIO two decades earlier. He has been the pastor of Fourth Presbyterian Church in South Boston since 1991 and has served on many civic boards of directors.

Larry Gordon (born 1948) was the lead organizer of GBIO at the time of these events. He began his organizing career with the National Welfare Rights Organization (NWRO) in New England during the civil rights movement and has been organizing with the IAF since 1990 as lead organizer in the San Francisco Bay Area with the Bay Area Organizing Committee (BAOC), the San Fernando Valley in Los Angeles (VOICE), Congregations Organized for a New Connecticut (CONECT), and as the supervisor for Marin Organizing Committee (MOC). He is the supervisor of Greater Cleveland Congregations (GCC), an affiliate of the Industrial Area Foundation (IAF).

"I used to pray that God would...do this or that, but now I pray that God will guide me to do whatever I'm supposed to do, what I can do.... Prayer changes us, and we change things."

Saint Mother Teresa of Calcutta

There is power in prayer, and a special power when it rises from an organization united for the common good in the public square. We call this "public prayer." Let us tell you a story. In 2006, during the administration of Gov. Mitt Romney, the Greater Boston Interfaith Network (GBIO) worked with a statewide coalition to secure universal health care in Massachusetts (see Cheri Andes' "Birth of the Affordable Care Act" in this book). While those on the national stage would eventually debate whether the ACA was "Obamacare" or "Romneycare," we knew in our hearts that more than anything this was "GBIO Care." Indeed, it was OUR care. So we in GBIO have kept organizing, kept fighting, and kept our seat at the statewide health policy table.

Here is the context. After (1) the Massachusetts health care expansion had been in place and proven itself successful for several years, (2) Massachusetts had elected a new Governor, Deval Patrick, (3) President Obama's election, and (4) the financial crisis of 2007-2009, GBIO got invited into a serious face-to-face meeting with Governor Patrick. Both of us were in that meeting, along with ten other top GBIO leaders. It was then that something happened that never happened to any of us before: The governor asked if GBIO would organize for a campaign to go after the health care industry and slow down the rampant increase in health costs.

The national "attack dogs" (our choice of words, not the Governor Patrick's) were trying to defeat the Affordable Care Act's passage in the U.S. Congress and were making the case that in the only state where this experiment was being tried (i.e., Massachusetts) health care costs were going through the roof. In fact, there was no cause and effect, but in such a partisan political climate that distinction got lost in translation.

This meeting with Governor Patrick was already pretty interesting, but the best was yet to come. Gov. Patrick said that he "needed" us. GBIO had proven many times our ability to organize. We had a large committed constituency that stood ready to go into action, fight a good fight, and negotiate a deal once we were at the table. We had by that time established our political credibility as the most powerful non-partisan political organization in the state, seriously engaging, among others, tens of thousands of ordinary health care consumers; and we were the only organized players in the system not making money off of the rising costs of health care. Indeed, we were organizing both those who were literally *paying* these higher medical expenses through insurance premiums, co-payments, and other out-of-pocket costs, as well as those completely cut out of the health care system because of increasingly higher health care and health insurance prices.

■ ■ ■ ■

Notwithstanding that the Governor's case on its merits was compelling and that we too were concerned that our previous success in achieving access to health care for millions of Massachusetts' resident would be undermined by rising costs, we initially resisted his invitation. Here is how we thought: *Our campaign to initially get health insurance and access to care had been "issuable." We could engage a large constituency, which we did.* In contrast, costs of health care are always hidden and obscured behind insurance premiums, co-pays, deductibles, out-of-pocket maximums, and actuarial computations and algorithms. Consumers never see the real costs, and even if they do it's a maze. Did you ever try reading a hospital bill? Or figure out why an aspirin during a hospitalization can cost as much as a month's rent? It's enough to drive you to re-read Dicken's *Little Dorrit* to get reminded of his "Office of Circumlocution." Nothing is more publicly obfuscated in our time than health care costs and pricing. We told the governor all this.

"So," he responded (we're paraphrasing here), "I get it. Your understanding of the nature of our relationship is that you expect that when you are here with me in my office with three, a dozen, or thirty of you, or you have me out to one of your actions with multiple hundreds or even thousands of your supporters, you expect me to agree to do what you ask of me. Which, by the way, over the past few years, is what I have done often. You just don't happen to believe in reciprocity."

We were all taken aback. No one with whom we had built such a constructive relationship had talked to us that way before. Governor Patrick wasn't just *pushing* us; he was *teaching* us what it meant to not just fight to get to the table but what it takes to participate in the people's ongoing business once we got there. He was about to end the meeting when one of our delegation (we don't remember who) asked for five more minutes.

We quickly caucused (as we have been trained to do) and came up with a counter proposal. "Give us some time," we asked the governor, "and we will have fifty or so of our top leaders and organizers invest the time in attending research actions with various decision-makers and medical experts to do a power analysis to decide whether we might be able turn the skyrocketing cost of health care and insurance from an insurmountably obscure problem into an issue or series of concrete issues around which we could potentially organize. And then we would get back to you within a month.

"It's a deal" the Governor of Massachusetts said.

■ ■ ■ ■

Through the next few weeks of research actions with health industry power players, providers, experts, and workers, we were able to cut through the obscurity and get to the power analysis. We discovered that as the higher-priced tier-one hospitals merged into larger consortia of hospital systems they were able to force the insurance companies to pay higher and higher prices for each and every medical procedure based on the percentage of the market that those providers controlled. It was not a competitive market, where costs were impacted by the quality of the care. It was a kind of monopoly, or at least a sweet deal: If you had the market share you could demand higher reimbursements, and you got them.

Using our hard-won seat at the public table and informed by this power analysis, we successfully worked on cost containment legislation that created a Health Policy Commission to oversee health care prices and transactions. We polarized; we disrupted; and then we prevented the largest (and most expensive) health care provider in the state, Partner's Health Care, from acquiring its eleventh hospital, saving the state $53 million a year in costs. And then from that seat of recognition we inserted ourselves again into a proposed merger of several other providers, led by health care giants Beth Israel Deaconess and Lahey Clinic. It was in this last fight that public prayer would have its powerful moment.

These two large hospital systems insisted they needed to merge together and with eleven other hospitals to create a new entity large enough to create real competition with the even larger Partners system. But our new set of research actions were telling us something quite different. This new merger would in fact increase costs even more, as well as take patients away from many hospitals serving low-income communities, rather than put price pressure on the Partners system. This merger would add costs unless either (1) desperately needed important conditions were imposed on the deal or (2) the merger was blocked. Primary among such necessary conditions were price caps, essentially unheard of in the health care market.

The public official in Massachusetts charged with regulating such a hospital merger was the state's attorney general, Maura Healey. She could not just "stop" it, but she could file a lawsuit and ask a judge to stop it on anti-trust and consumer protection grounds. However, over the last several decades those suits tended to be very unsuccessful, particularly in a state like Massachusetts where the medical industry has such out-sized political power.

But not unlike Joseph and Pharaoh of biblical fame, Attorney General Healy knew us and we knew her. She had seen us time and again stand up against the large hospital systems and insurance companies. She understood that we had learned that pricing was based on the hardball economics of market share and leverage, not competition in the marketplace over quality of care. She recognized us to be the organization with the largest and best-organized health care consumer constituency in the state and that we had taken the time to teach our members about these complex issues. She respected us as tough, nimble, flexible, and dependable. And she admitted we had a track record of success in producing results. We might disagree with her, but she knew we would say so and could deliver on what we promised. And in Healey's own ascendency to the attorney general position, we had observed her take a position on the right side of history—with us and against her prior boss—in our campaign against the Partner Health System's attempt to buy yet another large high cost hospital.

In this new battle of controlling medical costs, GBIO knew we could at least make our case to Healy and her staff regarding the conditions that would need to be imposed before she should sign off on the proposed merger. Indeed, she and her staff would have to construct the right legal approach and navigate the challenging political waters, but she was in position to be an effective ally, but only *if* she felt enough of a political push to engage. Our challenge was to create—and deliver—that sacred push.

Merger negotiations were reaching a critical point in the fall of 2018, and we had an action already planned with over a thousand people in New England's largest mosque to do work on a mix of issues. We invited Attorney General Healy to join us on that evening, which was only a few days before her final negotiations with the hospitals. It was our last chance to get her to push for the needed constraints on the merger.

Typically, GBIO would have tried to exercise our muscle on this issue by engaging in public action with the right people in power, addressing specific terms that led to negotiation and agreement, and winning the public promises we needed to then hold them accountable for what they had agreed to do. But the context we faced in this instance was very different. We had been negotiating with Healy's then chief-of-staff (the very able Michael Firestone) to make clear the importance of the A.G. preventing this proposed merger from making cost matters worse (the hospital CEO's protestations to the contrary notwithstanding). The rub was that because Healy would be moving into negotiations for the purpose of deciding whether she would sue them or not, it was not smart (and probably not legal) for her to come out to a large public gathering and negotiate, or even discuss, specifics of her legal strategy with us. It would "show her hand" prematurely. To get her to the action we had to make the wording of our questions much more general than we would typically prefer. We struggled with how we could still somehow convey the power of our 1,000 gathered leaders to give her the push to represent us strongly in the negotiations as "the people's lawyer" (one of her favorite campaign refrains) while avoiding specifics.

■ ■ ■ ■

We had been making good headway with her chief-of-staff on the conditions we wanted in the deal, but they weren't agreeing to anything yet. We had worked out that if the attorney general came to the action she could come up to the stage and talk in whatever way she felt appropriate. Finally, we proposed that before ending the event we would like to offer a prayer on her behalf. Her staff liked that proposal. They also knew us well enough to know that because our actions are "organized" and not "mobilized" (our language, not theirs) that our delegates would be well-briefed and disciplined.

That's when the power of public prayer became a tactic in the IAF pantheon. We re-acquainted ourselves with the inspirational biblical quotation from II Timothy 1:7 that "God did not give us a spirit of timidity but a spirit of power and love and self-control."[1] We decided we would end the action with a public prayer commissioning Healy to enter into the upcoming negotiations with the hospital CEOs not with a "spirit of timidity" but with a "spirit of power and love and self-control." It was the first time in history the two of us know of that the reaction the IAF was looking for was *silence*.

But once this idea was brought to our leadership team, there were concerns. "If we pray for her, shouldn't we pray for the other officials on

---

1 These words appear on the frontpiece of the IAF essay written and published in 1978, *Organizing for Family and Congregation*, which was the foundational document for what Saul Alinsky biographer Sanford D. Horwitt named the "post-Alinsky Modern IAF."

stage?" and "She was raised Catholic but may not be practicing anymore. Wouldn't that mean that this could make her feel awkward?" and "Aren't we missing an opportunity if she is in the room and we don't ask her to respond to our specifics?" The team eventually agreed that this approach could work, but only if I, [Burns Stanfield], agrees to be the one leading the prayer of blessing over Attorney General Healy at the end of her time with us. I was more than willing. I was eager and excited.

The evening of the action went well. The A.G. spoke in general and supportive ways, and our people applauded with support and appreciation. Then the co-chair of our health campaign, Bonnie Gilbert (serving with co-chair Michael Rubenstein) invited all attending clergy to gather around in prayer for Maura Healy as she prepared for her upcoming negotiations with the healthcare providers. We invited our 1,000 gathered citizens of all faiths and philosophies to extend their hands and join their hearts in this prayer:

Gracious God, Giver of Life, Spirit of the Ages—We give you thanks for our public servants….

…And especially our lawyer, the people's lawyer, Attorney General Healey. Grant her wisdom, courage, and strength. More than that, God, connect her heart to the hearts of those who are praying for her right now: people who raise children, people who manage households, people who pay the bills.

God, when she steps into that negotiating room, when she continues with this important work, hold her. Love her. Strengthen her. And give her a sacred, stiff resolve, the resolve of a warrior, the resolve of the people's—THE PEOPLE'S—lawyer.

Not everyone saw it, but some leaders in the front row recognized that the attorney general crossed herself at the conclusion of the prayer. Whatever her current view of organized religion, her liturgical instincts were intact, and there in the mosque she expressed her own Catholic version of "Amen" that affirmed she was indeed in the glow of a thousand prayers for her as "The People's Lawyer."

That prayer then informed her deed. She went into the negotiations a few days later. She won an agreement with the most important conditions even firmer than we had anticipated or hoped. The agreement allowed the 13-hospital merger to go forward, but with remarkable conditions and constraints in place. First among them was that for the first time the state-imposed caps on price increases for specific hospitals, going beyond the state's more general statutory guidelines for the industry as a whole for the next seven years. This calculated as a net savings in health care spending of $1.2 billion over the life of the agreement.

Other notable conditions included requiring that these merged hospitals and doctors expand their practices to include more patients on Medicaid; nearly doubling their financial investment in community medicine to $71.6 million per year; joint planning with community hospitals that were not members of the thirteen-hospital conglomerate; and the newly merged hospital system accepting an independent monitor who was charged with publishing a report each year for ten years on the hospitals' compliance with the terms of the agreement.

Her staff later told us that it was the push of GBIO that made this agreement possible. All those organized people. All those calls. All that attention to detail. All that hard work. All that discipline. All that tension with respect.

All that public prayer.

■ ■ ■ ■

Editor's Note: Rev. Burns Stanfield continues to serve as co-president of GBIO and pastor of Fourth Presbyterian Church, as a Strategy Team member of Metro IAF, and on various civic boards and committees. He has also taught at Andover Newton Theological School and Harvard Divinity School. Larry Gordon, now living in Los Angeles, has retired from full time organizing with the IAF but serves in semi-retirement as supervisor of IAF work in Cleveland, Ohio.

Questions for Discussion and Reflection

1. What is the difference between private prayer and public prayer? Is public prayer justified in an organization that is diverse in terms of faith or philosophy? Why? When? How is it done?

2. What is reciprocity? How do you feel if public officials ask you for something or to do something? Tell a story from your own experience or that of someone you know about how you or they responded.

3. Describe a "research action" or a "power analysis" you have participated in. If you have not, what do you imagine they might entail?

Nobody Likes a Know-It-All

by Amy Totsch

Amy Totsch (born 1978) is the lead organizer for United Power for Action and Justice (UPAJ), one of four affiliates of the Industrial Areas Foundation (IAF) in Illinois. Before that she was a leader and then the organizer of an organization of young adults related to the IAF, called Public Action for Change Today (PACT). That organization helped get young adults included on their parents' health insurance until age twenty-six (thirty for veterans in Illinois) in 2008, a policy that became the first change put into effect under the national Affordable Care Act in 2010. She is also a singer, once a part of the band Doko Benjo and now performing occasionally in the Chicago area.

Nobody likes a know-it-all. I know, because I've been one.

In Michael Specter's excellent profile of Dr. Anthony Fauci in the April 20, 2020 issue of *The New Yorker*, I learned about an expert who seemingly appeared out of nowhere—at least to me and to many Americans—with his daily media appearances during the pandemic of 2020, often as a backdrop and/or backup to the President of the United States of America.

Anthony Fauci didn't appear out of nowhere. He has a storied, thirty-six-year career at the National Institute of Health (NIH). He has worked under six different presidents. And at the height of the HIV/AIDS epidemic, Dr. Fauci dropped other priorities to become the government's lead researcher on that virus as it exploded and ravaged people throughout the United States and the world, most acutely within the gay community.

In the late eighties, AIDS activists, desperate to end the government's glacial response to addressing the disease, targeted the NIH—and Dr. Fauci specifically—to remove barriers to crucial clinical trials and development of life-saving medications. Specter writes: "I covered the AIDS epidemic for the *Washington Post*, and it was clear to me that Fauci was inclined to enforce the paternalistic medical tradition in which he had trained: Doctors and scientists were unquestioned authorities, and drug development had to follow a rigid process that included animal testing and rigorous clinical trials. Otherwise, the benefits and the risks of these drugs could not be adequately assessed."

Dr. Fauci was a classic know-it-all. But, eventually, he seems to have realized the fault in his ways and made a crucial pivot. He became a "listen-to-all," engaging especially with people who had experience (either as patients or healers or both) and therefore had worthwhile suggestions about what needed to be done to respond effectively. Eventually Fauci ended up building relationships with key people in the community most affected.

So, is Anthony Fauci an exception? A know-it-all who became a listen-to-all?

■ ■ ■ ■

In the midst of the Covid-19 pandemic in Illinois in April 2020, a colleague and I were on a phone call with the chief of staff to the state's attorney general. We wanted to discuss with her a set of measures that could be taken by the A.G. to address the emerging wild-west marketplace for personal protective equipment (PPE). For example, the *Chicago Sun-Times* had just run a story of a deputy governor of Illinois racing north on I-55 with a $3.4 million check to meet the deadline of one PPE supplier.

My colleague and I are organizers for the Illinois Metro Industrial Areas Foundation (IAF)—a network of 100 religious and civic institutions in the four most populous counties in Illinois—and we were hearing stories of shortages of PPE from our healthcare allies and our member institutions as well. One of our leaders was organizing people to make masks at home for non-medical workers at the local hospital, who were being offered only a single mask per week.

To address this issue, we simply wanted the attorney general (with whom we already had a relationship going back almost two years) to join us and, together, press the CEO of the 3M company—the world's largest manufacturer of the most critically needed surgical masks—to rein in their vendors from price-gouging.

The AG was too "busy" to take our call. We settled on a call with his chief of staff, with whom we had also been trying to develop a relationship. To make a painful story short, she told us: "We appreciate your concern; we've got this handled."

She then went on to report how "overwhelmed" they were with reports of price gouging on everything from hand-sanitizer to toilet paper.

And then in the next breath, she told us we'd be most helpful by "submitting any evidence" of price gouging in Illinois on the attorney general's website—the same website they were being overwhelmed by—so they could go after suppliers *on our behalf.*

Had she pivoted from being a know-it-all to a listen-to-all, as perhaps Dr. Fauci might have done, she would have heard our point: The A.G.'s office shouldn't spend its precious time and resources tracking down each and every venal price-gouger in Illinois, and neither should we. Still, the A.G. and the 100 religious and civic institutions in the state he was elected to defend and protect could call on one source of the profiteering, the 3M company in Minnesota. Together, we might leverage our combined power to stop the price-gouging and insane payment terms of 3M's own distributors.

This tiny action—a phone call, really—tripped a nerve inside of me. It reminded me again how some, if not most, of the top political people in our state approach democracy. They assume government is for them—a small group of specialists—and doesn't really need us—a powerful group of organized peoples' institutions. "Trust us, we'll handle it," the chief of staff told us. She might as well have said, "No one outside of our office could possibly have any useful input into what we are doing—other than to spectate and fill out a form and send it to us to take care of for them."

"If we aren't too overwhelmed at the time," she could have added.

■ ■ ■ ■

I recognized the know-it-all in this woman because I was one for many years. But fortunately, like Dr. Fauci, I reached a point in my life where I realized that patronizing other people was neither attractive, interesting, productive, nor meaningful.

I got good grades in school and made sure I knew the right answers to the questions on the test to get the same A's that the chief of staff always got. After I graduated from college with a degree in industrial engineering, I went into consulting as a twenty-two-year-old well-paid know-it-all. I analyzed data and would tell people who had been doing their job for twenty years or more that they were doing it wrong. The truth is I had no clue how to do their job. I was just trained to analyze data and believe that data doesn't lie.

But the data did lie. All the time. There were glitches and anomalies in the very systems that spit the data out. My know-it-all-ism ignored the human angles—the expertise, the nuances, the relationships among the people—that actually allowed the companies I "consulted" with to make a product.

To this day, I remember the faces and stories and some of the names of the people I worked with as a consultant. But relationship and listening to them was always superfluous to the expertise or technical knowledge I thought I was providing them. We rarely talked about how they got into the work they did or why it mattered to them. Or, what THEY thought the company should be doing and how they and I might solve the problems together.

I didn't enjoy consulting work, as you might have picked up by now. I quit to become an organizer with Metro IAF, where all of us could be experts: people from different walks of life; college graduates and those going to school part-time or not at all; the formerly incarcerated; the undocumented; poor, working- and middle-class people; every race; every religion or personal philosophy; people of every political persuasion and no political persuasion at all.

The IAF teaches organizers and leaders how to use our own lived experiences to develop a collective expertise and how to use it powerfully to make necessary change happen. We follow the IAF Iron Rule: "Never do for others what they can do for themselves." I got into organizing because I did not want to be a spectator, expert, or consultant. I wanted to become an agent of change. And I wanted to be respected, not patronized, by those with whom I am trying to work for the common good, including the chief of staff of the attorney general of Illinois.

■ ■ ■ ■

In *The New Yorker* article, Michael Specter revealed that Dr. Fauci used a pseudo-Latin expression to guide him: *Illegitimi non carborundum*, which translates roughly to "Don't let the bastards grind you down."

All right, Dr. Fauci, I won't let them grind me down. Instead I will spend my time teaching well-meaning public officials to realize they can no longer be know-it-alls, especially post-coronavirus. There is a role for organized people's institutions in helping those in government and business and education and not-for-profits respond to the challenges we will all face, together, for the rest of our natural lives.

Editor's Note: Attorney General Kwame Raoul of Illinois did in fact join A.G.s from twenty other states in pressuring the 3M company to control price-gouging during the Covid-19 pandemic of 2020. Upon hearing the news, Amy Totsch said, "Perhaps AG Raoul's chief of staff will become our new Dr. Fauci." Totsch is currently working on building and reclaiming housing at a large scale in the Chicago Lawn, North Lawndale, and Back of the Yards neighborhoods of Chicago. She is helping leaders to create an effective alternative to the incarceration of people facing mental illness or addiction challenges and force gun manufacturers to produce safer guns and locks and to sell their products only through responsible gun dealers as part of a national coalition led by Metro IAF. Called "Do Not Stand Idly By," the coalition was initiated at an action in 2013 of 500 people organized by United Power for Action and Justice at Chicago Sinai Congregation in response to the shooting of children and teachers at Sandy Hook Elementary School in Connecticut and the unending gun violence in Chicago. Totsch is married to Mark Staunton, and the couple live in the Irving Park area of Chicago.

Questions for Discussion and Reflection

1. Have you ever been patronized by someone? Describe it in detail. How did it make you feel? What did you do about it, if anything?

2. Why do you think so many people in power—from government officials to corporate leaders to academics to the media to philanthropists to "experts" of all kinds—patronize ordinary people and their institutions? What can be done about it?

3. Why do you think the Industrial Areas Foundation has taught for over eighty years that the "first issue" regarding power is always recognition? Give an example from history or current events.

Why Do Some People Ask Me about Looting?

by Richard Townsell

Richard Townsell (born 1964) is the executive director of the Lawndale Christian Development Corporation, a longtime resident of the North Lawndale neighborhood in Chicago, Illinois, and a founding leader in United Power for Action and Justice. He has held many other leadership roles in Chicago and has been a wrestling coach for a multitude of young men in Chicago. He is currently involved in leading an effort by United Power for Action and Justice to build 1000 new homes in Lawndale, modeled after the Nehemiah Homes in East Brooklyn, New York. This essay was written by Townsell in the aftermath of the national demonstrations in the summer of 2020 following the killing by police officers of George Floyd and many other Black people.

"But I know that the king of Egypt will not let you go unless a mighty hand compels him. So I will stretch out my hand and strike the Egyptians with all the wonders that I will perform among them. After that, he will let you go. "And I will make the Egyptians favorably disposed toward this people, so that when you leave you will not go empty-handed."

Exodus 3: 19-21

The Israelites did as Moses instructed and asked the Egyptians for articles of silver and gold and for clothing. The Lord had made the Egyptians favorably disposed toward the people, and they gave them what they asked for; so they plundered the Egyptians.

Exodus 12:35

don't know why, but many of my white brothers and sisters seem extremely bothered by the looting and property damage that occurred after brother George Floyd was murdered by the police last week.

If anyone should be angry about that, it should be me. We had looting and property damage once again in my community of North Lawndale in Chicago, just as we have had during many protests going all the way back to when Dr. Martin Luther King, Jr., was murdered. But I turned down some interviews with local press recently because they were fixated on it. They wanted to tour and see the "riots" up close and talk about what life was like "on the ground." It was as if they wanted to go on a safari in the wild.

I did do a piece on *Chicago Tonight* on WTTW, the PBS television station, which seemed largely respectful when it was filmed; but not as I watched it later. Over my words, they ran images and footage of stores that were broken into and looted on the south side of Chicago but were shown as if that "activity" had happened in my community of Lawndale. The casual observer would have inferred incorrectly that those stores were in our neighborhood. There was some damage here in Lawndale, but the media seemed intent on continuing the stereotypes about our community.

▪ ▪ ▪ ▪

The reactions I have seen and heard about the protests over the past week seem to fall into several categories. I will talk about them from the least to the most constructive in this moment:

- The least constructive come from the hard-core rule-of-law types. Apparently like President Trump, they are angry and want looters and anyone doing damage to property arrested and shot. They see all protesters as opportunists who do not really care about George Floyd and use it as an opportunity to steal some Nikes. This reaction, by the way, is not limited to white folks. There is a rainbow coalition who seem to hold this sentiment.
- The next level of reaction is from those who want to come in and "help." They wanted to do quick, feel-good service projects. These ranged from coming out and doing a clean-up (complete with selfies) for a few hours, or volunteering to help store owners fill out

insurance claims or donating fifty lunches for families or some other one-time activity. On Saturday, June 6, 2020, we had a community cleanup and I swear to you there were five white folks for every Black person. Hundreds descended upon our neighborhood to help us clean it up. Many I had never seen before nor expect to see again until the next "crisis" in our neighborhood. The problem is and continues to be that most of the damage from the few violent protesters had already been cleaned up by the time our helpers got there. We kind of appreciated the sentiment, but this help seemed aimed not so much for us as it was designed for them to ease their collective guilt and then go back to their largely homogeneous communities.

The last group of reactions that I experienced were the most helpful. These folks realized that anger and quick fixes are not the right solution. They are people who already have authentic and sincere relationships with us and realize that the best answer right now for them is probably just to listen and not speak. They are ready to pitch in when invited. Real friends are reciprocal, not paternalistic. Their response is informed by humility and not hubris, connection and not condemnation. I don't write this piece for them, and I apologize to them if it makes them feel badly; it shouldn't.

■ ■ ■ ■

The two Scripture passages at the beginning of this essay are an example of desperate people looting. You probably don't think of it that way, but I am going to try to help you understand that it is. It is a story from the Book of Exodus in the Bible. Moses is leading the Israelites out of Egyptian captivity, where they have been enslaved for over *400 years* (put a pin in that number) and lived in harsh conditions under a Pharaoh who exercised absolute power over them.

But after God's plagues broke Pharaoh and he decided to let them go, the people "borrowed" some silver and gold and Louis Vuitton robes (I mean some clothes and utensils and maybe a little food and drink) on their way out of town as they headed for the promised land. That is, they plundered the Egyptians. C'mon now, admit that is what the Bible says happened. But because of their harsh treatment for 400 years, we justify and understand the humble "requests" the Hebrews they made of the Egyptians to part with some of their wealth. Sounds a lot like "reparations," doesn't it?

Did not the God of Abraham, Isaac, and Jacob hear the Hebrews' cries, see their inhumane treatment, equip Moses to lead them out of captivity, and—oh, by the way—tell them it was ok to take a few souvenirs with them for their *400 years* of troubles?

If so, why would the Lord be ok when *they* looted, but be mad when a few of our people loot?

I know you are struggling with this, but I'm here to help give you some perspective. In 1968, when the riots that happened after Dr. King was assassinated tore through our community of Lawndale, not all of the stores were burned and looted. Mr. Edward Muldrow ran the Del Kar Pharmacy. His son, Edwin, has run the store since for the past twenty-eight years, and he tells the story that it was the Del Kar Pharmacy store where Dr. King bought his daily newspaper from when he lived at 1550 S. Hamlin in North Lawndale in 1966. Mr. Edward Muldrow senior was a Black pharmacist at a time when there were very few. He took care of everyone in the community. When the riots started, leaders of Lawndale organizations made sure that his store was spared.

Last week was very similar. Stores that were run by local shop owners who have respectful relationships with our community were mostly spared. But many of the stores in the neighborhood that take money out of the community and put next to nothing back were looted. Many of these store owners solicit and harass teenage girls every time they come in. They sell spoiled milk and bad meat at exorbitant prices. Their buildings look like they are abandoned, they serve us through plexiglass and throw our change at us because the workers don't want to touch Black peoples' hands. They sell drug paraphernalia and loose cigarettes and cover their windows so you can't see what's going on inside. They ring up our items but don't give itemized receipts.

■ ■ ■ ■

Do these insensitive businesses deserve to be robbed and looted? *No, they do not.* But if you have not experienced decades of exploitation and blatant disrespect at the hands of these store owners, then you don't understand why our people won't be crying over some stolen goods. I won't cry. Despite this daily reality for our people, the police are still more willing to guard these stores then care about the loss of life in our communities. The clearance rate on homicides in Chicago is the lowest in the nation. Black lives here clearly don't matter, certainly not as much as they do in more affluent neighborhoods. And you know it.

But we started this reflection talking about looting, and I want to finish there. This week we also learned that a study was done by WBEZ, the NPR station in Chicago, that showed the abysmal disparity in lending in black communities by major banks and mortgage companies. The report was titled *"Where Banks Don't Lend: In Chicago, lenders have invested more in a single white neighborhood than all the Black neighborhoods combined. It is modern-day redlining."* Google the story. Redlining means that banks and insurance companies draw a red line around communities where they won't make loans or write insurance contracts.

Black wealth has been stripped from our Black communities in Chicago since we began moving here in large numbers in the 1950s. It is estimated that the "contract buying" scheme in Chicago alone stole between $3.2 and 4 billion dollars in equity from Black families over two decades. There are so many examples of this kind of "looting and property destruction" of Black people since we were dragged here from Africa that I really don't comprehend the current fetish about looting. Could it have more to do with politics than any real concern for us?

My charge to you is this: Be upset with *ALL* the looting that has taken place, not just the latest incidents. Be upset about mass incarceration of Black men. Be upset with job losses due to globalization. Be upset about poor schools. From where I sit, the real looters are still looting....

■ ■ ■ ■

Editor's Note: Richard Townsell also tells this story. "There are volunteers, like me, who care about our families and communities and know that this system is built to divide and conquer through stereotypes and sensational media narratives about 'the other.' We are aware of our self-interests but also concerned beyond our narrow self-interests to enlightened self-interests (also called the 'common good'). Through our one-to-one relational meetings, patterns begin to emerge and collectively we decide to do research on a problem so that we can see if we can craft it into an issue. In North Lawndale, a local library named after Frederick Douglass was in shambles. Our team of leaders in the North Lawndale Homeowner's Association admitted they never went to that library anymore because it was decrepit and drugs were sold right outside the building. We decided to do what the Industrial Areas Foundation calls a 'power analysis' of the Chicago Public Library system. We began to understand who was on the board, when they met, what were their sources of revenue, how many other libraries around our neighborhood were going through renovations, and other pertinent information. We then decided to do a 'research action' and took a team of residents to inspect the Frederick Douglass Library. What we found was appalling: rat boxes in the children's reading area, mold and peeling paint in offices and meeting rooms, radiators too hot for a child's touch, elevators and fire extinguishers that hadn't been inspected in years. Our team took copious notes and pictures and put our research into folders. Next, we visited the new central Harold Washington Library in Chicago's Loop on a cold night in February of 2018 and attended a Chicago Library Board meeting. Our team watched and listened as the board members discussed a new, beautiful library they were building in a northside Chicago gentrified community, one that had been designed by award-winning architects, Perkins & Will. When it was our turn to speak, our spokesperson, Rochelle Campbell, walked the board through our inspection report with the precision of a trial lawyer. A few months later, we got a $2.5 million commitment from Mayor Rahm Emanuel and our 24th Ward Alderman Michael Scott, Jr., to completely rebuild the Frederick Douglass Library and make sure it was open seven days a week and had all the programming they have at other library branches in more affluent neighborhoods. In 2020, our leaders, including Ms. Campbell, got to speak at the grand re-opening of our library, and we vowed to make sure that it stays excellent."

REVEILLE FOR A NEW GENERATION

Questions for Discussion and Reflection

1. Have you observed times when those conducting or supporting a peaceful action or protest got accused of not following "the rules"? If so, give an example from your own experience or something you observed or read about. What to you think is the proper response to this accusation?

2. Why does organizing often create tension? Is that good or bad; necessary or unfortunate?

3. Why is it important for organizations to pick specific, immediate, and winnable issues (like the library issue described in the editor's note above) that people care enough about to act upon? How do such issues build an organization? Be specific

Organizing, Democracy, and the Iowa Caucuses

by Paul Turner

Paul Turner (born 1963) has been an organizer for over twenty-five years with the Industrial Areas Foundation (IAF). Beginning in 1995, he went to work for the IAF through their affiliate in Phoenix, AZ, the Valley Interfaith Project (VIP). From there he was hired as the lead organizer of the IAF affiliate in Nebraska, Omaha Together One Community (OTOC). His work in OTOC led to successful issue work in improving working conditions in Omaha's meatpacking plants, establishing an Office of Independent Police Auditor, and greatly increasing public investment in after-school and summer-enrichment programs for Omaha's poorest neighborhoods. He was the lead organizer of the IAF affiliate AMOS (A Mid-Iowa Organizing Strategy) from 2003-2014 and is currently co-director, along with Ernesto Cortes, Jr., of the Interfaith Education Fund. He wrote this essay right after the 2020 Iowa caucuses.

Winston Churchill said that democracy is the worst form of government...except for all the other forms. On Monday evening, February 3, 2020, all eyes were on Iowa. Or at least the eyes of the political pundit class and lots of energized American voters. It was caucus night in Iowa. For seventeen years, I've lived and worked in

Iowa as an organizer for the nation's largest and longest standing organizing network, the Industrial Areas Foundation (IAF), and I was eagerly awaiting the chance to participate in my local caucus.

I, and many Iowans, experience caucus night as one of the few authentic expressions of democracy left in our otherwise silly season of presidential politics. So on that cold night in February, I gathered with my neighbors in the gym of my children's middle school in Des Moines and caucused for my candidate for president.

Upon entering the gym, I was immediately confronted by neighbors whose passion for change was palpable. One neighbor who has spent a lifetime fighting for quality mental health care cornered me as soon as I walked in. Another approached me with real concerns about the electability of the candidates who were surging. A third was my neighbor down the street who lost his wife a few years back. We've lost touch. We promised each other to not wait another four years to reconnect.

We registered, rubbed shoulders, elected caucus officers, agreed to some rules, counted, re-counted, and lined up. The process was remarkably smooth given how many of us were jammed into the space. It was also loud, raucous, energetic, discursive, and in the end exhilarating—as every caucus I've attended over the last sixteen years has been, even the most disorganized ones. We mixed it up. We debated and we decided.

■ ■ ■ ■

Danielle Allen, political philosopher from Harvard, argued in the December 2019 issue of *The Atlantic* that if we are ever to regain a sense of union in our country, "Americans must recover the knowledge of how to create and operate democratic institutions, and put experts back in their places as advisors to a decision-making people." We were that decision-making people in the hundreds of caucus sites in Iowa that night. And we may never see them again.

The caucus process quickly came under attack both locally and nationally due to the failure of technology to deliver credible instant results. It seems an app didn't work right. So even as the caucuses themselves worked exactly as intended, the failure of an app may spell their doom. And as the media and the outside world grew increasingly angry at the botched results, their criticisms quickly turned to the caucus process itself as arcane, confusing, messy, and—most damning of all—undemocratic.

This last critique is the hardest for me to stomach. *Caucus* is an interesting word. It defines a group of people united to promote a common cause. It is a distinctly political word that is an antidote to polarization, because it is a process that requires persuasive speech, face-to-face conversation, negotiation, interruption, and argument. It is about power. Who decides? Who benefits? All critical questions and skills that ordinary citizens need to make our republic more democratic, and all are vanishing from our modern mass-market Pepsi-v-Coke presidential election nonsense.

■ ■ ■ ■

The more "democratic" alternative, we are told, is thousands of voters going alone—anonymously and without public debate—into a private voting booth behind a curtain, checking a box to indicate their preference (like choosing yogurt at the grocery store), and slinking back home to the privacy of their living rooms. That is what "real" democracy is apparently supposed to look like.

After listening to a solid year of contempt for the caucus process from every conceivable corner of the pundit class, it has left me wondering: Do we even know what democracy looks like anymore? Would we recognize it if we saw it? Some new technology malfunctioned, so the national media couldn't declare a "winner" before everyone went to bed. Twitter was alit with snark on caucus night and for days after, with lots of pictures of Iowans in gyms and meeting halls fighting to make their candidate viable; but those pictures most often were accompanied by 280 characters of contempt. 'What a ridiculous process,' they opined. 'Look at those buffoons (read rural hicks) ruining our democratic process! How can we trust our democracy in the hands of such a messy and confusing system?'

But isn't a healthy democracy by its very nature messy? Is it not an arcane and much maligned system of governance that dates back to antiquity (read the Greeks) and dares to tell ordinary people they should have a say in their own governance? Winston Churchill was right: It is the worst form of government. Except for all the others.

■ ■ ■ ■

I'll grant the homogeneity of Iowa as the first state to weigh in for president is a real problem, but I will defend the caucus system itself as inherently, authentically, and profoundly democratic. To caucus is to gather up. To caucus is to work in small groups towards a common cause. To caucus is to argue, defend our choices, take into consideration the opinions of others. To caucus is to organize and compromise. Contained within the expectations of caucusing is everything I've learned and attempted to teach to ordinary citizens in my years as an organizer.

Compromise may be the dirtiest of word of all in our current hyper-polarized environment. "I will not compromise" are the words of those who do not respect anyone's interests but their own. Autocrats and some tenured college professors can afford to make such a statement, says John Herman Randall in his classic essay, "The Importance of Being Unprincipled." The rest of us have to live in the real world.

■ ■ ■ ■

Every four years in Iowa since 1972, tens of thousands of voters leave their homes, say no to things they might otherwise do, get a babysitter, give up a shift at work, go out in the cold, and spend 2-3 hours arguing over who they think is the best presidential candidate for their country. Yes, the Democratic Party officials messed up the results in 2020. Yes, caucuses only represent a sliver of eligible voters. But can you name any other comparable experience like it, on its scale, anywhere else in our presidential election process?

Over 170,000 voters participated in a caucus in Iowa in 2020. Over 200,000 participated in 2008. It is the only time that many citizens ever have to engage face to face with their neighbors, defend their political choices, and become the decision-making people our democracy requires. Like a jury, democracy demands we reach judgment, and the Iowa Presidential Caucuses places you on a jury with tens of thousands of your fellow citizens.

For over twenty-five years as an organizer with the IAF, I've seen firsthand the creativity and imagination that comes from that kind of face-to-face deliberation. I've seen what is sparked when we cross lines of race, class, geography, religion, and sexual orientation and find common cause.

I witnessed three pastors whose theological and cultural differences couldn't have been greater, work together on a daily basis for more than four years. A Pentecostal African American pastor, a white Unitarian Universalist pastor, and a Seventh Day Adventist African American pastor working side by side to build one of the most successful job training organizations in the state of Iowa. For four years they spent countless hours as fellow leaders in AMOS, fighting to gain the funding and employment commitments necessary to make Project IOWA (Iowa Opportunities for Workforce Advancement) a reality. Today, Project IOWA lifts over 100 graduates a year into career-track, living wage, full benefit jobs. Everything about our current political culture would suggest those three pastors could never work together on anything, let alone become life-long friends.

■ ■ ■ ■

It would seem we Americans now prefer a more consumer-friendly democracy where everything is individualized and anonymous. Where decisions are made for us. Where we can remove ourselves from all interactions with our fellow citizens, vote our preference in secret, and return home to our echo chamber of MSNBC, CNN, or Fox News and feel good about our "participation" in the life of our country.

Given what happened in Iowa in 2020, that wish is about to come true. We will likely see in the future (if we haven't already) the elimination of the caucus process from every state in the union. Then, we will finally be able to vote everywhere without ever having to interact with anyone. Maybe there's an app for that?

■ ■ ■ ■

Editor's Note: In 2014, Paul Turner began work in Colorado to build an IAF affiliate in metro Denver and across the Front Range of the state. In 2017-2018, he was given supervisory responsibilities for IAF projects in Dallas, Colorado, Oklahoma, Nebraska, and Iowa. Turner has been married to his wife, Paula, for thirty-four years and the couple have three grown children.

Questions for Discussion and Reflection

1. Are community organizing and partisan politics complementary or antithetical? Explain your answer.

2. What do you think about the importance of being "unprincipled"? Read John Herman Randall's essay "The Importance of Being Unprincipled" (available online) and take a position on the need for compromise in a democracy.

3. How do you interact face to face with others? Where do you do so? Give examples, including some from the Covid-19 pandemic of 2020.

EPILOGUE

The Heartbeat of Wounded Knee

by David Treuer

David Treuer (born 1970) is Ojibwe from the Leech Lake Reservation in Northern Minnesota. His 2019 non-fiction book, *The Heartbeat of Wounded Knee: Native America from 1890 to the Present*, from which this excerpt is taken, was a *New York Times* bestseller and a finalist for both the Carnegie Medal and the National Book Award. It is included here at the end as a reflection on how the assumptions and perceptions of oppressed people's powerlessness has permeated the American consciousness from the beginning of our nation to today. (Note: Truer uses the word *Indian* throughout his book to refer to all those of tribal heritage within the United States. He says, "I also use 'indigenous,' 'Native,' and 'American Indian.' My choices of usage are governed by a desire for economy, speed, flow, and verisimilitude. A good rule of thumb for outsiders: Ask the Native people you're talking to what they prefer.")

By the time I graduated from high school I was ready to leave the reservation and never come back. In my mind, nothing good came from or of my Indian life, and I was exhausted by all the drama and trauma. I was tired of the poverty and the dusty roads that no one saw fit to pave. I was sick of the late-night calls and the trips to the hospital to witness the damage we were doing to ourselves. I looked ahead to the green, leafy excellence of Princeton University, to a future as a composed and

Olympic fencer. Nothing was clearer to me than the conviction that my past lay behind me, on the reservation, and the future awaited me beyond our borders, in America, so I left.

As soon as I was gone, I missed it. I missed what I hadn't known was my Indian life, our collective Indian life. I missed the Mississippi, which flows through my reservation as a tiny thing, little more than a stream I could walk across. I missed the ways the pine scratched the window screens at night. I missed my uncle Davey's antics, and I missed his love and I missed how he loved me completely, without judgment, without measure, without censure. I missed the Memorial Day gatherings at the Bena cemetery with my aunt and uncles and cousins, the sandwiches of canned ham mixed with Miracle Whip and relish and white dinner rolls. The yearning for home was rooted in nostalgia, but I was also trying to grow beyond it, toward a place approaching true knowledge.

As kids do when they leave home, I began to see my parents more clearly. I saw how my mother, born into the meanest of circumstances, had gone to nursing school and then to law school and then—quietly, without self-promotion—had returned to the reservation to practice law a block from the high school that had not thought much of the wiry Indian girl she had been. She represented all sorts of Indians for all sorts of reasons: divorce, DUI, theft. Indians had been appearing in court for centuries, but for most of my mother's clients it was the first time they had shown up in court with an Indians lawyer by their side, arguing for dignity, for fairness, for justice.

I saw, too, how my father—who was Jewish and had just barely survived the Holocaust—had adopted the reservation as his home and had adopted our causes as his own. I asked him about that. I asked him how he had come to feel so comfortable on the reservation. "I was a refugee," he said. "I was an outsider. I was told throughout my life I wasn't enough, I wasn't good enough, I didn't belong. When I came here I felt at home. I felt like people understood me." He taught high school on the reservation and then worked for the tribe, and when I was in high school he worked at Red Lake Reservation, where he had helped get the high school bonded and built in a way that made the tribe proud of their own accomplishments....

■ ■ ■ ■

I also started—in my own haphazard way—to think about our collective Indian past and present, and how the story of it was told. I decided on anthropology as my undergraduate major, a choice complicated by the way the discipline had created itself partly in relation to, and often at the expense of, indigenous people around the world. In the 1980s and 1990s, anthropology was reckoning with its colonial past, interrogating itself and its past practices, and the reflexive and self-appraising turn felt right to me. Anthropology was also a great place to have arguments, and for better or worse, I loved having arguments....

Around that time, I launched my life as a fiction writer. In that, too, I was oppositional: I abhorred the publishing industry's pressure to make multicultural fiction engage in cultural show-and-tell. As a result, I wrote novels where the characters never, ever, talked about their spirituality or culture, where nary a feather was to be found. Instead I tried (and often failed) to create complex, fully realized characters. Characters who, in Philip Larkin's phrase, had been pushed "to the side of their own lives" and had decided to push back. I went on to get my PhD in anthropology and to publish a few novels and eventually to write a nonfiction book about reservation life, a hybrid like me: part history, part reportage, part memoire.

Through it all, I came to see, we Indians often get ourselves wrong. My lack of regard for my own origins and those of my community began to trouble me, and troubles me still. If I could not see myself and my homelands differently from how many non-Indians do—more expansively, more intimately, more deeply—then how could I hope that the future of my people, in the broadest sense, would be any different from the story we kept being told, and kept telling ourselves?

■ ■ ■ ■

One of the mantras of the women's liberation movement in the 1970s was "The personal is political." This is undoubtedly true. But the political is also personal. Many of us have lived bitter and difficult times, and we have brought the ghost of our modern afterlife inside ourselves, where it sits judging us, shaping us, putting its fingers over our eyes so that all we can see, all we can feel, is that we were once great people but are great no more, and that we are no longer capable of greatness. We may feel that Dee Brown was right in his 1970 bestselling book *Bury My Heart at Wounded Knee*: What we Indians have now is not a civilization, not a culture, nor even real selves, but rather a collection of conditions—poverty, squalor, hopelessness—and that these are the conditions in which we live, and the state of our spirit.

This, too, is a narrative that must be laid to rest. I came to conceive of a book that would dismantle the tale of our demise by way of a new story. This book would dismantle the tale of our demise by way of a new story. This book would focus on the untold story of the past 128 years, making visible the broader and deeper current of Indian life that have too long been obscured. It would explore the opposite thesis of *Bury My Heat at Wounded Knee*. The year 1890 was not the end of us, our cultures, our civilizations. It was a cruel, low, painful point, yes—maybe even the lowest point since Europeans arrived in the New World—but a low point from which much of modern Indian and America life has emerged....

My book is not a catalogue of broken treaties and massacres and named and dates of moments when things might have turned out differently. There are, of course, treaties and battles and names and dates; my book is a history, after all. But facts assume a different place in this narrative from that in previous histories, because the project of my book is to do more than bend the broad lines of narrative true. It also tries to tract the stories of ordinary Indian people whose lives remind us of the richness and diversity of Indian life today and whose words show us the complexity with which we Indians understand our own past, present, and future.

So my book is a work of history, but it also includes journalism and reportage, and the deeply personal and deeply felt stories of Indians across the country, mine among them. In the telling, I have done my best to bring

Indian life into contact with the larger themes and trends in American life…. I have tried to show the ways in which Indian fates have been tied to that of the country in which we find ourselves, and the way that the fate of America has been and forever will be, tied to ours.

■ ■ ■ ■

Editor's Note: David Treuer splits his time between the Leech Lake Reservation in Minnesota and Los Angeles, where he teaches creative writing and literature at the University of Southern California. He is the author of four novels and three books of non-fiction, including *The Heartbeat of Wounded Knee*, about which a reviewer on National Public Radio said: "Chapter after chapter, it's like one shattered myth after another." Truer has written for the *New York Times*, the *Los Angeles Times*, the *Washington Post*, and many other publications.

Questions for Discussion and Reflection

1. What stereotypes do people have about a group to which you belong? How do you react to those stereotypes? Be specific.
2. There are approximately five million people of Native American descent in the United States today. What groups of fellow Americans do you not know well? What will you do about that?
3. Is writing a way of exercising power? Explain your answer, with examples.

ACTA PUBLICATIONS COMMUNITY ORGANIZING SERIES

Action Creates Public Life
Edward T. Chambers

Effective Organizing for Congregational Renewal
Michael Gecan

Freedom From and Freedom For
Michael Gecan

Going to the Well to Building Community
Deacon Timothy E. Tilghman

How to Raise Money for Community Organizing
Robert Connolly

Mixing It Up in the Public Arena
A. Zeik Saidman

Public Friendship
William L. Droel

Raising Money for Your Congregation
Robert Connolly

Rebuilding Our Institutions
Ernesto Cortes, Jr.

Reflecting with Scripture on Community Organizing
Reverend Jeffrey K. Krehbiel

The Body Trumps the Brain
Edward T. Chambers

The Power of Relational Action
Edward T. Chambers

**Using the Tools of Community Organizing to Build
Your Union's Strength in the Post-Janus Era**
Jonathan Lange, Amy Vruno, Ben Gordon

What Is Social Justice?
William L. Droel

Available from ACTA Publications • www.actapublications.com
800-397-2282